Stigma and Social Welfare

Paul Spicker

CROOM HELM
London & Canberra
ST. MARTIN'S PRESS
New York

©1984 P. Spicker
Croom Helm Ltd., Provident House, Burrell Row,
Beckenham, Kent BR3 1AT
Croom Helm Australia Pty Ltd, 28 Kembla St,
Fyshwick, ACT 2609, Australia

British Library Cataloguing in Publication Data

Spicker, Paul
    Stigma and social welfare.
    1. Social security − Great Britain
    2. Welfare recipients − Great Britain − Attitudes
    I. Title
    368.4   HD7165
    ISBN 0-7099-3313-4

Library of Congress Cataloging in Publication Data

Spicker, Paul.
    Stigma and social welfare.

    Rev. ed. of the author's thesis (Ph. D.) − University of
London.
    Includes index.
    1. Public welfare − Great Britain − Psychological
aspects. 2. Welfare recipients − Great Britain − Psychology.
3. Stigma (Social psychology) I. Title.
HV245.S67   1984   361   83-40194
ISBN 0-312-76200-3

Printed and bound in Great Britain

Contents

List of tables

FIGURE.

Acknowledgements

This book is an edited version of a Ph.D. thesis presented in the University of London. The debts incurred in the process of researching a study of this kind are considerable. The research was funded for two years by the Social Science Research Council, and completed while I was employed by Trent Polytechnic. The work was supervised by Professor R.A. Pinker, whose influence in its construction has been pervasive. I owe him my deepest thanks for his encouragement and personal support. I should also like to thank Mike Reddin, for access to data on the school meals survey; John Tomasen, for advice on statistics; Robert Pinker, Karen Stubbs, Professor N.Crisp, Julian Fullbrook and the Department of Health of Social Security, for permission to use material; most of the people in the Department of Social Administration and Social Work Studies at LSE, whom I have pestered at one time or another; the long-suffering staff at the British Library of Political and Economic Science; Alison, who put me up to this in the first place; Nicole, for help with filing, and both Nicole and Howard, who had to move my possessions around London five or six times before I finally moved in with them.

It goes without saying that I take full responsibility for the contents of the thesis, and that any mistakes are my own.

Paul Spicker

Foreword

by Robert Pinker

In this book Paul Spicker re-examines the nature of stigma in the context of social welfare. Whether it is regarded as a regrettable but necessary feature of social service provision or as an avoidable social evil, stigma is a permanent and contentious element in all decisions about universality and selectivity and all policies affecting the care of dependent people.

Spicker begins by challenging the conventional belief that the phenomenon of stigma originated in the British Poor Law. He goes on to discuss the relationship between stigma, the quality of social services and the demand for social services. In asking why some social services are more stigmatised and stigmatising than others he concludes that, although

> the reasons for stigma may lie with the nature of the users of the service rather than with the service itself (p.55),

some of the people who resort to services of low status are not themselves stigmatised. This leads to a discussion of stigma from the perspective of service users.

In part 2 Spicker examines the attributes of individuals and groups who are most vulnerable to feelings of stigma and social rejection. He distinguishes physical, mental and moral stigma and the stigma attaching to poverty and other forms of dependency. While recognising that his analysis can only be provisional, he convincingly argues that some form of classification is essential to a better understanding of the implications of stigma for social policy. This is elaborated in his subsequent analysis of the connections between stigmatic characteristics such as physical or mental deficiencies, poverty, dependency and lack of power. The context is then broadened to include the processes of exchange, the norm of reciprocity and the notion of altruism. Spicker argues that

> dependency is the defining characteristic distinguishing

social services from other forms of public provision
(p.100)
and that
if dependency is stigmatising, the association of stigma
with the social services is unavoidable. (Idem)
On this basis Spicker goes on to consider some of the ways in
which social policies could reduce the effects of stigma by
attempting to reduce the number of experiences associated with
dependency.

A fundamental dilemma of social policy is illuminated by
Spicker's method of enquiry:
collective action may have advantages for poor people
which it does not have for those who need rehabilitation;
rehabilitation, conversely, may not be satisfactory for
poor people. (p.119)
As long as social policy is concerned with redistribution and
rehabilitation, the dilemma will remain, and Spicker rightly
refuses to adopt the fashionable solution of excluding
rehabilitation from the ambit of social policy.

In the final sections of the book, Spicker examines stigma in
its social context as one part of a complex network of social
relationships. Not without qualification, he associates the
persistence of stigma with prejudice and with the social
careers of stigmatised people and the interactions of
stigmatised people with others. He finds little evidence to
support Goffman's thesis that the experience of stigma is
common to all stigmatised people. His own analysis suggests
that the experience of stigma is highly variable and in
addition that both the stigmatising and the status-enhancing
powers of social services are contingent on personal
experiences and structured social relationships which occur
outside the formal boundaries of social policy.

The roots of prejudice lie in the same processes of
socialisation that form our morality. The stigmatised person
is stigmatised because he offends against established norms,
and there are certain types of social service which tend to
accentuate the differences between recipients, leaving them
with a sense of inferiority. This process of association may
be irrational but it is nonetheless damaging and difficult to
forestall. Spicker does not end with a comforting moral
flourish or lay claim to a particular ideological virtue; he
follows the logic of his own analysis. If his conclusion is
rather bleak, that does not diminish his contribution to
social policy.

In reviewing the conventional models of residual and
institutional welfare and the methods of universality and
selectivity Spicker concludes that none of them is self-

evidently more likely to reduce stigma than the others. All forms of service provision identify their recipients, and the very fact of being identified as a dependent puts one at risk of stigma. Even in universalist services there is a risk of stigma spreading from those who are already stigmatised to those who are not. The question is how to legitimate the condition of dependency and how to reconcile redistributive and rehabilitative policies. It is arguable that stigma is functionally necessary to capitalist society and is therefore proof against all but radical social change, but this argument rests on questionable assumptions about the nature of capitalism, let alone the nature of alternative socialist societies.

This book extends the debate in a crucial area of social policy, including the individual and social dimensions of stigma and the relationship between the formal and informal aspects of social welfare. There are no simple answers to the complex problem of stigma, but Spicker's challenging and original analysis will add to our understanding of what causes the problem and what could be done to alleviate it.

Stigma and social welfare is the sort of book we need in Social Policy and Administration; it takes the spirit of impartial inquiry into a subject area that generates passionate convictions.

Robert Pinker
Greenwich

Introduction

THE NATURE OF SOCIAL WELFARE.

This book looks at the concept of stigma in the context of
social welfare. The idea of 'social welfare' is commonly
identified with the 'social services'. Both terms are
regrettably unclear. 'Welfare' can be taken to mean 'relief';
a 'welfare recipient' is someone who receives a monetary
allowance. Secondly, 'welfare' refers to individual well-
being; in economics, 'social welfare' refers to the overall
well-being of a society. Thirdly, it signifies a "pattern of
organised activities" equivalent to the social services
(Butterworth, Holman, 1975, 15). This is the principal use of
the term in studies of social administration. Social welfare
is an omnibus term used to cover a wide range of
activities in society. These activities are concerned
with the maintenance or promotion of social well-being.
(Ibid, 14.)
This is a very wide concept. 'Social wellbeing' covers
anything that could be argued to be good for society. "All
collectively provided services", Titmuss writes, "are
deliberately designed to meet socially recognised needs"
(1955, 39). ('Need' is used to signify those things which are
deemed essential for the well-being of individuals or groups.)
But not all services provided on this basis are social
services: the army is an obvious example. The needs that are
dealt with are of a specific kind. The services which are
most commonly accepted in Britain as being social services are
health, housing, education, social security and social work.
They have in common, not only that they provide for needs, but
that people receive directly a good or a service from them and
are therefore dependent.

Titmuss refers to "states of dependency" which are recognised
as collective responsibilities (1955, 42-3). These include
injury, disease, disability, old age, childhood, maternity and
unemployment. People in these circumstances rely on socially

provided goods and services, and it is this reliance which is the distinguishing characteristic of social welfare and the social services. Eyden writes that

A social service is a social institution that has developed to meet the personal needs of individual members of society not adequately or effectively met by either the individual from his own or his family's resources or by commercial or industrial concerns. (in Byrne, Padfield, 1978, 1.)

This definition implies, firstly, that the social services respond to individual need; and secondly, that they do so only when other methods have failed. This is true of some services, but not of others: education, or health, are accepted as social services, but are provided without regard to other resources which could meet the need.

Greve (1971), by contrast, cites a definition of a social service from a UN report: it is

an organized activity that aims at helping towards a mutual adjustment of individuals and their social environment. This objective is achieved through the use of techniques and methods which are designed to enable individuals, groups and communities to solve their problems of adjustment to a changing pattern of society, and through co-operative action to improve economic and social conditions. (Greve, 1971, 184-5.)

The definition, Greve notes, makes three points. The first is that

the provision of social services is not simply a transaction in which a passive person receives bounty (in the form of cash, kind or counselling) from the rest of the community. Nor, as many still think, is a social service concerned to get people to adjust unilaterally to society or to their possibly squalid environment. ... society must also adjust to the individual. (Ibid, p.185.)

The second point is that social services help groups and communities, not only individuals. Eyden suggested that social services were individual and residual. But dependency is not necessarily a feature of individuals: a group or community may be collectively dependent. The third point is that there is a 'positive, developmental function' pursued through 'co-operative action'.

This is a good definition, but it has its weaknesses. Its essential flaw is that it is prescriptive rather than descriptive. It puts great emphasis on self-determination - either by enabling people to meet their needs, or by co-operative action - when the relationship may be one of passive dependency. It emphasises mutual adjustment, whereas the reality may be a matter of social control. The concept of dependency does not in itself imply either adjustment or control, or determine a developmental function; but it is consistent with them, as it is consistent with other policies.

A social service can be defined as **a social institution which is developed to provide for those conditions of dependency which are recognised as collective responsibilities.** This is a restricted definition, but I believe it reflects the actual use of the term. Housing, health, social security, education and social work are social services because they deal with conditions of dependency. Urban planning, road building, libraries and the police force do not. This is the distinction between social and public services. The distinction may seem irrational, and in some ways it is. The study of social policy has moved increasingly towards treating them on an equivalent basis; but 'social policy', which takes in any policy affecting relations in society, is a wider concept than a study of the social services. The distinction is not completely arbitrary; states of dependency do present a distinctive set of problems, and those problems are central to this study.

'Social welfare' is not used quite synonymously with 'social services', although the terms are very close: references to 'social welfare services' can be found (e.g. Reisman, 1977, 50), which seem to mean, not services to promote welfare, but rather services which perform the function called 'social welfare'. Social welfare can be defined as **organised activity to improve the condition of people who are dependent.**

STIGMA AND SOCIAL WELFARE.

Stigma is an important concept in the study of social administration; it has been described as the central issue (Pinker, 1971, 136). A stigma marks the recipient of welfare, damages his reputation, and undermines his dignity. It is a barrier to access to social services, and an experience of degradation and rejection. "The imposition of stigma", Pinker writes, "is the commonest form of violence used in democratic societies." (1971, 175).

Although some sociologists have tried to claim it for their own (e.g. Lemert, 1972,15), 'stigma' is not an academic term; people who are embarrassed or ashamed of their dependency on social services use the word to describe their feelings. An unemployed miner talks about
> the stigma of going up to the dole every week, I think it's awful. (cited Gould, Kenyon, 1972,21.)

A tenant of a 'sink' estate says,
> It is stigmatised ... You felt ashamed to say you were from Abbeyhills, because of the stigma. (Flessati, 1978.)

A person who had been committed to a mental institution for three days in 1935 wrote to a Royal Commission more than twenty years later asking

> to get my name off your registers so that I no longer bear the stigma of being a certified person.   (Cmnd.169, 1957,97.)

And a recipient of Supplementary Benefit complains,

> It's shame, the stigma of it. (Richardson, Naidoo, 1978, 27.)

'Stigma' is a part of common speech; and, like many other common words, it has no precise definition, but is used in a way that assumes other people will understand it. Exposition of the concept has been limited, and the idea has been accepted, for the most part, uncritically. References to 'stigma' in studies of social administration tend to be made in passing; they are asserted, without the benefit of reason or evidence. I have built up an argument, in many places, on the basis of references like these - a short passage from one book, a phrase from another - in order to illustrate both the way the idea is used, and some of the underlying assumptions made about it. The result is, I hope, rather more than a selective review; it is an attempt to clarify the different uses of the word, to establish whether a coherent concept can be constructed, and to see what the implications of the idea of stigma are for social policy.

Part 1

Stigma and the social services

Chapter 1

Stigma and the Poor Law

The stigma of the Poor Law is legendary. For over a century, people who claimed poor relief were the objects of a policy intended to deter them from seeking help and mark them off from the normal members of society. When the Poor Law was abolished, there was clearly a belief that the stigma which accompanied it would also be wiped out (see Stevenson, 1973, ch.1). But in 1966, the Ministry of Pensions and National Insurance published the results of a survey of retirement pensioners (Ministry of Pensions, 1966). This survey showed that large numbers of people still felt a reluctance to claim which, if it was not attributable to stigma, was due to something very much like it. Among couples, for example, 30% had failed to claim because of pride, a dislike of 'charity', or dislike of going to the National Assistance Board; nearly 20% more said that they were 'managing all right', which could mean that they did not need help, but could also mean that they were too determinedly independent to ask (Ibid, 42).

The obvious implication was drawn that, particularly in the minds of old people, the stigma of the Poor Law had not died. The name of the Ministry of Pensions and National Insurance was changed to the Ministry of Social Security; National Assistance became Supplementary Benefit; and people were given a right to benefit, instead of receiving it at the discretion of a government agency. Douglas Houghton, the Minister responsible, claimed that this had had "a remarkable success. Some half a million more people applied within a few weeks." This view is disputed by Atkinson (1969), who shows that much of the increase in claims can be accounted for by an increase in the level of benefit that accompanied the administrative changes (pp.62-77).

The stigma of pauperism, which had seemed to be the result of a conscious policy, has proved greatly resistant to abolition. As time has gone on, memories of the Poor Law have dimmed, but stigma is talked about as much as ever. It is difficult to understand why, when deterrent policies have been abandoned, entitlement to benefits established, and the administration of benefits substantially changed, this should be so. A study of the history of the stigma of the Poor Law may help to explain the persistence of the idea.

THE DEVELOPMENT OF DETERRENT POLICIES.

In the middle ages, charity was given as a religious duty, intended more for the salvation of the donor than the advantage of the recipient (Fairchilds, 1976). This form of charity declined as feudal society developed. War, famine and disease drove itinerant beggars across Europe; men who spread the diseases they were trying to escape, and who were forced to rob if they could not receive charity (see Briod, 1926). Laws were made to restrict the movement of labour - the first in England was made in 1349. A recurrence of the problem in the sixteenth century inspired more draconian measures: mendicancy was punished by flogging and branding (Chambliss, 1964).

At the same time, the growth of the townships and the emergence of a new economic order provided the foundations of the Reformation (Tawney, 1936), a movement which destroyed both the ancient religious basis of charity, and many of the monasteries which dispensed it. The 'protestant ethic' - which was not confined to Protestant communities - emphasized labour as a mark of divine grace (Weber, 1904-5), and led to the treatment of idleness as sin. Calvinism favoured the teaching of St. Paul, that a man who does not work shall not eat. But charity was not abandoned altogether. Luther recommended the creation of a 'common chest' for the 'worthy' poor (Luther, 1536). Zwingli, another of the Protestant reformers, wrote ordinances on poor relief in these terms:
> The following types of poor persons and country folk are not to be given alms: any persons, whether men or women, of whom it is known that they spend all their days in luxury and idleness and will not work, but frequent public-houses, drinking places and haunts of ill-repute. ... But to the following folk poor relief **shall** be distributed, the pious, respectable, poor citizens. (Zwingli, 1525, 100-1.)

The Elizabethan Poor Law was conceived in less explicitly moralistic terms. An Act of 1576 had made provision for "setting the poor on work and for avoidance of idleness"; 'houses of correction' were established for persistent idlers. The Act of 1601 retained the concern with setting the poor on work; it made an implicit distinction between the able-bodied and impotent poor. The able-bodied became identified as time went on with the 'undeserving' poor, and identification which was strengthened by the growth of puritanism in the seventeenth century. The later development of deterrent workhouses - the first was set up at Bristol in 1697 - was a natural extension of a principle established more than a hundred years before.

The other main deterrent policy in use at this time was badging the poor. Zwingli commended the practice of fixing a badge to the clothing of a pauper to mark him out,
> in order that the poor who are in receipt of relief may be known, they must have a stamped or engraved badge, and wear it openly. (Zwingli, 1525, 101.)

This was enacted as law in England in 1697. Unlike the workhouses, badging fell into disuse, probably because it failed to distinguish the able-bodied poor from others. Alcock, writing in 1752, complained:
> And tho' Badges by the 8th and 9th of William, seemed rightly ordered to be fix'd as some public Marks of Shame, and to distinguish Parish Paupers from those industrious Poor that live by their own Endeavours: Yet these marks of distinction have had but little effect, and for that Reason, I suppose, have been almost every where neglected. (Alcock, 1752, 17.)

The editor of a report by John Locke, reprinted in 1791, gave a more convincing reason for the decline of the practice:
> The law which appointed the poor to be badged was, perhaps, meant for the purpose of deterring paupers from unnecessary applications for relief: but, by its universality, was more calculated to produce a contrary effect; and has, therefore, by common consent, gone into total disuse in most parts of the kingdom. Who can bear the idea of affixing a stigma to a child, and of introducing it to the world under a reproach, or at least with a mark of degradation, which it cannot have deserved? (Locke, 1791, 139.)

This is the earliest reference to 'stigma' that I have been able to discover in the context of the Poor Law; it seems to be an isolated instance.

THE MOVEMENT TO REFORM THE POOR LAW.

Over the course of the eighteenth and early nineteenth centuries, the Poor Laws operated in a climate of mistrust of the poor, and a growing concern about the increasing financial burden that pauperism represented. A belief that the poor had been corrupted by the Poor Laws began to be expressed in the mid-eighteenth century, and became more current from that time onwards. Alcock (1752) wrote that
> When the Statute of Elizabeth relieving the Poor first took place, the Burthen was light and inconsiderable. Few applied for relief. It was a Shame and a Scandal for

a person to throw himself on a parish ... but the Sweets
of Parish-Pay being once felt, more and more Persons soon
put in for a share of it. One cried, he as much wanted,
and might as well accept it, as another; the Shame grew
less and less, and Numbers encouraged and countenanced
one another. (pp.16-17.)

Porteous (1783) claimed that

It has been the experience of every country, that a
liberal provision for the poor has been followed by
sloth, prodigality, and neglect of their families. (p.1.)

Gascoigne (1818) stated that only thirty years beforehand,

A general feeling of self-dependence pervaded the
labouring class; that parish relief was considered as
disgraceful and disgusting; and that to apply for it,
even in old age, was to admit either idleness,
improvidence, or extreme misfortune. (p.8.)

Earl Grey (1834) believed that

It was aforetime a shame such as no man could bear, to be
dependent upon parochial aid - the name of 'pauper'
coming next, in the estimation of the peasant, to that of
'felon'. (p.20.)

Another writer in 1835 commented,

Poverty will leave its impress upon all men, both as
regards habits and manners, but it was left for the
pauper system of England to show that it might be
rendered available to the destruction of their feelings,
and strike out of the machine of man the mainspring of
his moral movements, namely - a sense of shame. (Anon,
1835, 4.)

These opinions represent an important strand of a complex
debate. (See Poynter, 1969, for other arguments.) It was
believed that pauperism had grown because men were no longer
ashamed to depend on the parish; it was essential to restore
in the poor a proper sense of degradation. The means of doing
this were provided by the model of the deterrent workhouse.
Joseph Townsend, writing in 1788, commented that the
workhouses

operate like the figures which we set to scare the birds,
till they have learnt first to despise them then to perch
upon the objects of their terror. (Townsend, 1788, 19-
20.)

It is difficult to know whether this is true, or whether it
belongs in a class with the general nostalgia for a bygone age
when people were more ashamed to be poor. Becher wrote, in
1828, that

the advantage resulting from a Workhouse must arise, not
from keeping the Poor in the House, but from keeping them
out of it; by constraining the inferior Classes to know
and feel how demoralising and degrading is the compulsory
Relief drawn from the Parish to silence the clamour, and

to satisfy the cravings, of wilful and woful indigence.
(Becher, 1828, 20.)
This passage was marked by George Nicholls, who on the
strength of his success as the overseer of a deterrent
workhouse was to become a Poor Law Commissioner; and Nicholls
gave the text, which is now in the British Library, to Edwin
Chadwick, the man principally responsible for the Poor Law
Report of 1834.

THE WORKHOUSE TEST AND LESS ELIGIBILITY.

The functions of the deterrent workhouse were interpreted in
different ways. Some people wished to make it as unpleasant
as possible: a letter to Chadwick in 1832 argued that
> The workhouse should be a place of hardship, of coarse
> fare, of degradation and humility; it should be
> administered with strictness - with severity; it should
> be as repulsive as is consistent with humanity. (Milman,
> cited Chadwick, 1833.)
However, according to Finer, Chadwick did not share this view.
> Chadwick, it must be stressed, never saw in the
> workhouse, as many of his contemporaries did, 'an object
> of wholesome horror'. Its food was to be nutritious, its
> ventilation and accommodation vastly superior to that of
> the independent labourer. It would deter by its stigma,
> its bleakness, its task work. (Finer, 1952, 85.)
Chadwick was strongly influenced by Jeremy Bentham, whose
secretary he was for a period. From Bentham, Chadwick learned
the doctrine of 'less eligibility' (Poynter, 1969, 126). The
Poor Law report of 1834 laid it down as 'the first and most
essential of all conditions' that the situation of the pauper
> on the whole shall not be made really or apparently so
> eligible as the situation of the independent labourer in
> the lowest class. (Checkland, Checkland, 1974, 335.)
Porteous had written, in 1783, that
> where the public maintains them as well as they were
> maintained by their own industry ... if they are better
> supplied, it is holding out a temptation almost
> irresistible to become poor.
> It follows, that no person maintained on charity
> should be raised **above** that rank which he held in the
> period of health and industry: - That every person on
> charity should descend at least one step **below** the
> station which he occupied in the season of health and
> labour ... (Porteous, 1783, 1-2.)
This passage is underlined in Bentham's copy of the tract
(although it is impossible to say with certainty that the
underlining was made by Bentham); the copy was later passed to
Chadwick. The argument contains the beginnings of the idea of
less eligibility; it would have appealed to Bentham, because
it was entirely consistent with his philosophy. Bentham

believed that man is motivated by the pursuit of pleasure or
the fear of pain, a principle that has been dignified by the
name of 'psychological hedonism'.   He argued that it is more
pleasant not to have to work, and therefore that pauperism
could only be reduced if somehow it was made relatively
undesirable.   Porteous had suggested that this could be done
by making a person's condition less desirable than the same
person's status in work; Bentham chose to compare the pauper
with independent labourers as a class, and concluded that the
pauper should be put in a worse situation - one less to be
desired - than that of the poorest labourer.

In a fragment on the subject of 'badging', Bentham outlines
his position.

> The expedient of a badge has experienced violent censure:
> it is a degradation of the human character; it is
> stamping infamy upon misfortune: it is confounding
> innocence with guilt.
>
> Answer. - Degrading a man is turning a man down from
> the class in which you find him, into another class which
> is below it. The badge marks the class in which it finds
> him: and there it leaves him.   Degradation changes the
> class; badging indicates it only ... If the mark for a
> pauper were the same as that for a felon, then indeed the
> affixing of it would be stamping infamy upon what would
> oftentimes be mere misfortune; then indeed it would be
> confounding innocence with guilt.   The mark branded upon
> the body of a felon certifies him to be a delinquent ...
> The Mark termed a Badge and locked to the garment of a
> pauper does not certify him to be a delinquent in any
> shape.   What it does certify is that he is poor, and so
> he is: that he is a burthen upon others; and so he is.
> (Bentham, 1831-2, 602.)

Pauperism, to Bentham, was a degraded status rather than one
on which degradation had to be inflicted.   At the same time,
he was prepared to defend the practice of badging on the
principle of less eligibility:

> The good ... consists in rendering the condition of the
> man of industry (in appearance) more eligible than that
> of the man of no industry: it consequently tends to
> dispose men to embrace the former condition in preference
> to the latter. (Ibid, 603.)

There is a nice distinction here between putting a pauper to
shame and degrading him.   A badge did not degrade, but it
humiliated, and Bentham did not think that humiliation was
undesirable.   His conclusion shows this to be a principle of
more general application:

> By all this, I do not mean to say that under the proposed
> system I would make a point of affixing a badge ... What
> I mean to say is that should that same effect follow from
> that or any other operation, with or without that view,

so much the better: that the principle upon which the
effect is grounded is a principle not to be censured, but
adopted with applause. (Ibid, 603.)

It is difficult to assess how far Chadwick was influenced by
these or similar arguments. It seems likely that he knew
Bentham's opinions, even if he did not know this particular
essay. In the event, he did not follow Bentham's reasoning
slavishly: it is clear from the report that he hoped as much
to improve the relative condition of the independent labourer,
by ending the depressed wages caused by the 'roundsman'
system, as to lower the condition of the pauper. It is
noteworthy, and perhaps surprising, that the Report did not
really argue for the imposition of a stigma. All it says is
that the labourer was tempted to abuse the system
> by the absence of a check of shame, owing to the want of
> a broad line of distinction between the class of
> independent labourers, and the degradation of the former
> by confounding them with the latter. (Checkland,
> Checkland, 1974, 377.)

This is framed in the same terms as Bentham's arguments. The
workhouse was not intended as an engine of degradation; it
would be shameful because it was the mark of a low status.
Rather than emphasising the disgrace of the workhouse, the
Report stressed its discipline, which would be "intolerable to
the indolent and disorderly" (p.338) but relatively a comfort
to the old and feeble. The 'workhouse test' would separate
the deserving from the undeserving poor.

This opinion was not shared by the Report's critics, who
objected that the pauper was to be humiliated. The Times
(1834), in a major editorial, commented that
> heretofore the employment given to paupers, or the relief
> extended to them, has not in many cases been attended
> with circumstances so irksome or humiliating as to mark
> with a line sufficiently strong the difference between
> the free labourer and the pauper.

- thereby identifying 'less eligibility' with circumstances
that were 'irksome' or 'humiliating'. In Parliament, Cobbett
opposed the reform vociferously:
> Mr.Cobbett said, the whole object of the bill was, to
> deter the poor from seeking relief. He had heard of an
> overseer in Sussex who cut off the hair of two women who
> applied to him for relief, put degrading badges on them,
> and in this condition marched them through the village to
> the parish church. (Hansard, 1834a., col.352.)

Badging was revived for a period by certain parishes. A
Guardian reported, in 1838, that
> In the Alresford, Andover, Portsea Island and
> Westhampnett Unions a badge of distinction has been
> placed on women of immoral character with Bastard

children with considerable effect, several left the
Houses in consequence ... (W.Hawley, cited Anstruther,
1973, 113-4.)

Unlike Chadwick, the administrators of some workhouses
evidently did intend to make their institutions 'the objects
of wholesome horror'.

'Less eligibility' was difficult to maintain in material
terms, largely because the condition of the 'independent
labourer' was so bad. Conditions in the workhouse could be
better than those outside (see Digby, 1978): Taine (1874), on
seeing a workhouse, wrote that "this was a palace compared
with the kennels in which the poor dwell". He understood the
reluctance of the poor to enter the workhouse to be due to the
loss of freedom they would experience; but I think it is fair
to say that more than this was involved. The sanction of less
eligibility, as Pinker (1971) points out,

> took a necessarily psychological form. It imposed the
> pain of humiliation and stigma. (p.58.)

Stigma became essential as a means of preserving the
distinction between paupers and labourers, and deterring the
poor from dependency. Abel-Smith (1964) cites, for example, a
statement by Longley in 1873: it was important that

> ... the stamp of pauperism is plainly marked on all
> relief given ... the words 'Dispensary' or 'Infirmary'
> should never be used in forms, advertisements and
> addresses without the prefix 'Pauper' or 'Poor Law' or
> 'Workhouse' ... (p.89.)

In Birmingham, patients at the infirmary were required to
enter and leave by the workhouse grounds to emphasise their
dependence on the Poor Law (Ibid, 131). The policy of
deterrence came increasingly to rely on measures of this sort.
Beatrice Webb (1948) quotes F.H.Bentham, who was with her on
the Royal Commission on the Poor Laws, saying in 1906 that

> We must mark off for stigma the dependents of the state -
> there must be no blurring of the lines between persons
> who were supporting themselves and those that were being
> supported out of the rates - whether on account of old
> age, sickness, or unemployment. (p.358.)

The Webbs record that, in evidence,

> The Chief Inspector and his staff had warned the
> Commission that medical relief was 'the first step to
> pauperism', and had insisted that medical treatment at
> the expense of public funds ought to be rigidly
> restricted to persons who were actually destitute, and
> accompanied by the stigma of pauperism through the
> disenfranchisement of the recipients. (Webb, Webb,
> 1929, 514-5.)

And the Boards of Guardians in 1913 favoured the retention of
a stigma on poor children educated as paupers, as a spur to
parents to take the full responsibility for them. With what

the Webbs call "a curious inconsequence", they also argued
that there was no more shame for a young poor parent to get
help through the Poor Law than from a Local Education
Authority (Webb,Webb, 1929, 748). These people were fighting
a rearguard action. The care of the sick ceased to be
pauperising in 1885; dependency by the old was widely
accepted. Charles Booth wrote, in 1893, that

> There are a few parishes where out relief is considered a
> disgrace, but in most places no stigma attaches to its
> receipt by the old. It is regarded as a matter of
> course, and often claimed very much as a right. (in
> Bruce, 1973, 119.)

Old age pensions were eventually to be introduced outside the
Poor Law in 1908, by which time they were "largely devoid of
controversy in principle" (Fraser, 1973, 139).

THE STIGMA OF PAUPERISM.

The use of the term 'stigma' in the context of the Poor Law
seems to have gained gradual currency over a long period of
time. The idea was not associated with the old poor law. In
a 'Table of cases calling for relief' drawn up in 1797,
Bentham wrote of "stigmatised hands" as paupers who became
dependent on the parish through criminal activity - people
like robbers, cheats, forgers and thieves (Bentham, 1843, opp.
p.360). They were not the only people who Bentham believed
were pauperised by virtue of their bad character, but the idea
of 'stigma' is confined to them. Stigma to him was
specifically the mark of the felon - a mark distinguished
clearly from the status of the pauper.

The word was used more at the time of the Poor Law report, but
it had not yet developed the particular connotations it was
later to have. In 1834, on the subject of bastardy,

> Lord Wharncliffe said, that if it were possible to fix
> any mark of shame on the father, to stigmatize him with
> any part of the disgrace attendant upon the transaction,
> he, for one, would gladly impose a penalty of that kind.
> (Hansard, 1834b, col.782.)

The use of the word 'stigmatize' is tentative. In the
following year, a pamphleteer expressed the hope that

> under the influence of the society, together with the
> force of example, and the stigma which will then be
> attached to idleness, that the number of those men who
> would prefer living upon a fund, to work, will be
> considerably lessened. (Anon, 1835, 15-16.)

A protest against the Poor Laws in 1837 referred to the method
of burying paupers as a

> foul stigma on the ashes of the humble dead (Bowen, 1837,
> 5-6)

and complained of the linking of pauperism with crime rates:

This attempt to poison the sources of mercy, by stigmatising the Poor as a band of criminals, and the Poor Laws as the cause of their criminality, has been successful in an alarming degree. (Ibid, 19).

Kay, in 1838, referred to the "taint of pauperism" that might attach to pauper children (cited Henriques, 1979, 51). In 1840, Dr. Alison complained that

There is just sufficient aid given to stamp the person as a pauper, and so to destroy his independence. (Alison, 1840, 20.)

The idea of a brand, mark, taint, stain, stamp or stigma seems to have been widely accepted, but the phrase 'the stigma of pauperism' was not yet current.

The idea continued in this form into the 1860's. In **The Woman in White,** published in 1859, Collins has a character say:

No pauper stain - thanks to my firmness and resolution - ever rested on **my** child. (Collins, 1861, 487.)

Rawlinson refers to

the dole of charity or the taint of pauperism. (Rawlinson, 1864-5, 160.)

The first use I have found of 'the stigma of pauperism' as a set phrase is in W.E.Forster's speech introducing the Education Bill in 1870: the School Board was to have the power

to give free tickets to parents who they think cannot really afford to pay for the education of their children, and we take care that those free tickets shall have no stigma of pauperism attached to them. (Hansard, 1870, col.455.)

This has the ring of a cliché; presumably it had become accepted in the years immediately preceding the speech. Certainly, from this time on, 'stigma' becomes a common expression in discussions of the Poor Law.

The Fabian essays of 1889 included, as an object of the Society, the intention to encourage the State

To provide generously, and without stigma, for the aged, the sick and those destitute through temporary want of employment, without relaxing the 'tests' against the endowment of able-bodied idleness. (S.Webb, 1889, 51.)

This was written by Sidney Webb, who evidently thought it was possible to preserve the workhouse test without stigma. This reveals a touching faith in the principles of the 1834 report. Although the Fabians made the 'stigma of pauperism' a focal point of their criticism of the Poor Law, it was not completely clear what they meant by it. J.F. Oakeshott wrote, in a Fabian pamphlet of 1894, a call for better laws under which

The worn-out, deserving worker will be maintained in self-respect in his old age; the temporarily disabled will be helped without pauperisation; the children will

be started in life without stigma; the professional
shirker will be forced to earn his own living; the
vicious and criminal will be put under restraint.
Pauperism will be blotted out; Poverty will be a social
disease; and Idleness will be a social crime. (in Bruce,
1973, 118.)

'Stigma', to Oakeshott, seems to mean unfair blame, or
possibly disadvantage. Bernard Shaw, writing in 1928,
referred to it as the loss of the vote: the Guardians, he
wrote, must look after the pauper, but

> they may do it reluctantly and unkindly, they may attach
> the most unpleasant and degrading conditions they can
> think of; ... they can attach a social stigma to the
> relief by taking away a pauper's vote ... (Shaw, 1928,
> 77.)

The Webbs, by contrast, stated that

> Whatever may happen to the 'stigma of pauperism', the
> legal pauper status is indelible and irremovable. (Webb,
> Webb, 1929, 995.)

The Webbs seem rather confused about the use of the term: they
do refer to it as a disqualification from the vote (1929, 335-
6n) but go on to say that

> This pauper status, while affording a definite legal
> basis for the 'stigma of pauperism', is a matter of
> greater moment than any sentimental feeling or
> manifestation of disgrace or disapproval (Ibid, 992).

The 1909 Royal Commission on the Poor Laws severely criticised
the term, not least because of the emphasis the Minority put
on its importance. The minutes of evidence illustrate their
attitude. Mr. T.H. Nunn is asking the questions of the Chief
Inspector, J.H.Davy.

> 2230. Does ineligibility consist of these three
> elements: firstly, of the loss of personal reputation
> (what is understood by the stigma of pauperism);
> secondly, the loss of personal freedom which is secured
> by detention in a workhouse; and thirdly, the loss of
> political freedom by suffering a disenfranchisement. Are
> those the main elements of ineligibility, or have I left
> any out?
> - I think those would be the main elements.
> 2231. Those are almost absent in nearly every form of
> relief which is now being given by boards of guardians,
> are they not?
> - I should not say so at all.
> 2232. For instance, take medical relief in infirmaries:
> no one minds being detained in an infirmary so long as he
> is ill, and if he does not have to pass through the
> workhouse he suffers no stigma of pauperism, does he?
> -   I think only a small proportion of relief is given in
> infirmaries.

... 2234.   With regard to most of the out-door relief
there is very little personal stigma, there is no
detention, and there is, on the part of the women, at any
rate, no loss of enfranchisement?
- That is so. (Cd.4625, 1909, 125.)

When the Majority report was written, the criticism of the
idea of the 'stigma of pauperism' was directed at its
relevance to children:
    The transference of the children by the Education
    Authority is sometimes supported by the plea that it is
    desirable to remove from the children 'the stigma of
    pauperism'.   We wish to protest against the way in which
    this term is loosely applied by critics of the Poor Law,
    without consideration of its justice.   It can only mean
    one of three things: (1) That the person to whom it is
    applied is disenfranchised; (2) that some blame attaches
    to the person in the mind of the speaker; (3) that the
    person labours under some disadvantage as compared with
    others of his class outside the Poor Law.   In the first
    two senses it should be obvious that the term has no
    possible application to children, and in the last sense
    it has ceased, as we have seen, in the great majority of
    cases to be true. (Cd. 4499, 1909, 197.)
Although it is possible to disagree with this argument, the
criticism of the concept is well founded.   The 'stigma of
pauperism' was a feature of the political rhetoric of the
time; it was unclear exactly what it was meant to be.   The
recipients of public assistance were not, in later years,
deprived of the vote, and 'stigma' came, in consequence, to
refer to other elements of the condition of the poor.   It was
not, however, confined to the loss of reputation a person
might incur in claiming benefit.   The index of Titmuss's
Problems of Social Policy (1950) has several references to
"Poor Law, stigma of": most of them describe, not the loss of
reputation suffered by the poor, but the indignities and
humiliations inflicted on them.   Titmuss, as Reisman notes,
associated stigma "primarily with denial of access and with
entry barriers to a service" (Reisman, 1977, 54).   The idea of
stigma had come to be firmly bound up with less eligibility
and the deterrent principles of the Poor Law.

This view has been imbibed by modern writers.   When Abel-Smith
writes about health care that
    the services provided for the poor are generally poor
    services and the process of applying for them is made
    stigmatising (1976, 42),
or a writer in **New Society** asks about food vouchers,
    surely, something so entirely stigmatising should by now
    be abolished? (Orlik, 1978),
they imply that stigma stems from the humiliating practices of

the social services. The Members of Parliament believed they
could abolish this humiliation with the Poor Law, and it
seemed reasonable to suppose that a problem apparently created
by a conscious policy could be resolved in the same way.

THE SURVIVAL OF STIGMA.

There are three possible explanations as to why this did not
happen. The first is that there has not in fact been a change
in policy: that stigma is still used to ration scarce
resources, and keep people from claiming welfare.   But it is
difficult to believe that the efforts governments have made to
alleviate stigma - including the abolition of the Poor Law -
were dishonest, and the differentiation of dependent groups
that followed the reform of the Poor Law makes it irrational
and unnecessary to stigmatise all of them.

A second explanation is that in important ways - the use of
old workhouses as institutions (P.Townsend, 1963; Cmnd. 7357,
1978), the legacy of attitudes of a previous generation, and
the persistence of selective services for the poor - the Poor
Law has not been abolished. The Seebohm Committee, which
reviewed the structure of social work departments, wrote that
        Historically the aim has been to deter people from
        seeking ... help and stigma has been attached to those
        who did.   It is not surprising therefore that many are
        prejudiced against seeking the help of services they may
        need and to which they are entitled ... (Cmnd. 3703,
        1968, para. 145).
It would follow from this view that, as time goes on, the Poor
Law becomes more distant, and services gradually change,
stigma will become less important. The Supplementary Benefits
Commission, for example, suggested in 1978 that the increasing
number of applicants shows a reduction in feelings of stigma
(p.8).   It seems to me to reflect rather an increase in the
number of potential dependants, especially pensioners. There
is in fact very little evidence concerning the influence of
age on attitudes to services, and it is difficult to say
whether old people do feel more ashamed of claiming.   Old
people are often more secure financially than young people,
because their income on social security is higher, because
benefits do not meet the cost of a child on an equivalent
basis to the cost of an adult (Piachaud, 1979), because their
resources are often greater even if their income is not, and
because they have lived through periods of greater material
hardship than younger people.   The statement of old people
that they can 'manage' on benefits may be true, rather than a
profession of independence and a dislike of charity.   On the
other hand, an aversion to dependency is not confined to old
people. Ritchie and Wilson (1979) found that
        people under 25 and over 60 rarely commented on the

atmosphere in the office or on the other people there.
These feelings were almost entirely confined to the
middle age range ... who talked about it in fairly
emotional terms. (p.7.)
Research for the SBC found that, of the opinions of 121 male
claimants between the ages of 21 and 50, 37% had been
reluctant to claim (Richardson, Naidoo, 1978, 25). Few people
under the age of 45 can remember the Poor Law at first hand;
the War, and evacuation, made it irrelevant to a generation of
children, and afterwards it was abolished. However, these
people are not immune from shame or embarrassment. It is
possible that we have fallen prey to the same illusion as the
writers of the eighteenth century: to believe, in the absence
of any real evidence, that people are less ashamed of
dependency than they used to be. No research has been done to
compare the attitudes of people to dependency over an extended
period of time.

A third explanation is that stigma is not, in fact, the result
of the Poor Law. The problems of degradation, humiliation and
reluctance to accept social services are the results of a much
deeper process. The Poor Law existed for a long time, and
laws punishing the poor preceded it. It was shameful to claim
relief before the 1834 Act, despite the common opinion that
paupers in England were shameless: the report of 1834 quotes a
worker who told the Commissioners,
    I know that none but the worst characters would ever
    think of applying for parish relief; and that the
    respectable workmen consider it disgraceful. (Checkland,
    Checkland, 1974, 391).
Dependency was also considered reprehensible in other
countries. The Poor Law Commissioners (1834) recorded that,
in Holland,
    such degradation attaches to the idea of obtaining
    relief, as is sufficient to stimulate a labourer to the
    greatest exertion and frugality to avoid it (p.584);
and in Norway,
    it is still considered disgraceful to have recourse to
    parish relief. (Ibid, 697.)
The Poor Law was to influence poor relief in other countries
than Britain, notably the US, and evidence that is not tainted
directly by contact with the Poor Law or by a similar
deterrent system of welfare is hard to find. But there are
some indications that the problem did come before the Poor
Law. In the Talmud, which was written down at some time about
the fourth century A.D., there is the following incident:
    When Rabbi Yannai saw somebody giving a zuz to a poor man
    in public, he said, 'It were better not to have given
    rather than to have given and shamed him'.
    (Encyclopaedica Judaica, 1971, V:342.)
Maimonides wrote in the same vein about the virtues of the

gift where both recipient and donor were unknown to each other, thereby pre-empting Titmuss by about eight hundred years (Encyclopaedica Judaica, 1971, 342-3). A scheme of poor relief in Ypres, Belgium, ran across familiar problems:

> For as moche as we se many so naturally abashed and ferful that they wyl rather hide their nede than disclose and open it ... these secrete and preuy nedyons shalbe serched out and such shalbe visyted as ar ashamed to be sene and to them that shalbe gyuen that are abasshed to take any thing. (Vives, 1531, 58.)

This seems to me to establish the existence of stigma in contexts entirely divorced from the Poor Law, and a strong indication that stigma is not simply the consequence of either the Poor Law or the principle of less eligibility. It helps to explain why stigma was not removed when the Poor Law was abolished: it was, and is, a more fundamental problem than it was believed to be.

THE EFFECT OF STIGMA ON THE DEVELOPMENT OF SERVICES.

The reaction to the 'stigma of pauperism' was significant in its own right: it became a major factor in the development of social services in Britain. With the abolition of the Poor Law, the services were reorganised to break their connection with its administration. The National Health Service was formed: social work was separated from social security; social security was redesigned about the principles of national insurance. These changes extended beyond those services which had been governed under the Poor Law. Middleton and Weizman (1976) write:

> Although the Poor Law never had control of education, the tenets of the period, influenced by the doctrine of **laissez-faire** and a mandate of complete parental responsibility for children, ensured that the elementary schools remained in their minds a form of poor relief. This was a stigma that remained, particularly as regards education over the age of eleven, to be largely dispensed only by the 1944 Act. (p.538.)

It was in fact one of the principal intentions of the 1944 Act to end this stigma. R.A.Butler, the Minister responsible, recorded:

> It was ... possible for the Act to cut right out of the educational vocabulary the word 'elementary', to which the stigma of an inferior kind of schooling for children of the poorer classes had continued to cling ... It was ... equally important to ensure that a stigma of inferiority did not attach itself to these secondary institutions – and they were bound now to be in the preponderant majority – which lacked the faciles and academic prestige of the grammar schools. (Butler, 1971, 25.)

The concept of stigma has broadened as time has gone on, so that now it encompasses almost any case in which a person is likely to be ill-treated, humiliated or degraded; and awareness of the problem has shaped the development of the social services since.   The reform of National Assistance in 1966 is the outstanding example, but there are others to note. The reform of the law of mental health in 1959 was made after an active consideration of the stigma relating to committal, and the labels attached to mental illness and handicap (Cmnd. 169, 1957).   The development of community-based services was intended to avoid the stigma of individual provision (Cmnd.3703, 1968, 147-8); Pinker (1971) argues that the case for 'positive discrimination' rests primarily on the desire to overcome stigma (ch.5).   In education, the debate in the UK on streaming has not been concerned explicitly with stigma, in contrast to the US where

> One of the central issues in achieving effective differentiation is how to avoid stigma.   The less 'normal', less 'typical' tracks tend to become stigmatised.   In turn, stigma leads to degradation and low-quality education ... (Miller, Riessman, 1968, 105.)

Inferior education results from

> low expectations by teachers, damaged self-esteem because of the stigma attached to lower tracks, poor peer models, dull subject matter, and ineffective and uninspired teaching in the lower track. (Schafer, Olexa, 1971, 12.)

The same argument has been made in Britain in a different terminology:

> once allocated, the children tend to take on the characteristics expected of them and the forecasts of ability made at the point of streaming are ... self fulfilling. (J.Douglas, 1964, 114-5.)

Stigma has been important in the development of services because people have believed it is important. This belief has affected the form that the services have taken.   It is difficult to say whether the effect of this has always been to the good. There is, for example, a case for the separation of social work and financial assistance: Handler (1973) has argued, in the US, that it

> removes the compulsion thought to be inimical to a sound casework relationship, but also allows for the opening of the door to the nonwelfare poor by removing the welfare stigma. (p.144.)

But I am not convinced this is true: social work in Britain is still confused with 'welfare', after a separation of more than thirty years.   There are, on the other hand, advantages in allowing caseworkers finanical powers: it enables them to deal with problems that have a financial basis.   Conversely, it would be useful to social security officers to equip themselves with social work skills for those cases where the problem is not solely financial. The reform of certain agencies in the US provides a unique opportunity for comparison of separated and combined services. Piliavin and Gross (1977) found that

> under the circumstances of separation, recipients tend to reduce requests for services and to perceive social workers as less helpful. (p.403.)

This is not altogether surprising: if caseworkers cannot give financial assistance, they are less helpful.

Stigma may be a myth; but, if it is, it is a powerful one, with important implications for social welfare. The measures taken to avoid it have had important consequences, and may conceivably have acted to the detriment of services.

CHAPTER 1: SUMMARY.

'Stigma' has not been clearly defined. The word became a cliché in describing the effects of the Poor Law in Britain. Critics of the old Poor Law, who wanted to impose deterrent policies on the poor, argued that paupers had lost the sense of humiliation they had felt in previous years. The workhouse was not designed to maltreat paupers, but only to be austere; it was to deter by restoring a sense of shame. In practice, stigma became the principal method by which deterrence was maintained.

However, when the Poor Law was abolished, the stigma of welfare remained. Stigma is not simply a survival of the Poor Law, but a more basic problem underlying the working of the social services. Although its precise meaning is still unclear, it has been influential in the determination of policies, and it is important to understand its nature in order to establish whether these have been appropriate.

Chapter 2

The effect of stigma on services

Stigma is associated with two problems fundamental to social welfare. The first is the **quality** of service provided. The second, closely related to this, is its effect on the **demand** for services. Stigma has been represented as a form of rationing; under the Poor Law, it was used explicitly to hold down demand to a manageable level, and reduce the burden on the ratepayer. But this does not imply the best or most efficient use of resources to achieve the aims of the social services (if these aims are not merely to hold the cost of a service to a minimum), and the effect stigma is supposed to have on demand nullifies the efforts of the services to reach people in need.

THE QUALITY OF SERVICES.

"Whatever the individual's needs and capacities", Holman argues,

> once defined as 'undeserving' or 'unworthy' they are awarded services inferior to others. (1973, 414.)

This does not have to happen - people with venereal disease are not necessarily treated less well than others - but where it does, it arises in three main ways. Firstly, the attitudes of staff towards them are likely to be condemnatory, in part because they share the opinions of the rest of society, but also as a reflection of unpleasant experiences. Willis (1978), reviewing the literature, finds that

> helpers' perceptions of a given target are considerably less favourable than lay persons' perceptions. (p.981.)

He gives several reasons for this. The attitudes of helpers are coloured by practical problems; a person who makes their job more difficult is not likely to be appreciated. Helpers (like other people) prefer clients whose attitudes and characteristics are most like their own. This is not true of many stigmatised people. It is easier to remember cases where a client has done something unusual, which is often something bad. This is no less true because nuisances are time-

consuming.   Helpers tend to dislike clients who resist their
influence. Lastly, helpers are inclined, like others, to look
for   faults   in   people's   characters   rather   than   their
circumstances.   Goffman (1961) adds a further reason.   An
institution runs by a logic of its own; the staff treat
people, not as individuals, but in a way that is determined by
their formal and informal roles. The views that staff members
express are as much a justification of the situation as a
cause of it (p.84).

Secondly, because stigmatised people are 'undeserving', they
tend to lack the political influence that is needed to divert
resources towards them.   In cases where their stigma is
morally reprehensible, as it may be, for example, in the case
of unemployment, they may have resources diverted away from
them; it is more likely, though, that they will simply be
ignored.

Thirdly, within the context of the service, stigmatised people
may be treated as inferior individuals.   One of the most
degrading features of the old people's homes described by
Townsend (1963) was the lack of privacy the inmates were
allowed - few personal possessions, inadequate places to put
them in, and large, impersonal dormitories (chs. 13, 14).
Morris (1969) found, in a survey of hospitals for mentally
handicapped people, not only a lack of personal possessions
and storage space, but lack of anywhere that was private - a
proportion had toilets without doors, and others had them
without partitions (pp.89ff).   Institutions affect   the
behaviour and character of the residents.   Goffman suggests,
in **Asylums,** that much of the behaviour of people in mental
institutions can be understood as a reaction to a situation
where sanity seems to have been abandoned, rather than
pathological madness (Goffman, 1961).   And Barton (1959)
describes one effect of institutional life as a clinical
syndrome, which he terms 'institutional neurosis'.   Many
residential institutions are insufficiently protected from
these problems.   The buildings are physically isolated, the
staff - especially untrained staff, who are substantially in
the majority - tend, for their own convenience, and because
they are severely overburdened, to favour methods that
facilitate the control of residents rather than their care,
and the residents are not in a position to protest (see
K.Jones et al., 1976).

The provision of services reflects an underlying attitude to
the people who use social services.   They are supposed not to
care about the quality of service they receive.   Privacy,
personal possessions and consideration for personal needs are
thought of as dispensable luxuries.   The recipient is treated
as something less than human, and this treatment both implies

and encourages his degradation.

THE DEMAND FOR SERVICES.

The reactions of people to ill-treatment are complex.
Masserman (1943), in an interesting if distasteful experiment,
subjected cats to blasts of air in their faces, or electric
shocks, while they were feeding (ch.4). The cats reacted very
much as individuals. Some cats preferred to starve. Some
waited until they were driven to feed by hunger. One cat
paced up and down, refusing to eat. Two became passive and
immobile at the time for feeding. One snarled when the signal
for food was given. It is possible to recognise in the cats'
behaviour some analogy with the beneficiaries of social
services. But people are more complicated than cats. They
can express their feelings; they are able to rationalise their
behaviour; they can communicate their attitudes to each other.
People cannot be expected to react in a simple or uniform way.
Demand, as Parker notes (1967) depends on what people think
about a service. This is affected by the experience of the
previous generation, and
       whether or not they feel the service carries the stigma
       of social inadequacy, failure, or charity. (p.206.)
This section tries to assess the implications of these
feelings for demand.

The failure of demand.

The recipients of certain services do show a marked reluctance
to claim. The Ministry of Pensions survey (1966) gave strong
indications of unwillingness to claim benefit because of the
shame or embarrassment that people felt. These feelings are
evident in many subsequent studies. A survey in Coventry of
over a thousand elderly people found 281 eligible non-
applicants for Supplementary Benefit (Coventry Social
Services, 1973). Common reasons for not claiming were dislike
of charity, humiliation, resentment of the means test, and the
reinforcement of negative opinions by the attitudes of staff.

This reluctance is not confined to old people. Moss (1970),
questioning 184 people in Liverpool, found that people were
reluctant to apply because they preferred to be independent,
they were afraid, in the case of education benefits, that
their children would be jeered at by other children, they felt
that there was too much 'red tape', or they had applied before
and weren't prepared to be 'humiliated' again. In Ireland,
Clifford (1975) found that 42% of his sample of 110 people
confessed to shame or embarrassment when approaching Home
Assistance, a state agency which gives residual income
maintenance, or St. Vincent de Paul, a charitable institution
(p.46). In the US, Stuart (1971) found between one and two

thirds of a small sample of welfare recipients felt uncomfortable about making their application. This depended crucially on the type of benefit claimed (p.167). In another small survey, Horan and Austin (1974) found only 18 out of 48 people prepared to say that they never felt ashamed or bothered to be on welfare (p.652). Podell (1968), in a survey of 2179 mothers on Aid to Families with Dependent Children (AFDC), a form of residual income maintenance given to female single parents, found that 58% were bothered by being on welfare; 56% agreed that people on welfare feel ashamed (pp.31-33). Handler and Hollingsworth (1971) found that nearly half their sample of AFDC recipients were sometimes or often embarrassed to be with people not on AFDC (p.167).

The takeup of many benefits has been low. Official estimates suggest, for example, that one quarter of people eligible for Supplementary Benefit, and one half of those eligible for Family Income Supplement, fail to take them up (DHSS, 1981, 253). A number of explanations have been given for the failure of demand which this represents. In a survey in Islington, Meacher found both a marked ignorance about benefits, and a certain diffidence when it came to claiming: for example,

Table 2.1: **Knowledge of non-recipients about means-tested benefits.** (from Meacher, 1972, 22.)

	% unaware of benefit	% unaware if eligible	% aware eligible but not claiming
Free milk	45	10	13
Free prescriptions	67	5	12
Rate rebates	39	25	17
Free school meals	6	11	15

It is clear from these figures that ignorance has an important effect on demand; but it is not clear how far, if at all, the residual failure of demand is due to stigma rather than to other factors. There are a large number of other factors to consider. The Supplementary Benefits Commission (1978) attributed reluctance to
some mixture of pride, ignorance, a sense of stigma, reluctance to make the efforts which a claim calls for, a desire for self-sufficiency on the part of an individual or family, an unwillingness to become involved with a government agency and a feeling that the whole business is not worthwhile. (pp.7-8.)
Klein (1975) suggests that stigma is an excuse for an

explanation. It is
> the phlogiston of social theory: a label attached to an
> imperfectly understood phenomenon - when low take-up of
> means-tested benefits can be explained just as well,
> perhaps better, by the information costs involved, by the
> fact that expense in time, trouble and travel may
> outweigh the value of small benefits, and by the ability
> of some people to manage on a given amount of money
> better than others. (p.5.)

Some impressive evidence for this contention comes from a
study of the takeup of free school meals made in 1968, written
up by Davies some years later (Davies, 1978).   I have been
fortunate to be given access to some of the results by Mike
Reddin, who collaborated with Davies on the original survey,
and the following argument is based in part on my analysis of
their results.

Stigma as myth.

There was little direct evidence in the school meals survey to
show that stigma was important in affecting people's decisions
to apply.   "The major reasons for non-uptake in the English
free school meals systems", Reddin writes,
> were more evidently related to information than stigma.
> Stigmatising factors **were** identified extensively   by
> survey respondents (mothers) as accounting for the lack
> of uptake of benefit by 'other people'. It was, however,
> only referred to by a small minority as affecting their
> own decisions.   Thus stigma may be a piece of folklore:
> part of that popular mythology which avows work ethics
> that are not manifest, moralities that are not observed,
> hostilities that are not felt - and explanations of Their
> behaviour but never Ours. (1977, 67.)

The same conclusion is reached by Davies (1978, ch.5), and on
the face of it the figures certainly support this argument.
Davies defined 'stigma' to include the attitudes of other
children and of teachers, a feeling of charity, a dislike of
stating income, and a dislike of telling an employed that one
was applying - a wide definition of the term (p.256).   Of 226
people who did not receive free school meals, only 15 felt
that 'stigma' affected their decision. 15 felt that there was
no stigma at all. The remaining 196 said that stigma was felt
by other people, not by themselves.

However, there are grounds on which to question this
interpretation.   Firstly, it is possible that an admission of
stigma is itself stigmatising.   People may be eager to deny
that they feel any stigma.   The parent of a mentally
handicapped child claims,
> I let everyone know we've got a daughter like it and that

there is no stigma (Cooper, Henderson, 1973, 119) ;
the assertion seems to contradict itself. Tucker (1966) asked
a man who lived on a council estate whether he felt any
stigma, and received the reply:
> Certainly not. Why should you say that? Do you think
> we've all got some terrible disease here? (p.35.)

The same person continued to express the fear - irrationally,
in view of his denial - that if there was any stigma, it might
harm his daughter. The reason for denial is not difficult to
establish: a person who complains of stigma is admitting to
degradation,   the contempt of others, a loss of social
standing; it may be a truth he would rather avoid.

Secondly, it is widely accepted that statements about what
'other people' think are indications of the respondent's own
opinions. For example, one technique for measuring attitudes,
'facet analysis', rests in part on a distinction between a
person's behaviour ('personal interaction'), his beliefs about
his behaviour ('hypothetical interaction'),   and   his
perceptions of group attitudes (the 'norm')   (Guttman, 1959).
The perception of a group norm may be 'projection', which is
simply a reflection of the subject's own values.   Richardson
and Naidoo (1978) interpret their results in this way. 83% of
their sample thought that other people felt bad about being
unemployed and on Supplementary Benefit, and 61% felt bad
themselves.   They suggest that the discrepancy (which is much
smaller than in the school meals survey) probably conceals
some true feelings.

Davies' figures show that people who pay for school meals, in
particular, are more likely to attribute stigma to others than
recipients are:

Table 2.2: Attribution of stigma to others by users of school
meals. (from Davies, 1978, 82.)

	Payers agreeing	Recipients of free meals agreeing.
Eligible families don't claim because of stigma	86	59
Other reasons	72	90

(Chi-square = 4.3, p<.05)

In the US, by contrast, Wyers found that users of different
benefits consistently ascribe more stigma to other people than
non-users do, although this is statistically significant only
in the case of public assistance.

Table 2.3: Attribution of stigma to others by users and non-users of public assistance, food stamps and free school meals (US). (from Wyers, 1975, 135.)

Those who agree that others feel stigma about:	Users (N=72)	Non-users (N=72)	
Public assistance	49	34	(p<.05)
Food Stamps	52	41	
Free school meals	41	29	

The difference in results is, I think, explained by the difference in the questions. Davies is asking about claiming; Wyers, about shame and embarrassment in relation to the benefits. The people who have claimed may be embarrassed, but they have not been deterred. The results are consistent with the view that opinions about other people reflect the subject's own feelings; the claimants attribute embarrassment to others because they feel it themselves, but do not necessarily expect others to be deterred by it, because they were not. Conversely, it may be true that some payers have been deterred, and therefore more likely to attribute the same behaviour to others.

Thirdly, it can be argued that school meals are not typical of other benefits. A CPAG study found much in practice which might upset a child - the collection of 'dinner money' in class, the use of different coloured tickets for those receiving free meals, segregation from the others at meal time, or restriction of the choice of food for those on free meals (Bisset, Coussins, 1982) - but it is the child who experiences humiliation as a result, and the parent, who makes the claim, may be less concerned. This may mean that the claimant is less sensitive to the potential embarrassments of receiving benefits. Like Davies and Reddin, Wyers found a marked discrepancy in the numbers of people who said they felt stigma in relation to school meals and those who thought others felt stigma:

Table 2.4: Stigma and school meals in the US.
(from Wyers, 1975, 135.)

	Users (N=72)	Non-users (N=72)
Feel stigma	12	3
Others feel stigma	41	29

However, analysis of his figures shows a significant difference between the attitudes of non-users towards school meals, food stamps and public assistance:

Table 2.5: Feelings of stigma by non-users of certain benefits in the US. (from Wyers, 1975, 135.)

	Feel stigma	Feel no stigma
Public assistance	20	52
Food stamps	16	56
Free school meals	3	69

(Chi-square = 14.83, 2 d.f., p<.001. Chi-square is used as a test of goodness of fit, not of independence.)

The attitudes of users are not significantly differentiated, although there still seems to be a tendency to attribute less stigma to free school meals:

Table 2.6: Feelings of stigma by users of certain benefits in the US. (from Wyers, 1975, 135.)

	Feel stigma	Feel no stigma
Public assistance	18	54
Food stamps	13	59
Free school meals	12	60

(Chi-square = 1.8, 2 d.f., n.s.)

It is not possible to be certain that these results apply to conditions in Britain, but they do give some indication that it would be unwise to accept the apparent unimportance of stigma in the British survey on school meals as representative of attitudes to other benefits and services.

Stigma, low take-up, and lack of information.

Davies found
> no shortage of evidence to suggest that the absence of information, taken together with mothers' inability to devote time and energy to coping with a complex system, was probably the most important factor causing the shortfall in uptake. (1978, 129.)

This does not exclude the possibility that stigma plays a part. A person who feels that benefits are stigmatising is not likely to make an effort to find out about them; it is possible that the ignorance of those who are eligible and not claiming is a consequence of their feelings about benefits.

This argument cannot, without further research, be much more than a speculation, but there is some evidence to reinforce the idea.   In an unpublished paper, Pinker (1973) recorded that people who were disabled seemed to know less often about registers than people of the same social class who were not disabled.   The paper offers the tentative suggestion that illness

> leads to a denial process and avoidance of services suspected of being stigmatising. (p.36.)

Similar questions arise from a survey of disabled people which showed substantial confusion about registration of blindness. 2% of the sample believed they were registered as blind, and half of these actually were.   5% were registered (CCETSW, 1974, 48). So, 4% - four-fifths of the people on the register - said that they were not on it.   Is this only confusion, or is there an element of denial in the answers?

These studies give at least some reason to look again at the evidence that ignorance causes low take-up.   The survey of pensioners by the Ministry of Pensions and National Insurance found, even after people were told they were entitled to benefit, that a number still refused to claim (1966, 49). Moss (1970) found a small number of people who would not apply for benefits even if they were eligible: 22 people of 184 would not apply for school uniform, and 4 would not apply for Family Allowances (the former name for Child Benefit) (p.10). Age Concern (1974) found 341 old people out of 2700 who had not claimed Supplementary Benefit when they thought they were eligible or didn't know if they were (p.63). 23% of these did not want to claim because they considered the benefit to be charity; 11% were reluctant to reveal personal details; 30% more were vague about their reasons.   Of the few eligible people in Davies' and Reddin's survey who did not know about free school meals, it may have been that some would not have claimed even if they had known.   The survey into school meals was done at a time when there was extensive publicity, and a 'personal' letter had been circulated from the Department of Education to every parent.   The circular led to a substantial increase in takeup (Davies, 1978, 128-9).   Illiteracy, mentioned as a problem by Davies, may account for the failure of some parents to respond. But the number of people who said they had not received information is high - a fifth of the whole sample - and it seems quite possible that people were ignoring information they didn't want to know about.

Attitudes and demand.

There is no doubt that some people are reluctant to claim benefits and services, and that some feel embarrassed or ashamed on making an application for help. This is influenced by the attitudes of other people.   The Ministry of Pensions survey, covering several thousand respondents, found large numbers unwilling to claim because of pride or dislike of charity; but proportions ranged from 19.7% of single males to 29.8% of couples (Ministry of Pensions, 1966, 42). The higher proportion of couples is an indication of the effect of one person's negative attitude on the spouse.

Bellin and Kriesberg (1967) examined why some people on low incomes applied for public housing in the US when others did not. Their sample was small - 75 out of 80 young families responded - but it is possible to rearrange their figures to get some interesting results. The approval or disapproval of relatives or friends was an important factor in deciding to apply.

Table 2.7: **The relationship of the approval of relatives and friends to application for public housing in the US.** (Bellin, Kriesberg, 1967.)

	Relatives and friends:	
	Approve	Disapprove
Applied	22	9
Didn't apply	12	32

(Yates chi-square = 12.3, p<.001)

Further analysis shows a relation between the interest that a person has in applying for rehousing and the decision to apply:

Table 2.8: **The relationship of interest in applying for public housing to application.** (from Bellin, Kriesberg, 1967.)

	Interested	Not interested
Applied	26	5
Didn't	16	28

(Yates chi-square = 14.66, p<.001)

This is hardly surprising. But what is most intriguing is the relation of a person's interest in applying with the attitudes of relatives and friends:

Table 2.9: The relationship of personal interest in public housing to the attitudes of relatives and friends.   (from Bellin, Kriesberg, 1967.)

	Interested	Not interested
Relatives and friends:		
Approve	30	4
Disapprove	12	29

(Yates chi-square = 23.89, p<.001).

The expression of 'interest' seems to depend on the respondent's view of other people's opinions - which may be accurate, or may in turn depend on his own views.   Whichever is true, it is clear that attitudes and opinions are important factors in the demand for public housing.

The effect of stigma on demand.

The pensioners in the 1966 survey were far more likely to explain their reluctance to claim as pride or dislike of charity than as dislike of the service: only 6.8% said they didn't want to claim because of their feelings about the National Assistance Board, compared with 29.8% who were too proud to claim or did not want to ask for charity (Ministry of Pensions, 1966, 42). However, once a claim has been made, it appears that the claimant's experience of applying for assistance becomes the crucial factor. For example, people who receive free school meals are more likely than non-recipients to agree that children don't receive free school meals because parents don't like to state their income:

Table 2.10: Persons agreeing that people are reluctant to claim free school meals because they dislike stating their income.

	Recipients	Non-recipients.
Agree	112	183
Disagree	37	120

(Yates chi-square = 8.97, p<.01)

This implies both that recipients did not like to state their income, and that they did so.

On the other hand, non-recipients are far more likely to agree that people were put off because the application was too complicated - a view which recipients, if they ever shared it, seem to have forgotten.

Table 2.11: Persons agreeing that people are reluctant to claim school meals because the application is too complicated.

	Recipients	Non-recipients
Children not receiving because:		
Application too complicated	43	153
Not for this reason	106	149

(Yates chi-square = 18.43, p<.001)

Klein seems to be justified in saying that the trouble it takes to apply is an important reason for not claiming. But it is less important than dislike of the means test:

Table 2.12: Non-recipient's reactions to statements that children don't receive free school meals because of either a dislike of stating income, or because the application is too complicated.

	Dislike of stating income	Application too complicated
Agree	183	153
Disagree	120	149

(Yates chi-square = 5.42, p<.05. Chi-square is again used as a test of goodness of fit.)

I have already reviewed some of the evidence which suggests that shame, embarrassment and dislike of benefits are felt by many welfare recipients. These results do not contradict that evidence, but they emphasise that people who feel embarrassed are not necessarily deterred from claiming. For the most part, these studies concentrate on people who are in receipt of benefit. One old woman told Glennerster that, when she claimed,

I felt awful going to post it, and when I put it in the letterbox I felt as if I had signed my death-warrant (1962,7).

Another recipient was

afraid of someone coming in and seeing me that I knew. Degrading. (Stevenson, 1973, 29.)

But they still applied. Richardson and Naidoo (1978) found that, of the 61% of claimants who 'felt bad', 31% were more ashamed to be unemployed than they were to be in receipt of benefit.   The   37% who had been reluctant to claim had, of course, claimed anyway; they would not otherwise have been included in the survey (p.26).

Weisprod (1970) argues that the decision to claim a service balances the benefit of receiving help against the costs of claiming a service, which include the stigma associated with it.   If a person is already stigmatised, a little more matters less than it would to someone who is not stigmatised at all:
> the marginal stigma costs associated with accepting welfare or other aid may be negligible even if the total stigma costs of being poor and accepting other types of poverty aid are substantial. (p.7.)

By this moael, stigma is not so much a barrier to access as a price one has to pay. The price may be acceptable to some and not to others.   This implies that stigma may be a problem for applicants, and yet have only a limited effect on the demand for services.   Stigma may, than, be a more widespread problem than it appears at first.   Firstly, even if stigma does not deter claims, it can have an effect on the claimant's attitude to services.   Pomeroy et al. (1970) found, in research in New York, that people who were less willing to ask for help also had more negative attitudes to the services, and were less willing to talk about their circumstances with their caseworker (pp.21-2).   Secondly, the cost in stigma which recipients are forced to pay may be inconsistent with the functions of a service, if these are intended to produce a benefit for the people they serve.   Although stigma seems to deter only a minority of claimants from applying,   its implications extend far beyond that.

CHAPTER 2: SUMMARY.

Stigma affects both the quality of services, by affecting the attitudes of providers and the provision made, and the demand for services, which has been an area on which much research has been concentrated.   It has been argued that stigma is a myth, that low take-up is due to other factors, but the evidence for this is open to differing interpretations. There is some reason to believe that embarrassment is felt by more people than are deterred from claiming, and that stigma should be taken into account as a cost imposed on people who use services.

Chapter 3

Stigma and the social services

'Stigma' refers to many things. A service is stigmatising when it degrades the recipient, or undermines his dignity; when it embarrasses or humiliates him, and makes him feel guilty or ashamed; when it deters him, or makes him hesitate to seek help; when it deprives him of rights, or treats him with contempt; when it marks him out from others, or identifies him as someone who is socially rejected.

At the same time, the social services are also described as 'stigmatised', as if it was the service itself which was tainted. It is possible to talk, for example, about a council estate with a "bad reputation" (Griffiths, 1975, 10); Supplementary Benefits, Donnison writes, are in danger of becoming

> a stigmatised second-class service for stigmatised second-class citizens. (1976, 358.)

It is fairly common to talk about a stigma in a way that makes it uncertain whether the stigma is a part of the service, or something the service inflicts on its beneficiaries. It has been said that stigma "surrounds the occupation of a council house" (NALGO, undated, 10). The personal social services (Jordan, 1974, 179), or public wards in US hospitals (Duff, Hollingshead, 1968, 155) have been said to "carry" a stigma. In schools, stigma is "attached to the lower tracks" (Schafer, Olexa, 1971, 12). In practice, 'stigmatised' and 'stigmatising' are used interchangeably. It is difficult to imagine a service that could be one without the other; Armstrong (1975) comments, for example, that the reputation of an estate

> undoubtedly results in the population itself **feeling** stigmatised (p.21),

a pattern which is reflected in other services.

There are many reasons why a service can be described as stigmatised. It is impossible to discuss these problems without referring to specific programmes; I intend, as a basis for analysis, to outline the contexts in which stigma is attributable to different services, and subsequently to look at some of the explanations that are commonly given for stigmatization.

STIGMATISED SERVICES.

As a general proposition, housing, social work and social security are stigmatised, and health and education are not. But the services are diffuse, performing different functions in many ways; generalisations like this are difficult to maintain. The division breaks down when it is examined in more detail; reactions to individual services are not uniform.

Housing.

"All council estates", according to Griffiths (1975, 10), "carry a social stigma". Stigma is not confined to council estates - Spencer (1964) describes the same process in a private estate, and Schifferes (1978) writes that in Ireland, private rented housing is stigmatising - but it is often associated with them (p.179). Stigmatised estates are distinguished by a reputation which attaches to the people who live in them, sometimes (though not by any means always) coinciding with poor physical conditions and high indices of social deprivation. But, as one Social Services officer commented to Griffiths (1975) ,
>It's mainly the stigma that comes through, not the actual problems. (p.36.)

Corina (1976) comments,
>It seems that some residents are acutely conscious (one tenant used the word 'ashamed') of being given a tenancy which is tantamount to a housing 'caste mark'. (p.44.)

On the other hand, some council estates are highly desirable and much sought after. I worked in a housing department where many owner-occupiers applied for council housing because it was superior to their own. Huttman (1969) argues that, if council housing was really stigmatised, there would be a lowering of the social class of occupants, more reluctance to apply, shorter waiting lists, a high turnover of tenants, people wouldn't go out of their way to get a council house, and adult children would try to move away from the estates. It would be more difficult to find sites for council housing, particularly in the outlying suburbs; property developers would not mix their private buildings with council estates; and there would be more consideration of the alternatives to council housing. She suggests that these things are not, in general, true of Britain in the way they are in the US, and this leads her to believe that there is not a severe stigma on council housing (ch.9). However, there are certain estates

which do have a high turnover of tenants, which are not
accepted willingly by applicants for council housing, which
are regarded with suspicion by owners and other council
tenants alike. These are the 'ghetto' or 'sink' estates which
are the worst kind of council housing (see Corina, 1976); they
are clearly stigmatised.

There are also specific provisions which are stigmatised. Cox
(1971) refers to the 'stigma of homelessness' attached to
large units intended to provide for homeless families (p.19);
Huttman (1969) refers to the closure of units in Lewisham
"because of the workhouse image and stigma that they created"
(pp.310-311). A report by BASW in Kent complains of the
"stigma-inducing treatment" to which homeless families are
subjected, "even if this amounts to no more than being dealt
with by a social worker" - which says something about the
reputation of social work - "but which usually includes
admission to temporary accommodation of some kind" (BASW,
1974, 57-8).

Provision for housing may be made in cash rather than in kind.
Housing benefits, which are payments to tenants on low
incomes, may be stigmatising (Taylor-Gooby, 1976); on the
other hand, there is no evidence to suggest that this is true
of other financial assistance with housing - subsidies on the
interest paid for mortgages, the purchase of council houses at
a discount, improvement grants or assistance to first-time
buyers.

In housing, therefore, some services are stigmatising, and
others are not. The type of service provided - whether
financial or material - does not seem to make the difference.
It is not immediately clear what does.

Personal social services.

In the personal social services, the position is just as
confusing. Like housing, these services are generally assumed
to be stigmatising: "the personal social services", Jordan
writes, "always carry a stigma" (1974, 179). Holman (1974)
argues that intensive casework treatment publicly marks
'inadequate' clients as 'problem families' (p.610). Shenton
(1976) comments that
    Agencies such as social services ... add to the stigma of
    an area by their very presence. (p.31).
Glastonbury et al. (1973) found that 30% of their sample
believed social work departments to be for the 'lazy and
feckless' (p.194). And Rees (1975) reports that, in a survey
he conducted,
    the only respondents who denied feeling some sense of

shame or guilt at being referred to a social worker were either those few who had been in contact with social security officials for years and had resigned themselves to the situation, or those who had sought advice and help with difficulties - such as applications to become adoptive parents, or aids to the disabled - which did not reflect on their position in the social structure. (pp.65-6.)

The functions of local authority social services departments are complex, and it is difficult to draw dividing lines between a social worker's fields of activity. Having said that, it seems fair to say, in the absence of statements to the contrary, that aids for the disabled, fostering and adoption do not seem to be stigmatised. There are, conversely, other provisions which are stigmatising. The reception of children into care, with its attendant implications of neglect, abuse or criminality, can be seen as a stigmatising function, primarily but not exclusively of parents. Social workers are still in part responsible for the compulsory detention of mentally ill people, an action which labels a person formally, deprives him of certain rights, and discredits him socially. Local authority social services administer old people's homes, which I have already commented on. And lastly, the department is responsible for maintaining a register of disabled people, which is not well regarded. As one writer put it,
However much the caring services deny it, there is a stigma - or a special look in the visitor's eye - when your name is on file. At least one local authority runs a register of disabled people who don't want to be included on a register of the disabled (New Society, 1978, 3).
Again, the pattern is diverse, and there is no evident rationale in the attribution of stigma to services. In part, this is the result of a collection of tenuously related responsiblities into one administrative department; but it also reflects the subtle distinctions made between different provisions in different groups.

Social Security.

In the study of social security, the problems of stigma have been more thoroughly discussed and analysed than in other fields. Traditionally, a distinction is made between benefits which are means-tested and those which are not. Meacher (1972), for example, describes among old people
A proud sense of self-respect which saw the receipt of means-tested benefits ... as a stigma. (p.40.)
The means test is believed to be, and often is, demeaning. But there are exceptions: Pinker (1971) points out that grants

for educational purposes are not stigmatising (pp.170-1), and Blaxter (1974) found that, where means tested benefits were used for the purpose of providing health care, they were accepted by the recipients without embarrassment.   They felt quite differently about 'welfare'.   By contrast, benefits which are not means tested may still be stigmatising.   Lynes (1979) suggests that

>   One explanation of the low takeup of the child benefits
>   premium (paid to single parents in addition to the basic,
>   universal allowance) may be that a benefit payable only
>   to lone parents carries a stigma even if it is **not** means
>   tested.

The take-up of this benefit is about 60% (personal commmunication from the DHSS, 1980).   It is difficult to evaluate this figure, for three reasons: single mothers on Supplementary Benefit have nothing to gain by claiming it; being a fairly recent introduction, some ignorance can be expected; and it is paid nominally as part of Child Benefit, which has relatively little stigma attached to it.

Attitudes to National Insurance benefits are also difficult to assess. I wrote to the DHSS to ask for figures about take-up, only to be told that there weren't any, because there was no reason to suppose that there was any problem.   The extent of ignorance alone makes this arguable; but I also feel that the assumption there is no stigma is open to question.   In Denmark, according to Kai Westergaard (who was Director-General of the Ministry of Labour there), people on unemployment benefit are well provided for in comparison to their British counterparts - they receive more than three-quarters of the average wage in benefit - but there is a strong social sanction attached to unemployment, and people are ashamed to admit it (Westergaard, 1979).   In the UK, the level of unemployment is now officially measured by the numbers of people claiming benefit, but many who are unemployed do not claim.   Some of these may think they are ineligible - like married women who believe (rightly or wrongly) that they are not entitled to benefit; but it would be surprising to discover that no-one had failed to claim Unemployment Benefit because of pride or embarrassment.

The analysis of these problems has been hampered by the uncritical acceptance of a received wisdom, which has caused administrators and researchers to ignore the stigmatising potential of benefits that are not means tested.   In reality, the stigmatising effects of social security provision are no less complex than those of other services.

Health services.

Certain functions of the health services are stigmatised

because of the reaction to the conditions they treat.   VD has
been argued to be morally stigmatised, with the effect that
the provision made for VD patients is below standard:
> With few exceptions, the clinics' premises are physically
> unattractive, congested and uncongenial (Singha, Donnan,
> 1980, 151)

This criticism, which I think is an isolated one, may be
interpreting the quality of   provision in the light of
attitudes to V.D..   The same complaint could be made of many
other forms of health care, for conditions which are not
morally reprehensible.   More important is the possible effect
of stigma on the use of services.   Alcoholism is another
disease with negative connotations.
> While more people with drink problems were coming forward
> to seek help ... many suffered in solitude, either
> because they did not know where to go for help or because
> they were afraid of the stigma. (Shore, 1981.)

Mental illness has powerful implications for the patient. "You
mention St. Elizabeth's", one woman said about a mental
institution, "and they throw up their hands in holy terror."
(Yarrow et al., 1955, 34.)   The institution itself has the
power to stigmatise: an article by Phillips (1963) shows how
the rejection of mentally ill people tends to be greater when
medical help is sought, or a person goes to mental hospital.
The effect may be to deter people from seeking help.

Within these limitations, it is commonly accepted that the
British health service is not stigmatising - a view which is
supported by the attitude to financial provisions for 'health'
described by Blaxter.   Mechanic (1974) asserts that health
care
> can foster dependency or encourage self-reliance. It can
> respect and enhance the dignity of persons or contribute
> towards stigmatizing and humiliating them. (p.12.)

The National Health Service appears to have avoided the
problems which occur in other countries.   It has sought to
provide equal standards of care for all - in contrast to the
US, where public wards (Duff, Hollingshead, 1968) and clinics
(Stoeckle, 1975) represent a different standard of treatment
for the poor.   Duff and Hollingshead describe the aversion of
patients to the ward:
> Admission to the wards was not easy and it was not
> accepted willingly by those who could avoid it. (p.117.)

In some (admittedly limited) circumstances, the provision for
poor people in Britain is different in kind from the service
received by others.   NHS spectacle frames, Simpson (1978)
records,
> were frequently rejected as carrying with them a social
> stigma. 'I may be poor but I don't want to look poor'.
> (p.42.)

In another case, the Campaign for the Homeless and Rootless

comments that single homeless people find it difficult to get
medical care:
> The mobility and stigmatisation of the homeless poor
> reduce their chances of registering with a general
> practitioner. (cited Beacock, 1979, 130.)

It is surprising that the Health Service appears to have none
of the taint of other services.   Unlike housing, the health
service was administered under the Poor Law, but it seems to
be altogether dissociated from it - in contrast to the
position in Ireland, where the removal of the health services
from the control of the county councils in 1970 was intended,
among other things,
> to take away the stigma of the poor-law system. (Stephen,
> 1979, 97.)

In Britain, the infirmaries were administered under the Poor
Law until 1930.   A disabled person, writing in 1926,
complained about the degrading practices of these
institutions:
> A man who goes into the Infirmary has all his clothes
> searched to start with; he is cross-questioned as to his
> past ... His relatives, if he has any, are written to and
> asked to contribute for his maintenance.   In an ordinary
> hospital they are content with just your medical history,
> and if you cannot pay anything no steps are taken.   That
> is the difference between the two. (Cripples' Journal,
> 1926, 291.)

The aversion to this form of health care is assumed to have
disappeared without trace.   Cartwright, in a survey published
in 1964, found a possible exception: a private patient told
her,
> I thought, of course, it's a terrific amount of money for
> working people, but if it's the last halfpenny I have I'm
> not going into the Infirmary. (p.199.)

His reluctance to go there may have been because of its
associations with pauperism; on the other hand, it may be that
he thought the Infirmary in question was just a bad hospital.

There is some reason to question the general assumption that
health care is not stigmatising. Cartwright (1964) found, for
example, that delays in seeking medical care were often caused
by the reluctance of patients to approach the doctor.
> We're not a family for bothering the doctor. (p.14.)

Research for the Royal Commission on the NHS remarks on a
similar reaction. One patient said,
> I don't like to go unless it's something bad.   (Simpson,
> 1978, 19.)

An old person commented,
> I don't like bothering the doctor with simple things. My
> wife has rheumatism, but doesn't bother the doctor about
> it. (Ibid, 19-20.)

These statements can be taken in many ways: they are generally
regarded as deference to busy doctors, but they might
conceivably be taken as an assertion of independence, of the
sort made by pensioners in the 1966 study of National
Assistance.   If people said this sort of thing about social
security - 'I don't really need it', 'I don't like to bother
them' - it would be interpreted as a feeling of stigma.

There are other reasons for reluctance to visit the doctor
besides deference.   A patient has been put off by the doctor
on his last visit; "the receptionists are off-putting ... they
think you make things up, you exaggerate"; "there's always a
problem and I just can't put up with a fight every time I go
there" (Simpson, 1978, 22). This, again, can be compared with
a feature of the social security system - the reluctance of
people to claim benefit after they have been refused once.
There seems to be an active deterrence of 'malingering'; many
doctors consider that consultations are made for trivial,
inappropriate or unnecessary reasons.   Papper (1970), writing
in the US, describes the features of the 'undesirable' patient
in a way that seems to be equally applicable in Britain.   The
undesirable patient is alcoholic, aged, dirty, uneducated, or
very poor; he is ungrateful, wants to know too much, or
already knows too much; he is not ill, or has an illness which
the doctor thought he didn't have, or he does not respond to
the correct treatment; and he comes late to appointments.   A
patient with these features is unlikely to be well received
anywhere.

In health care, as in other fields, the social services have a
potential   to   stigmatise which seems   to   have   been
underestimated.   I do not want to say that health care in
Britain is stigmatising to the same extent or in the same way
as social security; I think that would be unfair.   But there
does seem to be a process similar to what is called
'stigmatisation' in other services.   The fact that it has not
been described in these terms says something about the
received wisdom of social administration in Britain.

Education.

Education is another service which is not apparently
stigmatised.   Schools
      are institutions which are acceptable to the community,
      in contrast to other social agencies which may be
      stigmatised. (Smith, Smith, 1974, 189.)
But here, as in the health service, there are exceptions to be
made.   In the US, it has been argued that 'streaming' in
schools is stigmatising, because it degrades certain pupils in
the lower streams (Pink, Sweeney, 1978, 374). Jensen
criticises minimum competency tests for high school

graduation:
>It appears to me to be an unnecessary stigmatising practice with absolutely no redeeming benefits to individual pupils or to society. (cited Cookson, 1980.)

Lynn (1969), writing in Britain, talks about "the stigma of having failed the eleven plus" (p.295). These uses seem to be founded in the view that a person is stigmatised if he is treated as an inferior, which is a weak interpretation of the idea.

There is more force in the argument that special classes for the mentally retarded are stigmatised. Jones asked teachers about the reactions of pupils to the classes: more than four-fifths were aware of pupils being ashamed of being in a class for 'slow learners' in junior or senior high schools (RL Jones, 1972, 562). Similarly, boarding schools for disadvantaged children may be stigmatising, because in their attempt to provide special facilities they also mark the children out from others.

>'Residential care' is the posh word for a situation of stigma and shame. (M.Miles, cited St.John-Brooks, 1980.)

A further source of stigma in education lies in the links of certain schools with deprived areas. "No education authority", Freeman argues (1979),

>however inspired or resourceful, could have escaped from some of the stigma which inner city dereliction imparts to the public services.

Berg (1968) describes how parents from a 'respectable' school objected to a move to a disreputable one:

>It was a bad district, and they did not want their children to inherit the stigma. (p.196.)

The Plowden report (Central Advisory Council for Education (England), 1967) called for 'positive discrimination' in favour of schools suffering from the conditions of greatest deprivation. This led to the creation of 'Educational Priority Areas' (EPA's). The reaction to this provision was not universally favourable. Anne Corbett (1968) wrote that

>There is wide support for the view that to be classified as an EPA is a slur. 'It sounds more like Poor Law charity than an opportunity for innovation', said one teacher. Many (local education authorities) seem to agree. There is at least one which is going all out not to get designated. (p.787.)

Acland (1971), similarly, suggests that the classification of EPA's is based on a distinction between 'good' and 'bad' schools.

'Good' and 'bad' schools are distinguished by their reputations rather than their educational merits. A 'bad' school may be an excellent teaching establishment with a bad image: Berg (1968) argues that Risinghill, in Islington, was a school of this sort.   There are schools to which parents are reluctant to send their children, which teachers are reluctant to work in, and which give the child a bad name in the local community. A teacher in a priority school described to me the problems the school had in recruiting teachers, and the reactions of other people who assumed that no competent teacher would choose to work in such a school.   Berg, in her case study, suggests that parents can be deterred from putting their children in a secondary school by administrators, teachers and the head of a child's primary school (1968, 162-3). It does not seem unduly forced to call these schools 'stigmatised'.

THE REASONS FOR STIGMATISATION.

In every branch of the social services, some provisions are stigmatising and others are not; but the reasons for the pattern of stigmatisation are not immediately clear.   Council estates, means-tested benefits, mental institutions, registers for the disabled and priority schools have little in common that would explain why they should be thought of as stigmatising.   A number of arguments have been put forward to identify the factors in the services which lead to stigma.

Degrading treatment.

One of the principal explanations is the ill-treatment which is a continuing feature of contact with the social services. Hilary Rose (1975) remarks, acidly, that

> The 'gift relationship' which exists in Supplementary Benefit is one of an exchange of public cash for personal humiliation ... (p.152.)

and that to succeed in a Supplementary Benefit Appeal Tribunal,

> the applicant must adopt a suppliant role, like a medieval leper exhibiting his sores. (Ibid,p.152.)

As a representative at these tribunals, I have watched people in these tribunals hold out articles of clothing for examination, interrogated as to their moral worthiness, or faced with queries about their sex life.   Rose calls them "rituals of degradation"; the term seems to me entirely appropriate.   (The law governing these tribunals has recently been reformed. It remains to be seen what effect the reform will have.)

A common reason for not claiming benefits is the reaction of people who refuse to be 'humiliated' again.   It may be that they are being oversensitive to an impersonal process which, in times of stress, they see as hostile.   But their comments tend to be a little stronger.

They make you feel like dirt. (Wyers, 1975, 138.)
If I could be treated like something other than an animal. (Ibid, 139.)
They treat you as though you were muck. (Richardson, Naidoo, 1978, 28.)

Stuart (1975) found significant correlations between feelings of stigma, the opinions that a service was inadequate, and perceptions of favouritism in the operation of a service: which, he thinks, suggests that

feelings of stigma are associated with negative perceptions of how one is treated. (p.85.)

The relationship is unsurprising: inferior treatment implies a loss of esteem, or contempt, which is bound up with the idea of stigma.

One example of the process of degradation is the treatment of people in residential institutions, to which I have already referred. Another is the treatment of people on 'welfare' - residual income maintenance. Briggs and Rees (1980) comment that

In most respects, the evidence we collected did not support the view that transactions with supplementary benefit officers would be felt to be unpleasant or stigmatising. Some experiences regarded by claimants as humiliating were recounted to us, but they were not very common. Spontaneous favourable comments about the last interview and the manners and helpfulness of officers greatly outnumbered unfavourable ones. (p.73.)

At the same time, there is a striking difference in their figures between the expression of general difficulties by pensioners and those of other groups. For example, only seven pensioners out of 285 complained about officials, in contrast to 61 unemployed people out of 395. This may reflect preferential treatment, a reluctance to complain by pensioners, a willingness to complain among unemployed people, or simply a reaction to the differences in the operation of the scheme for pensioners and unemployed people; it is difficult to know which. Whatever the explanation, their impression of attitudes is not easily reconciled with the views expressed by others quoted above.

Coser (1965), writing in the US, identifies three aspects of the treatment of recipients which he considers particularly degrading: the denial of privacy, intrusion into their home, and the limits on freedom to choose how to spend their money (p.145). The intrusion on privacy may be substantial: a welfare recipient does not have the right to keep personal information to himself. Obviously, the agency must have some information to work on. A number of welfare recipients told Handler and Hollingsworth (1971) that their financial affairs were none of the agency's business, which is a surprising view

to take about a means-tested benefit (p.83). But other
resentments seem legitimate; a similar proportion said they
were bothered 'much' or 'moderately' by caseworkers discussing
their social life (p.113). Some social services - in
particular, social work and medicine - put a strong emphasis
on confidentiality. It is a widely held principle, but not a
universal one. The Jenner Amendment in the US, passed in
1951, opened welfare rolls to public scrutiny in the hope of
checking welfare abuse (Cohen, Berman, 1952); but it is
something of an exception. It is more common to find a lack
of care taken with confidential information. I have heard
receptionists in social security and housing offices broadcast
details about a person's claim across a crowded waiting room.
This shows a certain insensitivity to a recipient's feelings,
rather than a specific loss of esteem - although of course,
insensitivity could be taken as an indication of the
recipient's loss of status.

Intrusion on the home is, similarly, a mark of lowered status.
Handicapped people complained, during a CCETSW survey, that
they were

> visited without notice by helpers who did not identify
> themselves or their purposes in calling on them. (CCETSW,
> 1974, 15.)

Their resentment is a reaction to a practice which is
demeaning, rather than degrading; the behaviour of the
officials is a mark of the same insensitivity to a persons's
feelings. In the local authority where I worked, the housing
investigators refused to make appointments to visit people.
They reasoned, firstly, that people would clean up before they
arrived, which would make it difficult to assess their
standard of housekeeping; and secondly, that it was essential
not to make appointments so that they could catch people out
who were not living where they said. This indicates an
attitude towards clients, which, although it is not directly
hostile towards them, does not recognise a need for civility.

Handler and Hollingsworth (1971) remark that it is disturbing
how few people are bothered by unannounced visits from welfare
investigators (p.172). The practice has been challenged in
the US courts; the Constitution offers protection to citizens
against searches, and a group of mothers on AFDC complained of
"unreasonable searches, harassing surveillance, eavesdropping
and interrogation concerning their sexual activities". The
court held that a welfare recipient had a perfect right to
refuse entry to an investigator - but she could hardly
complain if, when she did, she was cut off the welfare rolls
(Piven, Cloward, 1971, 166-7). Offensive intrusions have also
been known in Britain: the work of social security
investigators chasing cohabitation has gained a certain
notoriety. Julian Fullbrook has told me of the time he

questioned a visiting officer at a tribunal how he could make
with such confidence the assertion that a couple were sleeping
together.   The officer replied that he had climbed a gable
below their bedroom and looked in.   It is worth noting that
intrusion into a person's home is nevertheless less degrading
than removal from it - a point which Goffman shows is
particularly important for people who become mental patients
(1961, 130ff), but which is clearly just as important for old
people forced to go into a 'home'.   It is an additional
problem in relation to institutional care.

The third factor Coser remarked on was the lack of freedom
people had to choose how to spend their money.   In certain
cantons of Switzerland, for example, a person in receipt of
assistance is not allowed to enter a bar (Sales, in ICSW,
1969, 150).   Sarbin (1970) writes that
> to degrade an individual's social identity, one need only
> remove from him the opportunity to enact roles that have
> elements of choice. (p.41.)

A person who is not free to spend is not a full member of
society. This is the substance of the reaction against relief
in kind, or against payment tied to particular purposes, like
food vouchers (see Orlik, 1978).   Stuart (1971), however,
found on the basis of a small sample that marginally less
stigma was attached to food stamps in the US than to public
assistance (p.183).   This is perhaps because food stamps are
less significant in limiting a person's total range of
activities than public assistance is.   A person who is
stigmatised also finds it more difficult to take part in
normal economic transactions.   Griffiths (1975) describes how
people living on a stigmatised council estate were unable to
get goods on credit, get newspapers delivered, or get a taxi
to come to the area (p.37).

The limitations on a person's freedom of choice may go beyond
economic matters, not least because the social services
themselves, which work on criteria outside the economic
market, are not always geared to give someone a choice.
Preferences are, nominally, taken into account in the
allocation of council housing; but mobility between areas is
not provided for, and if someone is deemed to be 'adequately'
housed, he has little hope of a transfer.   It is probably
putting it too strongly to say that these things are
stigmatising in themselves. Denial of privacy, intrusion into
one's home, or a lack of choice are important, as they imply a
lack of status; but this is not necessarily the same thing as
stigma.   They complement the process of stigmatisation, and
probably form a part of it, but they do not account for it.

Loss of rights.

A second explanation is based in the loss of rights which a person experiences by claiming social services.   Julia Parker (1975) refers to stigma as a "denial of citizenship" (p.146). Citizenship is composed, not only of formal rights, but of informal ones –

> the notion of citizenship postulates that similar respect be accorded to those who are dependent and poor. (Ibid, 146.)

Rights and respect are bound up with each other.   A loss of formal rights is a mark of disrespect; the person who loses them ceases to be regarded as a proper person.   The most obvious case of legal disability in the social services is the treatment of people committed to mental hospitals.   Goffman (1961) refers to the process as "civil death" (p.25).   A recent British government document suggests that the removal of legal disabilities

> would be a significant step towards removing any stigma associated with admission to a mental illness or mental handicap hospital. (Cmnd. 7320, 1978, 2.)

The establishment of rights has been a major element in the protection of vulnerable and dependent groups. In the US, old people have a decalogue of rights (Bergman, in ICSW, 1969, 430).   In a legal case in the same country, Wyatt v. Stickney, it was decided that a psychiatric patient has a constitutional right to, amongst other things, a comfortable bed, adequate meals, and a television set in the day room (cited Sutherland, 1976, 225).   In England and Wales, disabled people have been given rights – by virtue of duties placed on others – to certain facilities, like telephones, under the 1970 Chronically Sick and Disabled Persons Act.   These duties are subject to administrative discretion, and are not perhaps to be taken as real obligations. Homeless families have a right to temporary accommodation, and perhaps permanent accommodation (which the local authority has a duty to 'secure the provision of') under the Housing (Homeless Persons) Act 1977.   The rights under this Act are residual; they do not apply to all citizens, but only to people who find themselves without an alternative.   They do not imply a right to a home.

These things go beyond the rights of a normal citizen; but they cannot be taken as evidence that mental patients, old people, disabled people or homeless families have been fully restored to citizenship. They seem, rather, to respond to the disadvantages of these groups.   There is no reason to suppose that these laws have overcome any stigma attached to these people; legal reform may be a necessary step, but it is not a sufficient one.

Entitlement and charity.

There are services to which a person is entitled, and others
which are given on a discretionary basis, comparable to
'charity'.   Blaxter (1974) suggests that this distinguishes
'health' and 'welfare' services, at least in the public mind:
> 'Health' was a basic universal entitlement: medical
> services were seen as a 'right'. (pp.47-8.)
Welfare, on the other hand, is paid not by right but by need.
It is, in consequence, less acceptable.

'Dislike of charity' is a recurring theme in surveys which
identify feelings of stigma.   The 1966 survey of pensioners
classified 'pride' and 'dislike of charity' together (Ministry
of Pensions, 1966, 42, 44-6); so does Taylor-Gooby (1976), in
a study of the take-up of rent benefits (p.44-5).   But
Clifford (1975), in his survey in Ireland, separated the
factors, and found an interesting variation in people's
reasons for reluctance to claim from Unemployment Assistance
(a   means-tested benefit   for   unemployed people),   Home
Assistance (a means-tested residual benefit), and St.Vincent
de Paul (a charity). Pride and independence featured strongly
in reasons for not taking the state benefits, but less
strongly in reaction to the charity.   Shame and embarrassment
were less pronounced in reaction to Home Assistance than they
were to the charity or to Unemployment Assistance. Similarly,
Stuart (1975), testing people's feelings about various means-
tested benefits in the US, found no discernable relationship
between the opinion that a benefit was 'charity' and the
stigma that a respondent felt was attached to it (p.86).   One
unemployed man told Briggs and Rees (1980) that
> there is a certain stigma attached to crawling to the
> state for money that is a right (p.151)
- which indicates both that he considered it a right, and that
he thought it stigmatising. A similar conclusion is indicated
by the failure of the 1966 Ministry of Social Security Act to
eradicate the stigma attaching to Supplementary Benefit
(Atkinson, 1969, 58ff). Entitlement is not enough.

Labelling.

Further explanations rest in the way a service affects the
relations of the individual to society.   One example of this
is the problem of labelling. The recipient of social services
is identified as a different kind of person through his
contact with the services.   The services have a tendency, in
common with any bureaucratic structure, to rationalise their
activities by the classification of their clients.   A label,
in this sense, can be seen as a stigma - a mark of shame that
the recipient is forced to bear.

Proponents of 'labelling theory' - better described as the 'labelling perspective' - argue that labelling is the critical act in the process distinguishing a person from the rest of society. The definitions imposed by social agencies become a part of that person's social identity. Holman (1974) argues, for example, that

> Problem families are not separate from the rest of society ... What most distinguishes them is to have been designated a problem family by a social agency. (p.609.)

According to Szasz (1971),

> Individuals categorised as mentally ill labour under the handicap of a stigma imposed on them by the State through Institutional Psychiatry. (p.207.)

Shoham (1970) writes that

> name-calling, defining, tagging is not stimulating reality; it is reality itself. (p.130.)

This is true in so far as the label defines the situation of the labelled person, and changes the opinions and actions of other people towards him; but it is only a half-truth at best. Many people are labelled as a result of receiving benefits - like 'pensioners' - who do not seem to be stigmatised because of it. And, even in those cases where the recipient is stigmatised, labelling does not account for all the rejection he experiences. Phillips (1966) found that the fact a normal individual had been in mental hospital would cause substantial rejection by other people, which can be seen as evidence of the importance of categorisation in forming other people's opinions; but he also found that rejection increased with disturbing behaviour (p.761). The label conveys an expectation of certain types of behaviour, and the knowledge that someone has been in mental hospital creates uncertainty about his behaviour. But Pollack et al. (1976) found that the application of the label to a videotape of a person's behaviour made no difference to their subjects' response to the tape. Segal (1978), in a review of the literature on attitudes towards mental illness, concludes that

> The behaviour itself, or the pattern of behaviour, is the major determinant of the positive or negative character of the public's attitudes towards mental illness. (p.213.)

Nunally (1961), putting the case a little more strongly, says that

> People would be no less afraid of a lion if we hung a sign around its neck saying 'pussycat'. (p.148.)

The label can have a detrimental effect. Denzin and Spitzer (1966) note that the formal legal status of a mental patient makes the attitudes of staff towards him more negative, and this can act to his disadvantage. Equally, the label can have advantages, because it encourages people to make allowances.

Budoff and Siperstein (1978) found that children were less likely to express dislike for a child who couldn't spell if that child was labelled mentally retarded. The label causes people to make assumptions about the person who is labelled. It is, therefore, potentially but not necessarily stigmatising. It does not explain the reactions associated with rejection, and it is not adequate as an explanation of the process.

Differentiation and selectivity.

More fundamentally, the roots of stigmatisation can be seen in the way in which social services set people apart from the rest of society. The tradition that health and education services in Britain are not stigmatising rests in the belief that they do not differentiate between different sectors of society. Holman (1970), for example, writes that
> No stigma is attached to receipt, as they are experienced by the majority of the population. (p.191.)
The main exceptions - mental health and special education - are exceptions precisely because they do separate their recipients from other people.

The stigma of public housing, and in particular of depressed estates, is founded in this process. In Paisley, Armstrong (1975) writes,
> The allocation policy of the Housing Department seems to have been effectively and consciously controlled in a way that segregates Paisley's 'bad elements'. In other words, social stigma has become an administrative device ... (p.20.)
Minns (1972) describes a similar process with homeless families:
> one of the norms of good housing management demanded that homeless families, because they exhibited objectionable traits, should be 'insulated' from settled housing estates. (p.7.)
From my own experience, I can say that it is not always true that homeless families are allocated the worst properties because they are not considered to deserve better, although this may happen. They are likely to get these places because no-one else will have them, and the houses have to be let. From the families' point of view, of course, the effect is the same.

Social security has similar problems. Selective benefits, Jordan (1974) writes,
> have contributed to the worsening situation of the poor by creating an enormous class of people whose circumstances have, by stigma and rationing, to be made less eligible than those of another group who do not

qualify for allowances. (p.14.)
In other words, differentiation and inferior treatment are
combined to the disadvantage of the recipients.   Other people
have argued that the residual nature of social assistance is
in itself sufficient to cause stigma. Beck (1967) writes that
> Residual welfare makes possible the   separation   of
> populations of persons who do and who do not use the
> programmes,   thus bringing the stigma of welfare use
> directly onto some people. (p.267.)

But the problem is not so simple. Jones et al. (1978) suggest
that
> the selective benefits for the disabled do not appear to
> be associated with stigma and the universal health
> service in many instances stigmatizes the way people are
> treated. (p.46.)

These points are open to argument, but they are not untenable,
and similar points can be made about other selective benefits.
Widow's Benefit, or Child's Special Allowance, are selective,
in the sense of aiming at a particular category of people in
need, but there is no indication that they are stigmatised.
The problem is not that there is a selection, but that certain
selective benefits carry a stigma while others do not.

Conclusion.

None of the reasons looked at so far - degrading treatment,
loss of rights, feelings about 'charity', labelling, or
selectivity - explains in itself why a service should be
stigmatised.   There are services which are stigmatising, but
which do not use degrading treatment (like social casework);
which do not cause a loss of rights (like special education);
which do not label the claimant (like rent allowance); and to
which there is an entitlement (Supplementary Benefit).   The
only exception is a service which is not selective; it seems
to follow from the concept of stigma as something that
distinguishes and discredits people that a service which is
not selective cannot be stigmatising.   Conversely, some
services do treat people badly (the regime of some hospitals
is oppressive); cause a loss of rights (like student grants,
which make an adult dependent on his parents); label people
(as doctors do); are selective (like medical benefits), and
offer services that are not entitlements (no-one is entitled
to adopt a child) - and yet they are not stigmatising.

It is probably true that the more of these features a service
has, the more likely it is to be stigmatised.   The Poor Law
had them all, and its stigma was vicious; Child Benefit has
none, and it is not, I believe, generally stigmatised. Most
services, however, fall somewhere between these two extremes,
and there are curious anomalies.   Wolins (1967) gives the
example of Old Age Security and AFDC in the US, which have the

same non-contributory base, the same eligibility and financing
provisions, and which were enacted in the same statute, but
are looked on quite differently - AFDC is stigmatised and OAS
is not (p.10). Wolins gives four reasons for this
distinction. Firstly, he argues that OAS has more clearly
defined aims and intentions than AFDC. This is questionable;
the objective of AFDC, to enable unsupported mothers to look
after their children without having to go out to work, is at
least as clear as that of OAS. Secondly, he says, OAS accepts
large numbers of people; AFDC deals with a scattered, isolated
population. I am not convinced that this matters; Widowed
Mothers' Allowances are given to a scattered population, and
Unemployment Benefit to a much larger number of people, but
Unemployment Benefit is more stigmatising. Thirdly, OAS
conforms to existing values; AFDC does not. Fourth, the
recipients of OAS are seen to be acting as upright, law-
abiding citizens, unlike AFDC recipients. Both of these
points beg the question: why should different services cause
such different reactions? If AFDC does not conform to
existing values, and its recipients are not seen as good
citizens, this is an indication of the stigma attached to it,
not an explanation.

The obvious conclusion - one which Wolins somehow manages to
avoid - is that the reasons for stigma may lie with the nature
of the users of the service, rather than with the service
itself. The reaction of people to a VD clinic, a leprosarium
or a tuberculosis sanitorium is a direct result of their
reaction to stigmatising disorders. There is no intrinsic
reason why a residential institution, set apart from the city,
should be stigmatised; public schools seem none the worse for
their physical isolation. It is not possible to explain the
stigma of these institutions by looking at the institutions
designed to deal with them. The social reaction to mental
illness explains both why mental institutions were built in
isolated locations, and why the institutions are stigmatised.
At the same time, it is true that confinement in a mental
institution is profoundly stigmatising; the asylum sets apart
people who are mentally ill, both physically and socially, and
this exacerbates a reaction which is already negative. But
the explanation of stigma cannot be given simply as a
rejection of recipients. There are services which are
stigmatised, which deal with people who are not stigmatised -
more than 60% of the claimants of Supplementary Benefit are
pensioners, and although pensioners do not altogether escape
from social rejection, they are not stigmatised in the way
that the stigma attached to Supplementary Benefit might
suggest. Stigmatised people may receive unstigmatised
services - disabled people receive non-contributory benefits
like Attendance and Mobility Allowance. The relationship may
be clarified only by examining the nature of the stigma which

affects the people involved.

CHAPTER 3: SUMMARY.

Social services are often described as stigmatised. As a general proposition, housing, social work and social security are stigmatised, and health and education are not; but this distinction breaks down when it is examined in more detail. In every service, some provisions are stigmatising and others are not.

A number of reasons have been put forward for this: degrading treatment, loss of rights, dislike of 'charity', labelling, and selectivity. None of these is altogether satisfactory. The stigma associated with the social services seems to have more to do with the characteristics and problems of the stigmatised people who use them.

Part 1: conclusion

The idea of 'stigma' has been traced from its origins in the
Poor Law to its current uses in the context of different
social services. Stigma affects both the quality of services
and the demand for services. The uses of the term reflect to
some degree a number of related problems, but its meaning is
often inconsistent and unclear. This suggests that stigma
cannot be understood in terms of the services alone. In Parts
2 and 3, the idea of stigma is looked at from the point of
view of the people it affects - both as individuals and groups
- in an attempt to clarify the concept.

Part 2

The stigmatised person

Introduction to part 2: the nature of stigma

Stigma has been identified with loss of dignity, ill-treatment, deterrence, degradation, the denial of citizenship, shame, embarrassment, disadvantage, an imputation of failure or inadequacy, the reluctance to claim benefits, labelling, and feelings of inferiority. I have, up to this point, avoided specific definitions of stigma. Although the concept was born out of the social services, it cannot be understood in terms of the services alone. It is only when it is related to people - groups and individuals - that it begins to make sense.

It can be argued that a stigma is essentially an attribute of the stigmatised person. A stigma is a mark of disgrace. The mark may be a physical one, or it may be something which attaches to the person, like a stain or taint. Goffman (1963) at first refers to stigma as

a failing, a shortcoming, a handicap (p.12);
an attribute that is deeply discrediting (p.13);
an attribute that makes him different from others ... and
of a less desirable kind (p.12);
and
a shameful differentness. (p.21.)

These definitions present stigma as a personal flaw. There is an implication, when we talk about someone who is stigmatised through homelessness and unemployment, that his condition somehow defines his character. George Orwell wrote about unemployed men in the following terms:

In their circumstances, it was inevitable, at first, that they should be haunted by a sense of personal degradation. That was the attitude to unemployment in those days: it was a disaster which happened to **you** as an individual and for which **you** were to blame. (Orwell, 1937, 86-7.)

An unemployed teacher writes to the Guardian:

One visit to get benefit is usually sufficient to make you feel stigmatised, a burden, a failure. (Vellender,

1980.)

A failure, a shortcoming or a handicap are features which
reflect on the person who has them. The idea that stigma is a
personal characteristic implies a pathological view of social
problems. This use is unsatisfactory. A mark cannot be
inherently discrediting; the marked individual is discredited
by the interpretation that is put on it. A stigma is socially
defined. Reddin (1977) quotes the definition of 'stigma' in
the OED: it is an

> imputation attaching to a person's reputation; stain on
> one's good name. (p.64.)

A reputation exists in the minds of others, not in the
character of the person; and the attitudes of other people are
clearly important to the stigmatised person. A stigmatised
person loses respectability, and the shame he feels is a
natural consequence of that.

People suffer a loss of esteem through the receipt of social
services. Clifford found that two-thirds of his sample
thought they would lose self-respect if they claimed benefit
(1975, 45) - which is equivalent to saying they do not respect
the people who do claim. People may become aware of this loss
of reputation in various ways. The taunts of children can be
extremely wounding: Moss (1970), researching in Liverpool,
found it was a major reason for not claiming education
benefits (p.9). And Land (1966) records a pathetic request
from an eleven year old child to his mother :

> Please pay ... 'cos if you're a free school meal child
> you're marked for life. (p.795.)

The stigmatised person may experience discrimination.
Mentally ill people, epileptics and coloured people may
experience discrimination in the job market; in a survey of
ex-mental patients, Miller and Dawson (1965) found that a
third of those who felt stigma felt it only because of the
discrimination they had experienced in this field (p.285).
The link between stigma and discrimination is a close one;
Cumming and Cumming (1965) actually call discrimination, or
the expectation of it, "situation stigma" (p.140). Thirdly,
there is the debilitating experience of being an object of
pity. Scott argues that it is demoralising and humiliating to
be pitied, because this implies that the object of pity is
inferior to the other person.

> The blind person comes to feel that he is not completely
> accepted as a mature, responsible person. As a second-
> class citizen, he must deal with the sense of inadequacy
> that inevitably accompanies that status. (Scott, 1969,
> 37.)

It is clear that these attitudes are not formed without
reference to the characteristics of the stigmatised person.

Goffman tries to explain the position by saying that
a stigma ... is really a special kind of relationship
between attribute and stereotype. (Goffman, 1963, 14.)
I think this places a little too much emphasis on the
characteristics of the stigmatised person; it would be more
accurate to say that the stigma consists of a negative social
reaction to a characteristic that a person is supposed to
have. However, the main failing of this definition is that it
fails to take into account the feelings of the stigmatised
person, which are an important part of the concept of stigma.
People feel embarrassed to use the social services; they are
ashamed to be in that position. These feelings are commonly
described as 'feelings of stigma'.

Some of this can be attributed to a sense of failure; Singer
actually identifies a sense of failure as an internalised form
of shame (in Piers, Singer, 1953, 52). A welfare recipient,
talking to Gould and Kenyon, complained:
There's always a stigma, there's always a comeback,
there's always an innuendo that you've been a failure.
(Gould, Kenyon, 1972, 35.)
Landy and Singer note that mentally ill people feel
the very fact of their mental illness marks them apart
with the stigma, not only of being different, but of not
being upto the demands of a competitive, status- and
achievement-conscious society. (Landy, Singer, 1968,
457.)
This interpretation is important for an understanding of
stigma because, in the way the words are used, failure itself
is a stigma. The idea of 'perception of stigma' is, in this
case, equivalent to a perception of failure, and an acceptance
that failure is discrediting.

However, a sense of shame does not have to be related to
anything so specific as failure. Clifford (1975) records that
loss of face before neighbours, the feeling of being
gossiped about, and the feeling of being misclassified
with low status recipients, seems to be what hurt the
recipients most and accounts, it seems, for much of their
shame and embarrassment. (p.46.)
These seem to be the effects of stigma, rather than the stigma
itself. In practice, when we say that people feel stigma, we
mean that people feel the effects of a stigma which itself
remains elusive and undefined. The important element in
'feeling stigma' is not the stigma but the feeling. Something
is assumed to exist to account for the feelings and reactions
which people experience, and that something is called 'a
stigma'. But 'stigma' in this sense is inseparable from those
feelings. It is possible to have a stigma, in the sense of a
mark of disgrace, or to 'feel stigma'; but it does not make
sense to talk of someone as if he 'had stigma' or 'felt a

stigma'. The 'perceptions of stigma' which figure so
prominently in the debates about takeup refer to something
quite different from the pathological view of social problems
implied by the view of stigma as a shortcoming or handicap.

In practice, the characteristics of the stigmatised person,
his feelings, and the attitudes of other people are bound
together in the idea of stigma. This complexity is
anticipated by the concept of 'facet analysis' (Guttman, 1959)
referred to before. This takes into account a person's
behaviour, his beliefs about his behaviour and about group
attitudes as composite aspects of his state of mind. Although
it is possible, and sometimes necessary, to distinguish these
factors, there are some cases in which they are too closely
intertwined to be separated. The 'stigma of poverty', in its
various uses, implies that the person is poor, which is a
characteristic (a handicap, possibly a failing); that because
he is poor, he is socially rejected; and, to some extent, that
he feels his poverty to be shameful.

Stigma must, then, be seen as a complex concept, which is
formed from certain discrete but interrelated elements. It is
not wholly possible to treat attributes, attitudes and
feelings in distinct sections, but I propose in the following
part to postpone consideration of attitudes and feelings, and
focus on the attributes which bring about social rejection, to
discuss some explanations for these attributes, and their
implications for social policy.

STIGMATISING ATTRIBUTES.

Goffman divides the forms of stigma into three "grossly
different" types: physical deformities, defects of individual
character (like mental illness and unemployment) and tribal
stigmas, including low classes and statuses (1963, 14). The
classification is based on his work in **The Presentation of
Self in Everyday Life** (1959). In that book, he looks at the
effect of social roles - 'performances' - for the individual,
for teams (small groups that have to co-operate with each
other) and for regions (different groups that share space with
each other). Physical deformities correspond to the problems
of an individual performance; defects of character, to a
position in a team; and tribal stigmas, to relations between
groups, which is equivalent to the 'regional' aspect. The
purpose of this classification is to relate stigma to the
context of an individual's roles. It seems to follow from the
analysis that lies behind the classification that any
discrediting attribute may be taken as a deformity, personal
defect or tribal stigma depending on the social context in
which it is viewed. The classification is, I think, intended
to emphasise the similarities between stigmas rather than to

distinguish them, and this limits its usefulness as a guide to
policy.   It is at times uncertain which group a stigmatising
feature belongs to: a black skin, for example, can be both a
physical stigma and a tribal stigma.   Defects of character are
difficult to distinguish from the stigma of status or class:
single parents, unemployed people, or welfare recipients in
general can be stigmatised as defective individuals or as
members of wider sectors of society.   People with physical
defects may be attributed defects of character.   And any kind
of 'tribal stigma' implies some kind of personal defect, or it
would not be stigmatising.

Pardo (1974) uses only a twofold classification, between
'physical' and 'moral' stigmas (p.1).   This distinction, for
reasons which are in part implied by Goffman's analysis, is
not as clear as Pardo makes it seem.   Physical stigmas, like
disfigurement or chronic disease, are socially defined: an
extreme example is that of the Kuba, who regard a certain
skin disease as normal (Bloom, 1963, 99).   Physical stigmas
are governed by social norms - generalised expectations about
health and appearance.   Moral stigmas are also governed by
social norms, but they are of a different kind.   Moral norms
are distinguished from others in three ways.   Firstly, moral
conduct is deemed to be responsible. It is possible to breach
expectations in ways for which one is not deemed to be
responsible - for example, by being crippled - and this is not
generally considered immoral.   Secondly, moral norms carry a
sanction. A generalised expectation that a person will behave
in a certain way, coupled with a sanction if he does not, is a
rule: it creates an obligation, and conveys rights to others.
There   are   certain   types   of   behaviour which breach
expectations, but which do not carry social sanctions - we may
not expect a senior politician to take a rubber duck into his
bath, but he would not be breaking any obligations by doing
so.   Thirdly, moral norms are valued more than other
expectations;   there is some rationale for them, either
religious, or to do with their effect on other people. Rules
for which there is no such reason are demoted to matters of
etiquette.

The distinction between physical and moral stigmas is useful,
but insufficient.   Both terms are too specific to cover all
the circumstances.   'Physical' stigmas do not really include
cases of mental illness, addiction and mental handicap, which
are as likely to be seen as aberrations of behaviour as they
are to be attributed to organic disorders.   Secondly, people
who are poor - welfare recipients, unemployed people, beggars,
homeless people or slum tenants - may be in breach of social
norms, but it would be wrong to suppose that poverty is
necessarily seen as immoral.   The attribution of
responsibility is unnecessary, and this means the norms are of

a different order.

It is possible to refine the classification to allow for these points. **Physical stigmas** need to be distinguished from **mental stigmas.**   Physical   stigmas   include   physical   illness, disability,   old   age,   and   race.   They   take   in   people discredited by loss of function, disfigurement, or infectious disease.   Clearly,   the   implications   of   these problems are diverse.   Illness has little that is evidently held in common with the problems of race; it is perhaps surprising to see old age   included   in   the same category.   However,   it   has been argued that

> Advanced   age   carries its own particular stigma.   In   a
> society marked   by   its concerns for consumption,   money,
> work and youth,   old people represent a special branch of
> deviance ... (Sussman,   1969, 392.)

The   reasons for this are complex,   and they extend beyond the physical features of old age - as the reasons for rejection of racial minorities extend beyond   their   physical features.   I have described them as 'physical stigmas' because the physical features are the immediate cause   of   rejection,   around which other problems are gathered.   A   physical stigma is simply   a physical   characteristic   which   leads   to   social   rejection. **Mental stigmas** are found in   the behaviour and mental capacity of   the   stigmatised person;   they   include   mental   handicap, mental illness and addiction.   It is not possible to describe a   mental stigma   in   exactly the   same terms   as   a   physical stigma, because mental stigmas are associated with patterns of behaviour, rather than personal characteristics.   However, the stigmatised behaviour is usually attributed to a mental state, rather than   immoral conduct,   and   the   mental state   may   be regarded as a discrediting personal characteristic.   Physical and mental stigmas are discussed in Chapter 4.

A distinction must also be made between the **stigmas of poverty** and **moral stigmas.**   The stigmas   of   poverty run the gamut of deprivation: unemployment,   low   pay,   financial   dependency, homelessness, and living in slums.   These problems are linked, simply, by a lack of resources which is socially discrediting. At the same time,   poverty may cause dependency on others, and in   particular dependency on   social services.   This leads to rejection that is greater than the stigma of poverty alone.   A degree   of   rejection is attributable to dependency in its own right,   and it follows from this that **the stigma of dependency** can   be   considered as   a   problem discrete from the stigma of poverty.   It is impossible to separate them completely, but it is easier, for the purposes of analysis, to make an artificial distinction between them. The stigma of poverty is considered in Chapter 5; dependency, in Chapter 6.

Finally,   there are **moral stigmas.**   The problems these present

are of a different kind to the problems of poverty or
dependency, although there are connections between them, as
there are connections between mental and moral stigmas.
Generally speaking, a person is stigmatised morally when he
does something that is seriously unacceptable and is believed
to be responsible for it.   Disability, illness, mental
handicap or epilepsy are not ordinarily thought of as the
result of a conscious decision or act of the stigmatised
person.   Mental illness, and the stigmas of poverty, may be
looked at differently; some people argue that no
responsibility attaches to them, while others say that it
does. A stigma is the result of a moral principle in so far
as resonsibility is attached to it.   It becomes distinctively
a 'moral stigma' when it is primarily the consequence of the
breach of a moral rule.   This includes sexual stigma, the
stigma of criminality, illegitimacy and divorce.   Moral
stigmas are the subject of Chapter 7.

The classification of stigmas I have outlined - physical
stigmas, mental stigmas, the stigmas of poverty and
dependency, and moral stigmas - is imperfect.   There are
substantial overlaps between the different groups.   A person
with a physical stigma may also be stigmatised mentally -
    'Does he take sugar?' (Ford, 1966, 41) -
and morally:
    'Get out of my house!' she shouted.   'Only bad, dirty
    people would have a child like that!' (Killelea 1952,
    cited Romano, 1968, 2)
as well as being poor and dependent.   Poor people and mentally
ill people may be stigmatised morally, because they are blamed
for their condition.   Poor people are 'lazy idle loafers on
the dole'; mentally ill people
    are regarded as relatively worthless, dirty, dangerous,
    cold, unpredictable, insincere and so on. (Nunally, 1961,
    45-6.)
The classification is, as a result, arbitrary to a degree; but
it is necessary to provide a framework for analysis of the
problems the stigmas present.

Chapter 4

Physical and mental stigmas

The rejection of people with physical and mental stigmas follows a pattern which is clear and fairly consistent, but difficult to analyse. In a study in the US, Tringo (1970) asked several different groups how acceptable these stigmas were to them. Rejection was measured by a modified form of the 'social distance' scale devised by Bogardus (1925). Bogardus had asked people whether they would marry a person with certain characteristics, accept them as kin by marriage, as a neighbour, a casual friend, and so on, using the answers to gauge the extent to which one person would reject or accept another. Tringo changed the items slightly, and weighted them according to their relative importance. He describes a 'hierarchy of preference' in their answers. There was a limited degree of rejection of people with arthritis, an ulcer, diabetes or asthma; greater rejection of those affected by heart disease, amputation, blindness or a stroke; still more rejection of cancer sufferers, old people, paraplegics, epileptics, dwarves, hunchbacks and people with cerebral palsy; and the strongest rejection of tuberculosis, mental retardation, alcoholism and mental illness. The only major discrepancy between the order of preferences of his different sample groups was in the attitude to epilepsy, which was much more strongly rejected by high-school students than by those with more education.

It is difficult to find any coherent explanation for this ordering. Tuberculosis is infectious, which may explain its rejection, but it is the only category which is. Some personal responsibility for the condition may be attributed to people with mental illness, but the same is true of people with heart disease or ulcers. Some attributes are more disfiguring than others, but cancer sufferers are rejected more than amputees, mentally retarded people more than hunchbacks. Some diseases are more disabling than others, but dwarfism is less acceptable than arthritis. Some characteristics make it difficult to maintain normal social interaction with a person, but epileptics are rejected more than deaf people. Some diseases lead to dependency, but a hunchback is rejected more than someone with a stroke. Some conditions cause fear and superstition, but alcoholism is rejected more than epilepsy. It is not sufficient, then, to explain the pattern of rejection solely in the terms that a disease or handicap is infectious, possibly self-inflicted, disfiguring, particularly disabling, intrusive on social contact, that it creates dependency, or that it engenders fear. The problem is that different handicaps and diseases have a variety of features that may lead to rejection. Rather than attempting to consider these conditions individually, it seems best to try to distinguish the different causes of rejection.

PHYSICAL STIGMAS.

There are many different types of physical stigma, and Tringo's results show that reactions to them differ. Siller et al. (1967) note that different disabilities conjure up different images in people's minds. Deafness seems to imply impaired communication, cerebral palsy suggests lack of control, paralysis is believed to lead to dependency, blindness to problems of mobility and cognition, and muscular dystrophy to helplessness (p.iii). These are all disabilities, but they are diverse, both in their nature and their effects.

The reasons for rejection are equally diverse. One is that a loss of function leads to **poverty.** A disabled person's capacity to earn is diminished. One analysis of the causes of poverty in Britain (Layard et al, 1978) has found that nearly one-third of disabled single men, and nearly two-thirds of disabled single women, are living at or below the level of Supplementary Benefit. Many of these people are old (p.29). Their age is a sufficient reason for their poverty: because they are unable to work, they are financially dependent, and because pensions are low, they are poor. Nearly two thirds of elderly people live on an income below 140% of the Supplementary Benefit level (p.29) (140% being a measure of poverty taken by Townsend and Abel-Smith, 1965). More than half the poor are elderly (Layard et al, 1978, 114). But among other families, too, disabled people were likely to be poor: more than half of all families in which the man was disabled received less than 140% of the Supplementary Benefit level.

Physical stigmas are also closely linked with **dependency.** When a limitation is severe enough, the handicapped person is forced to accept a dependent role. It is a role that takes different forms in different societies. Hanks and Hanks

(1948) described various treatments of disabled people. In India or Arabia, they were outcasts; to the Eskimoes, an undesirable liability; the Northern Blackfeet, or the Kiwai of Melanesia, tolerated them and occasionally used their services; the Trobriand Islanders, and the Maori, allowed limited participation; and the Bathonga allowed them to behave as normal members of society. In the developed countries, the writers suggest, there is not usually more than limited participation; handicapped people cannot always take on a full economic role.

It has been argued that dependency is a major factor in physical illness. Parsons (1951) describes physical illness as a socially defined role (pp.312-313). A role can be seen as a set of rights and obligations, or, more accurately, as "a typified response to typified expectations" (Berger, 1963, 112). In Parsons' model, the sick role is characterised by four principal features. Firstly, the sick person is discharged from ordinary social obligations. He is not expected to do the same as someone who is healthy. Kassebaum and Baumann (1965) emphasise not only the extent to which other people make allowances for illness, but also the way in which sick people demand special treatment from others. They note that men, older people, and those with low education are more likely to deny that they are ill; they see the sick role as demanding a dependence that they are not ready to accept. Women and those who are not employed are more likely to accept the role, to make allowances for others and to ask others to make the same allowances for them. Secondly, the sick person must not be sick by choice. A malingerer or a hypochondriac is someone who tries to manipulate the sick role, rather than someone who is genuinely of it; the fact that the illness is voluntarily assumed breaks expectations and alters the obligations of others towards the sick person. Third, though the sick role is an undesirable status, it is accepted as a legitimate one; and fourth, the sick person must seek help in an attempt to get better. "The stigmatising of illness as undesirable", Parsons writes,
> and the mobilisation of considerable resources of the community to combat illness, is a reaffirmation of the valuation of health and a countervailing influence against the temptation for illness. (1958, 117.)

These arguments are clearly intended to apply to acute illness. Acute illness, however, appears to carry little stigma; it leaves open the possibility that health will be re-established. The illnesses that lead to rejection - like heart disease, cancer, or tuberculosis - are all chronic. The 'sick role' does not really apply in the same way. Although there is an obligation to seek help at first, this becomes pointless over a longer period of time. Although allowances

will be made for a chronically sick person, there is a limit
to the tolerance of other people, and a prolonged state of
dependence is likely to cause a rift between the sick person
and others who are healthy. Further, the dependence of a sick
person extends beyond physical or psychological demands of
other people; it is also a finanical problem. Temporary
illness, Howe (1978) suggests,
     is less stigmatising than a long-term handicap since it
     does not reduce potential earning power. (p.185.)
Parsons emphasises dependency as the outstanding feature of
the sick role; but chronic dependence is qualitatively
different from the short term release from social
responsibilities that he is concerned with. The undesirable
features of illness no longer serve the function of persuading
the sick person to return to normality; instead, they work
against him, and lead to rejection and isolation.

A third reason for rejection is **disfigurement**. Disfigurement
is not the same as 'visible handicap' - a visible handicap may
be a visible loss of function. Goffman (1963) argues that
they are similar in effect - a wheelchair, or a white cane, is
a 'stigma symbol' that marks someone off for special treatment
(p.589). But disfigurement can cause a number of reactions,
ranging from strained conversations to repulsion and
hostility. Skin disease, which is disfiguring but not
disabling, provoked the strongest reaction by Siller et al.'s
subjects - stronger than the rejection of blindness, deafness,
cerebral palsy or muscular dystrophy (Siller et al., 1967, 59-
60). Disfigurement is not an objective quality; it is
socially defined. Skin colour can be a discrediting physical
attribute in a society where black is not beautiful.
Disorders which seem 'objectively' to be disfiguring are not
always seen in the same way: the reaction of the Kuba to skin
disorders again comes to mind (Bloom, 1963, 99). Ugliness,
and beauty, are social constructs. They convey more than
aesthetic properties. People believe that 'what is beautiful
is good': those who are good-looking are expected to be of a
higher status, and more pleasant, than others who are not
(Dion et al., 1977). Conversely, people who are ugly -
disfigured people - are thought to be base and evil. The
attitude is usually unthinking, a stereotype; this concept
will be discussed in detail later. The problem runs deeper,
though, than the repetition of unthinking prejudice.
Rejection is couched in terms of repulsion. One person
remarked to Siller et al. that
     lack of muscular coordination is rather repulsive. (1967,
     53.)
Someone else commented that cerebral palsy was "sort of
disgusting" (p.53). One woman described her reaction to skin
disorders as "repulsion, shock, fright" (p.59). Another woman
said, "it just nauseates me" (p.59). These statements go much

further than a naive association of the beautiful and the good. They suggest an element of **personal threat**.

Some illnesses are genuinely threatening. Tuberculosis, leprosy and syphilis are all chronic, infectious and potentially fatal. Understandably, they engender fear. The reaction to leprosy is compounded by the physical disfigurement the sufferer may experience; syphilis is rejected as much for moral reasons as it is for infectiousness. But fear is undoubtedly a major element in the reaction to these diseases. Having said this, epilepsy is also believed, in parts of Africa, to be infectious. Orley (1970) records that this belief has been found in Uganda, Tanzania, Ethiopia and Nigeria. Among the Baganda, the epileptic is rejected:

> Even after death the stigma remains and no-one will inherit from him for fear of also inheriting the illness. (pp.35-36.)

This belief may be false, but it illustrates an important point. It does not follow that, because a disease is infectious, the rejection of it is rational. Leprosy was not even recognised as infectious until the 17th century; lepers were rejected because they were unclean or contaminated, not because they spread disease (Richards, 1977, ch.6). The fear of leprosy is almost certainly exaggerated - it is an unpleasant and distressing disease, but it seems not to afflict everyone who is exposed to infection. (Gussow and Tracy state that it is not debilitating and probably not even mildly contagious: 1968, 320) This testifies to the strength of feeling against disfigured people, but it also illustrates the irrational element in rejection. Siller et al. found, from extended interviews with 65 people, that 22 expressed fears that a disability could happen to themselves, 19 feared ostracism by association with disabled people, and 12 were afraid they would somehow 'catch' the disability (1967, ch.5). There is some overlap between the answers, but they give a clear indication of the anxiety and fear generated by physical stigmas.

Satilios-Rothschild (1970) explains this prejudice in terms of 'body image'. A person has his own image of the 'normal' body, which is associated with the image of his own body. If someone does not conform to the norm, the observer feels threatened (pp.99-100). This theory also explains something of the reaction of the person who is physically disabled, who finds it difficult to reconcile himself to the difference between his body as it is and the image he has of what a body is supposed to be. This can be more difficult for someone with a slight deformity than another with a major handicap, because his body image is closer to other people's. Barker (1948) describes greater problems of adjustment for the

'marginally' disabled person than for people who are more
severely handicapped (pp.32-34).

MENTAL STIGMAS.

Like physical stigmas, the different mental stigmas provoke
some   very different reactions.   'Mental illness',   in
particular, is complex. It is conventionally classified into
psychoses and neuroses.   A psychosis is an abnormal or
pathological mental state, of which schizophrenia and manic
depression are the main examples.   Schizophrenia is likely to
be seen as odd or confused behaviour; depression may be seen
as 'giving up'.   A neurosis is a functional disorder, which
does not imply any organic change, but only a change in
behaviour.   Hysteria and anxiety states are the main types;
they are likely to be treated as weakness of character. There
are other types of mental illness: psychopathy, which falls
outside this classification, is a personality disorder which
may not be recognised as an 'illness' at all. People do, to a
surprising extent, recognise the diverse nature of mental
illness (Crocetti, 1973).   This fact has led Page and Page
(1974) to repudiate the idea of a 'stigma of mental illness'.
"Mental illness", they argue,
      is only conceptually stigmatising.   It is a semantic
      albatross.
Crisp has suggested that the diseases, and the reactions they
provoke, are sufficiently unalike for it to be possible to
speak of different stigmas of mental illness (London Medical
Group, 1979).

This argument can be extended to other mental stigmas.
Retardation is a matter of degree,   ranging from 'slow
learners' to people with substantial organic disorders.   The
problems of the most severely mentally handicapped people may
include   a   number of physical handicaps,   incontinence,
epilepsy, problems with speech, and behaviour disorders (Bone
et al., 1972, ch.4), which attract a variety of different
reactions.   **Epilepsy** may be minor,   with no loss of
consciousness; amnesic, causing confusion without convulsions;
or major convulsions, of which grand mal is the best known
form (see Linford Rees, 1976, 158-160).   It may not be
recognised as epilepsy at all, dismissed as a twitch or a lack
of concentration; or it may be a major handicap, causing fear
and revulsion.   **Alcoholism** takes a variety of forms: it may
involve sustained, regular drinking, a neurotic compulsion to
drink, or drinking in sporadic bouts (Kessel and Walton, 1965,
81).   Again, it may not be recognised as a problem, and the
range or reactions it can produce is considerable; in some
social circles, excessive drinking is even a mark of status.

The reasons why mentally stigmatised people are rejected are

diverse.   Firstly,   they are likely to be **poor**.   People with
mental   problems   may   be   actively discriminated   against   in
employment.   Ex-mental patients   are   regarded with suspicion
and   hostility,   based   in   the belief that they can never   be
quite normal again.   Epilepsy is still a reason for dismissal:
examples from   my   own   experience include   a   nursery teacher
dismissed because she could not   be   left to   look after young
children on her own,   which I think is a reasonable objection,
and   a   filing clerk   dismissed   from   government service   for
having fits,   which is not.   In France, epileptics are barred
from going into public service or   becoming priests (Bastin et
al.,   1977,   652).   Mental stigmas can also be disabling, and
disability leads to poverty. Mental retardation makes a person
less   competent   to   earn   a   wage: mental illness   tends   to
incapacitate a   person from maintaining social contact,   which
makes it difficult to work in a job.   Alcoholism,   Kessel and
Walton note,

> leads   to   absenteeism and unemployment,   debt ...   (and)
> social decline ... (1965, 21.)

Of   course,   not   all   people with   mental stigmas   are   poor.
Hollingshead and Redlich (1953) found that neurotic disorders,
in   contrast to   psychotic disorders like schizophrenia,   were
associated with higher social classes (pp.108-109).   Epilepsy,
too,   seems not to   be related to lower class.   It might have
been   expected that,   because epileptics   are   handicapped   in
finding jobs,   and because epilepsy is   associated with mental
handicap,   that there would be a tendency for epileptics to be
poorer than other people.   Gudmundsson (1966) however found a
greater incidence   of   epilepsy in the middle class in Iceland
than in the lower class (pp.112-113).   This is perhaps because
of under-reporting by lower class people,   but that is only   a
speculation, and the figures as they stand are intriguing.

Secondly,   mentally ill   people are likely   to   be   **dependent**.
Financial dependency follows from the   same root   as   poverty,
but   there   are   other   sorts   of   dependency.   Severe mental
handicap   leads   to   profound   physical   dependency   on other
people; some forms of mental illness, implying an inability to
cope,   may also lead   to   physical dependency.   Psychological
dependency   may   be   associated   with   certain neuroses.   The
concept   of   the sick role again gives some indication of   the
implications   of   this dependency.   A   person with   an   acute
mental illness is expected to seek help, he is condemned if he
does not,   and allowances will   be   made for him until he gets
better -   although this reaction is mixed with rejection if he
does   seek   help,   because   of   the   fear   that mental illness
generates.   A lingering implication remains, after this, that
he   cannot recover completely,   and the effect   is   similar to
someone   with   a   chronic disability: he   is   forced   into   a
dependent, and inferior, social role.

Thirdly, mentally ill people are rejected because of their
behaviour. "What psychiatrists see as mental illness",
Goffman points out,
> the lay public usually sees as offensive behaviour -
> behaviour worthy of scorn, hostility and other negative
> social sanctions. (1967, 137.)

There have been criticisms that the term 'mental illness' is
too often used as a rationalisation of antisocial behaviour
(Cohen, 1966, 66 ff.; Wootton, 1959). There is a **moral**
implication attaching to certain mental stigmas. Mentally ill
people may see themselves as 'sinners'. Alcoholism is seen as
a defect of character. This is because individual
responsibility is attached to the actions of the people
concerned.

Medical practitioners distinguish behaviour that is offensive
or unusual from 'mental illness' by their diagnoses. They can
take away moral responsibility by certifying that a person is
ill. But the name of mental illness itself is a cause of
rejection. Mental patients, and ex-mental patients, are more
likely to be rejected than those whose behaviour is simply odd
(Cumming, Cumming, 1957; Phillips, 1963). Criticisms have
been made - with some justification - of the importance
attached to diagnoses which are imprecise and too firmly
founded in organic medicine. But the labelling perspective is
not altogether satisfactory; all the indications are that it
is the behaviour of mentally ill people which is the main
cause of rejection.

Mental stigmas are disruptive of social relationships.
Mentally ill people fail to observe the rules of normal
conversation (Goffman, 1967, 137-148). Mental retardation, or
an epileptic fit, can be very intrusive in a conversation.
They prompt uncertainty and consternation; people don't like
it when they don't know what to expect. The feeling is well
expressed by the parent of an epileptic child:
> For the most part people are startled and flabbergasted
> and for some reason horrified because they've never seen
> it and they don't know what it's all about ... (Cooper,
> Henderson, 1973, 111.)

Novak and Lerner (1968) found that people were less keen to
interact with someone who had had a nervous breakdown if he
was like themselves. The trend was clear, if not
statistically significant. Lehtinen and Vaisanen (1978)
found, in a survey of a thousand Finns, that attitudes to
mental illness were less favourable when the person who held
them showed signs of psychological disturbance himself (pp.65-
66). These results, though obviously open to argument,
suggest that the reaction caused is not solely the result of a
dislike of the unfamiliar. There seems, again, to be a sense
of personal threat.

Mental stigmas, like physical stigmas, provoke anxiety and fear; and Lyketsos and Panayotakopoulos (1970) found that prejudice against mental illness was associated directly with the fear of it. Mental stigmas have been the object of superstition. Mentally handicapped children were believed to be 'changelings' - children exchanged by fairies or demons for real children. 'Changelings' were recognised not only by their ugliness, but by their inability to speak or laugh. Martin Luther wrote that

> The Devil sits in such changelings where their soul should have been. (cited by Wolfensberger, 1969, 71.)

This belief survived for centuries. Haffter (1968) notes eight recorded cases, in Germany, Scotland and Ireland, between 1880 and 1895, when 'changelings' were seriously maltreated or killed - perhaps burned alive - by their parents (p.60). Epilepsy has also been the object of superstition. The word itself derives from a root meaning 'to lay hold on' - implying possession by spirits or devils (Hudzinski, 1975, 27). And madness was also linked with possession. Lyketsos and Panayotakopoulos (1970) found that superstitious people in Greece were less likely than other prejudiced people openly to avoid, condemn, or show aggression to the mentally ill, but they were also much more likely to put off the time when mentally ill people would get help (p.181). This may be a reflection of a rural culture; or it may be that their fear causes them to prolong a period of uncertainty so that they will not have to know the worst. It seems to me that this superstition reflects the apprehension feel about mental stigmas, rather than being a cause of it. Superstition is a rationalisation of an experience that is not understood. The rejection of these stigmas is best explained in terms of the fear they cause.

Foucault (1961) suggests that madness filled a void when leprosy ceased to be important in Europe; madmen became the new lepers. The idea of 'mental illness' probably increased the rejection of madness, because the idea of illness conveys a further threat.

> All those forms of unreason which had replaced leprosy in the geography of evil, and which had been banished into the remotest social distance, now became a visible leprosy ... Unreason was once more present, but marked now by an imaginary stigma of disease, which added to its powers of terror. (Foucault, 1961, 205.)

Madness is beyond the bounds of normality. This is true in other societies besides our own. Jaques (1960) describes how, in Vietnam, mad people would be chained in one room and left there, even years after their madness had apparently subsided (p.12). Orley (1970) gives a fascinating account of the attitudes of the Baganda:

> In the old days mad people were put into the stocks until

they got better or died, but in these days there can be
few Baganda who have not heard of Butabika, the Mental
Hospital at Kampala, even though it was only opened ten
years ago. It is now regarded as a natural replacement
for the stocks of old. (p.30.)
This gives some support to Szasz's apparently extravagant
claim that the function of experts in psychiatry is
to justify the majority in rejecting and persecuting the
minority. (1971, 240.)
I do not think this is true - Szasz seems to me to confuse
effect and intention - but it would be wrong to pretend that
there is no case to answer.

REHABILITATION.

Certain problems are distinctive to physical and mental
stigmas - the problems of disfigurement, and the sense of
threat that physical and mental stigmas produce in others.
Both physical and mental stigmas disturb social interaction.
The main problem is one of social adjustment: how to make
these people acceptable to themselves and to society. This
process is called rehabilitation. It is an ambiguous concept,
which may imply three things: first, that a person's physical
or mental capacities should be restored, or at least developed
to their full potential; second, that his competence to fill
social roles should be established; and thirdly, that he
should be integrated into society.

Physical and mental stigmas spoil social roles by limiting a
person's capacity to fulfil them, or by opening a distance
between the stigmatised person and others. Rehabilitation is
a means of overcoming these problems, and the stigma which
accompanies them. Conversely, a sense of stigma could be
argued to improve the possibility of rehabilitation. A person
who recognises his condition as an undesirable one will make
an effort to get out of it. Chaiklin and Warfield (1973)
found that amputees who denied feeling stigma made slower
progress towards rehabilitation (p.164). This is analogous to
the position of the sick role, which makes temporary
dependency legitimate while encouraging a person to regain his
health.

The essential problem is to restore the dignity of the
stigmatised person. Safilios-Rothschild (1970) writes that
Often serious psychological problems become accentuated
after the completion of rehabilitation. (p.250.)
It is a strange concept of 'rehabilitation' that leaves people
with serious problems. This comes of seeing rehabilitation as
a development of physical capacity. Rehabilitation which
improves the psychological state of the stigmatised person
asks for rather more. Payne (1980) argues:

It is undoubtedly true that the individual social worker
can do nothing in everday work to affect the general
position whereby the client groups and the services of
his agency are stigmatised. In individual cases,
however, it may be possible to manage some of the
personal effects of stigma felt by clients, and this is
worthwhile for three reasons. First, stigma management
may reduce feelings of distress felt by clients. Second,
it may enhance the effect of interventions designed to
help clients by reducing the damage caused by stigma.
Third, it may have a cumulative effect on perceptions of
the social services and their clients. (p.44.)

I must confess to some scepticism about this. Although what
Payne says may be true of some individuals, it is questionable
whether it can be generally applied to people who are
physically or mentally stigmatised. The problems of
stigmatised people stem from a complex series of social
relationships. Casework can help some individuals to adjust
to their social circumstances, and perhaps revive the spirits
through a kind of faith healing; but where the problem rests
in those circumstances, it cannot deal effectively with the
problems that stigmatised people experience.

Another way of trying to deal with the problem is to encourage
participation in a self-help group. This may have the effect
of changing a person's social circle, and establishing
sympathetic people as 'significant others'. Self-help groups
are of two kinds. One is the type which, like Alcoholics
Anonymous, uses the knowledge and experience of rehabilitated
individuals to redirect others (Trice, Roman, 1970). The
other is the group which seeks to establish mutual respect and
support, and perhaps to establish a common identity in
reaction to a common experience of rejection. The problem
with either approach is that it rests in participation, and
participation may, for a stigmatised person, be difficult to
achieve. Firstly, it is necessary for him to avoid withdrawal
from society. It may be easier when the people he will
associate with are like himself, but it is never easy.
Secondly, he must admit he is like others who are stigmatised,
which it may also be difficult to do - or unreasonable to ask
of him, because he may have nothing in common with the group
apart from his stigma. Thirdly, there are often financial and
physical obstacles to participation in groups for which
assistance may be required.

A further method is to attempt to change the attitudes of
stigmatised people through a process of education. The
factors which affect this process are discussed in chapter 8.
In this context, the problem may be approached by the
education of individuals, so that in turn they will seek to
change the opinions of the people they meet. Gussow and Tracy

(1968) describe how certain sufferers from leprosy have become militant in correcting misapprehensions about the disease (pp.322-323). However, this requires a certain temperament which not everyone possesses.

CHAPTER 4: SUMMARY

Different handicaps and diseases have a variety of features which may lead to rejection. Physical stigmas may be rejected because they lead to poverty, or dependency, and because they cause disfigurement, which leads to repulsion and fear. Mental stigmas similarly may be related to poverty or dependency, but other grounds for rejection include the perception of behaviour as moral or disruptive, and the ability of mental illness to provoke anxiety or fear.

Policies for mentally and physically stigmatised people may be directed to reintegrate them into the community by restoring their capacity to function in society and by changing their perceptions of their role.

Chapter 5

The rejection of poverty

Although attitudes to the poor are often negative, a major survey undertaken in the nine countries of the European Community found substantial differences in the attitudes to poverty of people in different nations. People in Britain were far more likely than others to attribute poverty to laziness or lack of willpower - 43% of Britons said so, compared with 23% in West Germany, 16% in France, and 12% in the Netherlands (Riffault, Rabier, 1977, 72). There is no distinction in this between the deserving and the undeserving poor. Poverty is a sign that the person is not deserving, and it is therefore a cause of social rejection.

"There is absolutely no evidence", Handler (1972) writes,
>   to support the notion that the working poor have
>   deserving poor status. (p.152.)

He argues that it is not acceptable to earn only a part of what one needs to live. Matza (1967) writes of the 'disreputable poor' as

>   the people who remain unemployed, or casually or
>   irregularly employed, even during periods approaching
>   full employment. (p.289.)

This recognises in part that the working poor, as well as the unemployed, may be stigmatised. In a later version of this paper, he develops this idea into the concept of 'sub-employment'. Subemployed people may be working, but their work is not adequate to bring them the full respect and status accorded to other people in society. They are consequently stigmatised (Matza, Miller, 1976, 661-662). Support for this view can be found in Newby's study of agricultural workers (1977), or Walsh's description of dustmen in the US (1974). Those who are working may be less disreputable than those who are not, but they are disreputable nevertheless.

The idea of poverty itself is stigmatising. Marsden (1973) notes how

>   Mothers found the word insulting ... the words obviously

carried a stigma, and the mothers preferred to talk of being 'hard up'. (pp.59-60.)
Harvey (1970) gives the example of Potter Addition, a community in the mid-west US, which is the object of 'stigmatic labelling'. The community consists of the working poor and marginally employed. But they resist the imputation that they are poor:

> To be poor in their minds is to be useless, to be a relief cheater, and to be despicable ... To finally admit that they are indeed poor is to give up the last line of self-defence against degradation. (p.140.)

Blaxter (1974) found, by contrast, that

> People gave no impression of wishing to conceal, or being ashamed of, lack of money (p.50);

and it is perhaps possible to distinguish lack of money from poverty. As Bosanquet argued (1902),

> To have classified a man as belonging to the poor, or the residuum, or the submerged, means that we no longer expect from him the qualities of independence and responsibility which we assume as a matter of course in all others.

The rejection of poverty has important implications for the social services. Social services exist, in large part, to offer support to people in need. But need is often defined by poverty, and a resort to the social services - a request for help - is an admission that one is poor. "I wouldn't go within a mile of the Home Assistance", one person told Clifford (1974). "It has the brand of poverty on it." (p.494.)

CLASS, POVERTY AND POWER.

People who are poor belong to inferior classes in society. Classes, by Weber's definition,

> are groups of people who, from the standpoint of specific interests, have the same economic position... (1967, 31-2.)

This idea is closely linked with status. A status is a structured form of social identity which identifies the roles a person is expected to play, and the reactions of other people to those roles. But status

> is in the main conditioned as well as expressed through a specific style of life (Weber, 1967, 31-32),

which emphasises the material basis of status. Weber argues that

> Social honour can adhere directly to a class situation, and it is also, indeed most of the time, determined by the average class situation of the status-group members. (1967, 31-32.)

Stigma adheres to class, as it does to status. If status is a form of social honour, and low class implies low status, then poverty is associated with a lack of social honour. But this cannot be taken for granted; the association of social roles, social honour and economic circumstances is a process which needs to be explained.

Poor people, in general, lack power. It is not possible to talk meaningfully about power as a monolithic concept. Power is diffuse, taking a different shape in economic, social and political affairs. It is made up of different elements: notably, control, authority, and influence. A person has a degree of **control** over another when he has an effective sanction against him. He has **authority** when his commands are accepted as legitimate. He has **influence** when his opinions or desires are likely to be accepted by another. There is, of course, a great deal of overlap between these sorts of power, but they are not the same. Poor people lack power in every sense. They have no resources to command; they have no economic sanction, and little influence or authority. Their social power is restricted. They have no effective social sanction - rejection or condemnation by the poor distresses no-one but other poor people. They have no social authority, because poverty is not a legitimate status in society. They have little social influence, because they are less able than others to summon the resources needed to gain it. Similarly, their political power is limited. Their only authority, and their only effective sanction, is found in so far as they constitute a part of the electorate; there are few people to speak for them, and with neither sanction nor authority to support their arguments, they are able to exercise little influence.

Powerlessness is treated with contempt. Adorno et al. (1950), examining authoritarian tendencies, identified
> a desperate clinging to what appears to be strong and a disdainful rejection of whatever is relegated to the bottom. (p.971.)

Fromm (1942) follows a similar line of argument, and comes to the conclusion that some people like to be in a hierarchy. Put crudely, the great advantage of looking up to some people is that you can look down on others. This type of explanation is attractive, but even if there are psychologies common to different societies, they manifest these views in different ways - there are enormous differences in attitudes to poverty, even between countries as similar as the members of the European Community. The psychology of contempt reflects these social differences, rather than explaining them. Sociological explanations may seem tame by comparison, but they are also much sounder.

Shils (1968) argues that social honour - 'deference' - is a

function of power. We defer to those who are stronger than
ourselves, and we contemn poverty because it has no power
(1968, 104-108). But the process is more complex than this
suggests. Power and deference are associated through a
person's status. A status is 'a collection of rights and
duties' (Linton, 1936, 113), and people without power have few
rights because few people have obligations towards them. A
person with low status has little power. Status has elements,
though, not only of power, rights and obligations, but also of
expectations, honour, economic position, and life style. The
question remains why these things should be associated.

The simplest explanation is one which bases status in economic
circumstances. Money implies power, to the extent that it
gives control; in a society where status is deemed to be
achieved, it calls for honour; it determines life-style; and,
taken together, these things set social expectations. Poverty
in turn implies lack of power, dishonour (because poverty is
seen as a result of personal inadequacy) and a limited life
style. But it is not possible to be crudely deterministic.
Education and occupation affect life style and expectations; a
degree of status may be determined by birth. The getting of
money is facilitated by power, social honour, the appropriate
life-style, or by expectations. There is a constant
interaction between the different factors.

Power tends to be associated with high status; but, although
stigmatised people tend to have low status, not all
stigmatised groups are powerless. Pensioners, who are poor,
have considerable power as a lobby. They have legitimate
authority, both because they form a substantial proportion of
the electorate, and because respect for the aged is a demand
of our moral code. Groups of disabled people, like the
National Federation for the Blind, have been influential
although they possess neither authority nor control. Racial
minorities, especially in the US, have gained substantially in
influence because of riots in the ghettoes - a material
sanction. However, although many of the people affected are
poor, these groups are not primarily distinguished by their
poverty. They are all physically stigmatised. Other types of
stigmatised groups - people with mental stigmas, moral
stigmas, or welfare recipients - have failed to gain power.
Their lack of influence is founded in a belief that they are
socially inadequate. In cases where the assumption of
inadequacy has broken down, stigmatised people are able to
gain power. If this is correct, powerlessness is not so much
a cause of stigmatisation as a consequence of it.

SOCIAL CONTROL.

One part of the function of social services is to control behaviour that is socially unacceptable. The prevention of child abuse, the committal to institutions of mentally ill people, or the treatment of truancy as a social problem, are all cases in which the idea of welfare is strapped to a big stick. Stigmatisation has been represented as another form of social control, a deliberate policy to make people behave themselves. This is closely related to the question of power. It has been argued that power is concentrated in the hands of those who own the means of production, and poor people are controlled because the people who have the power wish to preserve it. But I do not think it is necessary to posit the existence of a conspiratorial ruling class to explain social control. Some behaviour cannot be reconciled with certain types of social organisation, whether because it breaches social norms, it hurts others, or it imposes a burden on others which they are not prepared to accept. Stigmatisation is, in part, a response to behaviour of this sort. It controls behaviour by punishing the offender and by acting as a warning to others.

"The stigma of being a claimant", Ginsburg (1979) suggests,
is an essential ingredient in a system designed to discipline claimants and to promote the values of insurance and individual and family self-help. (p.104.)
This discipline is seen most strongly in the attempt to make the able-bodied poor work. The Poor Law did this by means of a work test, administered at first in the workhouse, and then more commonly in special centres for people receiving out-relief (see Cmd. 3585, 1930). Those who received benefits outside the scope of the Poor Law were examined to make sure they were 'genuinely seeking work' (Deacon, 1976). More recently, the 'four week rule' limited the benefit to which a person was entitled if work was believed to be available (Meacher, 1974). Even now, it is generally a condition of receiving benefit that an able-bodied person is registered for work, and someone who becomes unemployed voluntarily or through 'misconduct' has benefit restricted for up to six weeks.

The object of these policies may be seen either as an attempt to force people to work, or to dissuade others from giving up work, in the belief that people will not choose to work if they have the opportunity to avoid it. This belief is highly questionable. Ideally, the person who is unemployed should return to stable work at the first opportunity. In practice, however, the intermittent employment which results from being pushed into marginal work is taken as evidence, when the person becomes unemployed again, that he doesn't want to work

- and, because he may not like to admit that he has no control over his own affairs, the unemployed man may reinforce this impression.   This disguises powerful social factors which cause people to work.   Marsden and Duff (1975) give an excellent example of the results of this process:
> 'I'm not bothered.   I never bother going for a job now. Aw, if you can keep your dole and make £10 per week on top of that, who's going to work?'
> Within four months this man had found a job and was back in full-time work. (p.189.)

Piven and Cloward (1971) argue that
> to buttress weak market controls and ensure the availability of marginal labour, an outcast class - the dependent poor - is created by the relief system.   ... Its degradation at the hands of relief officials serves to celebrate the value of all work ... (p.165.)

I suppose this is a tenable interpretation of the problems of unemployment, but I think it goes too far.   It may be true that the relief system serves the **interests** of employers, but it does not follow that this is its **intention**.   Jordan (1974) writes in the same vein:
> In order to retain the exaggerated respect for work (at any wage) which is considered an essential element in the market economy, the authorities devise procedures which stigmatise, ration and harass both those who are not working and those who cannot afford to live on what they earn. (p.59.)

This is inconsistent.   He cannot hold both that there is an exaggerated respect for work at any wage and that poor working people are stigmatised.   But there are more important objections.   Firstly, like Piven and Cloward, Jordan sees the problem as one of the market economy.   But work is vital to any economy.   Even in the Soviet Union, there is an Act to curb the activities of
> able bodied adult citizens who lead an anti-social, parasitic mode of life, maliciously avoiding socially useful work, and likewise living on an income not earned by labour. (Beerman, 1958.)

Secondly, it is unwise to attribute all the undesirable features of a service to the deliberate actions of the authorities.   Certainly, they have to ration - that is true of any service which is in short supply where the price mechanism is not in use.   (It is probably more true, in consequence, of non-market economies.)   But the harassment, ill-treatment and degradation of claimants by officials are as much attributable to the attitudes which the officials share with the rest of society as they are to the policies of the agencies.   It is simply not true that all the consequences of a policy are intentional.

It requires some explanation that people who are not expected
to work - pensioners, single parents, or disabled people - are
still affected to some degree by the stigma of not working.
Marris (1958) records that widows would still go out to work,
because

> they seemed less afraid of their children suffering from
> lack of their mother's company, than from the stigma of
> poverty. (p.110.)

Spitzer (1975) relates the rejection of stigmatised groups to
the needs of the capitalist system. Using the specific
example of mental retardation, he argues that the meritocratic
ideologies of capitalism sanction the stratification of
society, that the destruction of the extended family weakens
the traditional methods of assimilation of such people, and
that the use of unskilled labour by capitalist production is
threatened by the existence of mentally retarded people who
could do the job just as well (p.640). Along with other
'social junk' - the aged, the handicapped, and the mentally
ill - these people are therefore excluded form the process of
production, where they become

> a costly but relatively harmless burden. (p.645.)

He argues that deterrent policies are used because

> The social expenses and threat to social harmony created
> by a large and economically stagnant surplus-population
> could jeopardise the preconditions for accumulation.
> (p.643.)

It should be noted that old, handicapped, mentally ill or
mentally retarded people are rejected in societies that are
not capitalist. Societies that are not capitalist are also
stratified; the 'traditional methods of assimilation' include
burning mentally handicapped children (Haffter, 1968, 60),
chaining up mentally ill people (Jaques, 1960, 12), and
killing handicapped people who are a burden (ibid, 10).
Mentally handicapped people are generally less able than
others to participate in production in any society (Jackson,
1977); they are not excluded only in 'capitalist' societies.
Spitzer's argument is tendentious nonsense.

It can still reasonably be argued that the rejection of people
not expected to work is a result of the work ethic. Walker
writes:

> The generally accepted assumption that those who are out
> of work will be worse off than those who are in work
> follows directly from the overriding value that
> industrial society places on work. ... The same
> individualistic value also underlies the definition of
> the elderly and other groups which are in poverty as
> dependent on the rest of society, and it assigns the
> stigma that is part of this dependent status. (1980, 59.)

The problem comes down to a matter of social values - not of
the policy of the welfare agencies. At the same time, while

acknowledging the importance of the work ethic, there are other factors in the rejection of stigmatised people - particularly the moral rejection of single parents - which seem to be stronger. I think it is a mistake to overemphasise the importance of work as a source of stigma; it is only one element out of many.

POLICIES FOR POVERTY.

Poverty itself is a stigmatised condition. Rainwater (1967) argues that the only problem the poor have is lack of money (p.124). It has been assumed too often that they can be helped while they are poor, which is a treatment of the symptoms of poverty, not the causes. He believes that an attack on inequality is the only way out. But redistribution is not an answer in itself; it implies dependency, which is also a stigmatised condition. Moreover, the stigma of poverty is itself an obstacle to redistribution. "If the distribution was to be changed significantly", Howe argues, "the stigmatising values which supported it would have to be changed first" (1978, 186). This is Catch-22. People are stigmatised by lack of money; the stigma of poverty makes society reluctant to give them more money; and if they did give them more money, it would only lead to more stigma.

There are two possible approaches to take. One is to 'rehabilitate' individual poor people. By giving the individual the opportunity to escape from poverty, that individual can be redeemed. This was the approach of the Victorian reformers who favoured 'scientific charity' for the deserving poor. Octavia Hill, for example, wrote:
    As soon as I entered into possession, each family had an
    opportunity of doing better; those who would not pay, or
    who had clearly led immoral lives, were ejected. (cited
    Gauldie, 1974, 86.)
The problems of this approach are considerable. Many poor people are incapable of 'lifting themselves' out of poverty; they are often old, disabled, sick, or educationally disadvantaged. Pinker notes that
    When rehabilitative agencies identify 'success' with
    return to work an self-supporting status, they will be
    reinforcing the expectations and attitudes of their
    clientele. The consequences of using this criterion of
    'success' will be to elevate the morale of those who
    respond to treatment and lower still further the morale
    of those who do not recover. (1971, 210.)
One effect of this is to discourage the provision of services that are unlikely to be 'successful'.
    Wherever the criteria of the economic market prevail,
    those states of dependency with the worst prognosis will
    receive the poorest social services. (p.50.)

Scott (1967), for example, notes that services for the blind
are disproportionately concerned with young people when a
substantial majority of those affected by blindness are old.

Rehabilitative services can only be an answer for a limited
number of people. In any unequal or competitive society,
which includes virtually every society known to man, someone
has to come at the bottom. 'The poor ye have always with
you'. A policy of rehabilitation strengthens the divisions
between the deserving and the undeserving poor. It might be
argued that this distinction, like the work ethic, is
desirable as a motive force in society: if poverty is not made
unpleasant, then people will not attempt to avoid it. The
answer to this, I think, is that poverty is bad enough without
having to support the contempt of other people at the same
time.

An alternative to this approach is to attempt to improve the
position of the poor collectively. 'Positive discrimination'
has been seen as a way of overcoming the stigma of poverty by
diverting resources to poor people. But redistribution of
money is not enough, because it increases the sense of
dependency. The improvement of the condition of the poor
involves a redistribution of power. The poor need to
establish a collective identity - a rational step, Haggstrom
(1964) argues, when they cannot succeed as individuals (p.218)
- to overcome their social disadvantages. In the field of
social welfare, this implies that poor people must take
collective action in respect of the policies which affect
them. This has been the thrust of the 'War on Poverty' in the
US, community action, and of the trend towards participation
in the administration of services.

There are a number of difficulties inherent in these
approaches. It does not always help to have a collective
identity if the image of the group is negative and the group
relies on persuasion to gain influence. There is, as
Griffiths (1975) argues, a double bind: a group that says
nothing will get nothing done, but a group that forces itself
on public attention risks an identification that may aggravate
a stigma (p.31). Another difficulty is that since
stigmatisation implies isolation and a lack of participation,
those people most in need of assistance will not be touched by
collective action. This is true in part, but it is not a
strong argument. In the first place, I have argued that
'stigmatisation' affects more people than those who 'feel
stigma'. This means that many people affected by stigma will
not be isolated or prevented from acting because of it.
Besides, the actions of certain people - community or group
leaders - on behalf of others may still be to the advantage of
all. The Disablement Income Group, for example, has exercised

pressure on behalf of many disabled people for income support. On the other hand, this can work against a stigmatised group: the work of the Claimants Unions (**pace** Jordan,1973) has not unquestionably improved the lot of claimants, and I believe that in certain respects, notably by generating antagonisms within a service, may be said to have made it worse.

Formal participation suffers from the further disadvantage that it depends upon on administrative machinery. Arnstein (1971) describes a 'ladder' of citizen participation, ranging from manipulation and 'therapy' to citizen control. This model draws attention to another basic problem, which is the relationship of the community to the administration. It does not follow that, because there is a collective organisation, it will gain the influence necessary to redress disadvantages or change social attitudes. A further problem is that 'collective action' means something only if there is a community of interest - a problem which Arnstein's model fails to recognise. In real life, there may be a conflict of interests, or even numerous conflicts. 'The poor' are not a homogenous whole. The 'undeserving poor' gain status at the expense of the deserving poor. The unemployed in one area may get jobs at the expense of unemployed people in another area. There may be a conflict between slum tenants who want to be rehoused, and those who want the area improved and community preserved. Some single parents may want a guaranteed income; others would benefit more from the right to be maintained.

Despite all these reservations, there are some advantages in participation. It allows opinions to be heard which otherwise would not be. It creates social organisations which can support individual members, like Goffman's 'huddle-together self-help groups'. It can assist in establishing the influence of a client group, and helps them to put the case in their favour. Because I do not attribute stigma to a lack of power, I am sceptical about the potential of an increase in power to reduce stigma. But the influence gained can be used to change some of the conditions which lead to stigma.

An example of this is the effect of tenant participation in the management of public housing estates. Griffiths (1975) advocates this as a method of improving depressed estates, and illustrates this with a case study. Power (1979) gives a similar example. By co-operative action, the tenants were able to make a physical improvement in their area, reversing the cycle of decline and establishing a shared pride in their achievement. But this achievement, real as it is, must be seen in context. Co-operative effort has succeeded by diverting resources towards itself - which implies that they are being diverted from somewhere else - and often, Power's work suggests, by establishing itself as a form of deserving poverty, and excluding difficult tenants and problem families from admission to the community. There is reason to be cautious about the claims made for the process.

CHAPTER 5: SUMMARY.

It may be argued that the rejection of poor people reflects their lack of power, and that policies towards the poor are oppressive mechanisms reinforcing the 'work ethic'. The work ethic is important as a set of social values, but the attribution of a specific intent to oppress the poor is difficult to maintain, and other values besides the work ethic are also significant.

Policies dealing with the stigma of poverty have taken three main approaches. First, there is financial redistribution; but redistribution is resisted because of negative attitudes. Second, there is 'rehabilitation' - which may lead to a distinction between the deserving and the undeserving poor. Third, there are collective policies - positive discrimination and collective action - which seem to have limited scope.

Chapter 6

The stigma of dependency

Poor people are rejected, but people who are poor and dependent are rejected more. The distaste for dependent poverty is evident in the dislike people feel for 'charity', or social services which they see as a form of charity. This feeling is not, I have suggested, a major element in the failure of demand; nor is it a strong factor distinguishing types of service, because the reason for disliking a service, its association with dependent poverty, is the same for any sort of residual welfare. The emphasis people put on independence is almost certainly made for the same reason. The survey of pensioners in 1966 found, in addition to those who were too proud to claim or who disliked the National Assistance Board, a substantial proportion who said they were 'managing alright' - nearly 20% of couples, 30% of single men, and 37.7% of single women (Ministry of Pensions, 1966, 42). It is possible that many of these were not ready to become dependent, although the precise proportion is a matter for speculation.

The public rejection of dependent poverty is strong. Unemployment is one of the most disreputable forms, and one which is prominent in the public mind: in the European study, 'laziness' and 'chronic unemployment' were the most common reasons given by those in the UK who had seen people in poverty (Riffault, Rabier, 1977, 69). The two are closely linked: there was a time when unemployment was called 'idleness', which has pronounced moral overtones. In its consideration of social security, the popular press devotes a disproportionate amount of space to unemployment benefit - disproportionate both in terms of its cost and the numbers of people who claim it. Stubbs (1980) found, in a sample taken from the national popular dailies over six months, that out of 457.5 column inches on social security, 226.5 were given to unemployment benefit. (63.75 more went on Supplementary Benefit, of which a proportion goes to unemployed people.) Most of the stories were judged to be unfavourable.

The other main groups dependent on welfare benefits are people
who are old, sick, disabled, widows or single parents. In the
US, programmes for income maintenance are often related to
specific groups in need - unlike Supplementary Benefit in the
UK, which covers all these groups. The American practice
gives us some indication of the extent to which groups of
welfare recipients are rejected, and how that affects the
services that deal with them. Williamson (1974c) asked people
to rank several programmes according to how much stigma they
inflicted.   General relief was felt to cause the most,
probably because this benefit goes to the rump of the poor,
like tramps, who are not covered in other ways.   It was
followed by AFDC, which is specifically given to unsupported
mothers with children; Unemployment Compensation; Aid to the
Disabled; and Old Age Assistance (pp.217-220).   All of these
groups are, to some degree, rejected in their own right, and
it can be argued that the order in which benefits are placed
reflects feelings about the recipients.   At the same time, it
should be emphasised that the receipt of welfare carries with
it a stigma of its own. As one old man told Walsma (1970),
      I am a welfare case. I have humbled myself. (p.148.)

THE DEPENDENT PERSON.

There are three kinds of dependency.   The first is physical.
Ill, disabled, old and mentally handicapped people may rely
on the services of others for their basic physical needs, such
as mobility, food and hygiene.   The second is material
dependency,   which is associated most strongly with the
financial dependency of social security programmes, but which
includes those cases where a persons receives goods in kind.
Thirdly, there is psychological dependency - a dependent state
of mind. It is marked by
      resignation, helplessness, hostile pessimism, physical
      sickness for which doctors can find no organic base,
      passivity, and inability to mobilise the self to take
      necessary action or responsibilities. (Perlman, 1951,
      327.)
Psychological dependency implies more than the fact of
dependence; it is a need to rely on another person because of
an inability to act for oneself.   It is an aspect, for
example, of depression (Sutherland, 1976).   It manifests
itself in a dependent role - which may be clinging, demanding,
manipulative, pleading, or any number of these things by
turns.

There is some overlap between these forms.   Physical
dependency often implies financial dependency - many of these
people are poor as a result of their physical limitations -
and it may be bound up with psychological dependence, although
this is not a necessary consequence.   Physically stigmatised

people are often expected to fit into the sick role, to be dependent, and it may be necessary for a disabled person continually to assert his physical independence in order to keep himself out of the role. Traditionally, financial dependency has been believed to lead to psychological dependency. Franklin wrote in 1753:

> I have sometimes doubted whether the laws peculiar to England, which compel the rich to maintain the poor, have not given to the latter a dependence that very much lessens the care of providing against the wants of old age. (cited Williams, 1944, 77.)

Gladstone (1889) expressed a similar concern for the moral welfare of the pauper:

> If he loses his self-reliance, if he learns to live in a craven dependence on wealthier people rather than upon himself, you may depend upon it he incurs mischiefs for which no compensation can be made.

Financial dependency is believed to be a result of personal inadequacy as well as a cause of it. Social work clients, Marcus wrote in 1928,

> have fallen into the limbo of the dependent and are exposed to the social stigma which even professional case workers still attach to dependency, the stigma of suspected inferiorities - mental, moral and physical. (p.136.)

Professional workers may still take this view. Problem families, according to Soyer (1961),

> seek quick and tangible help. Over and over again one senses beneath a hostile veneer, an oral character; a client who never stops demanding, a mother who cannot give emotionally to her children but can only drain those around her of emotional sustenance. The dependency is pervasive ... (p.36.)

It is not altogether surprising to hear that some people who are dependent on social services are also psychologically dependent. Poverty is debilitating, and poor people can hardly be blamed if they try to get help from others; psychological dependency is an understandable response to an oppressive situation. At the same time, it would be absurd to suggest that everyone who is financially dependent is helpless, or that dependency inevitably leads to a degraded character. Perlman (1951) protests the confusion of psychological and financial dependency, which are logically distinct. A widow is not inadequate; an unemployed person need not be resigned to dependency; a pensioner is not a defective person. They are "sound citizens with empty purses" (p.328).

THE NORM OF RECIPROCITY.

There is a general obligation to make some return for things received. This is the norm of reciprocity. The norm of reciprocity was identified by Aristotle as an important element in social relationships (Thomson, 1953); Levi-Strauss (1958) has written,

> In anthropology, this theory continues to stand, as soundly based as the gravity theory in astronomy. (p.162.)

Gergen (1969) has suggested a simple psychological basis for reciprocity. Reinforcement leads to repetition, and so we reinforce behaviour which gives us pleasure and try to deter behaviour which does not. Exchange is a method of mutual reinforcement. Exchange, we learn from the theory of 'comparative advantage', has general benefits: by exchange, we can expand our potential both for production and for consumption (Kindleberger, Lindert, 1978, 16-23). This is enough in itself to explain the recurrence of the phenomenon in different societies. But exchange also has specific sociological functions. Exchange, Levi-Strauss (1949) writes,

> provides the means of binding men together. (p.480.)

The act of exchange is important in ritual: the Kula ring, the formal exchange of essentially worthless articles by the Trobriand islanders, is a classic example (see Mauss, 1925, ch.2).

Exchange is useful and desirable, and it has therefore in the course of time acquired, by the process Burke called 'prescription', the status of an obligation. Because prescription - the process by which a practice is tried, found good and accepted as a moral imperative - is determined by the nature of the society in which it takes place, exchange takes many forms. The workings of the principle are seen most clearly in the most extreme cases. Mauss, in his book on The Gift (1925), describes the potlach, which is a form of aggressive giving. By potlach, one person can gain dominance over another by pressing on him a gift that he cannot match. This is not generally practised, but it is an example of a process common to many, if not all, societies. Gouldner (1960) has argued that reciprocity is a fundamental principle of social organisation.

> The norm of reciprocity is a concrete and special mechanism involved in the maintenance of any social system. (p.174.)

Reciprocity is not the only norm governing gifts. The receipt of goods may be a mark of high status, rather than a state of dependency. In some societies, there have been tributes, which may be regarded as the opposite of the potlach: the aggressive demanding of 'gifts', sanctioned by war. The

legend of Theseus and the Minotaur centres around a tribute:
Theseus was sent with others as a tribute to Crete.   The
Romans took tributes from conquered countries.   It could be
argued that German 'reparations', or the 'protection' money
paid to gangsters, are a kind of tribute, although they have
the form of reciprocity. Another example in modern society is
the making of presents for a royal wedding.   Secondly, there
are norms of altruism. We are told it is more blessed to give
than to receive (Acts 20:35).   In **The Gift Relationship**
(1970), Titmuss argued that blood donation was an example of a
'pure gift' - a gift made by an anonymous donor to an
anonymous recipient, without penalties for not giving or
rewards for doing so, and without obligation or expectation
that a gift would be made in return (pp.84-85).

There is a conflict between reciprocity and altruism.   Where
reciprocity is the norm, there can be no such thing as a pure
gift: some return is demanded or expected. The effect of this
may be inconsistent with humanitarian principles.   Engels
(1845) inveighed against charity:

> Charity - when he who gives is more degraded than he who
> receives.   Charity - when those who dispense alms also
> insist that those who receive them must first be cast out
> of society as pariahs ... (pp.313-314.)

Frenkel Brunswick argues that

> From a social point of view, charity often has the
> function of keeping the underprivileged in their place,
> kindness acting in effect as a humiliating factor.
> (Adorno et al., 1950, 307.)

She explains this in terms of the aggression which underlies
charitable motives.   Exchange theory provides a model which I
find more convincing. In the first place,

> it is **morally** improper, under the norm of reciprocity, to
> break off relations or to launch hostilities against
> those to whom you are still indebted. (Gouldner, 1960,
> 175.)

Secondly, dependency implies a relationship in which the giver
is more powerful than the receiver, because he can control
aspects of the receiver's fate.   If an exchange is conceived
in a negative way, the imbalance of power inherent in
dependency may be used to the disadvantage of the dependent
person.   Charity may be humiliating, as well as being
degrading in itself.

All social services, Pinker (1971) argues, are systems of
exchange (p.153).   People are expected to give something in
return for what they get.   Dependency is only acceptable if
some contribution has been made, or is likely to be made, to
society, and a service is not respectable unless some element
of reciprocity can be established.   Steiner (1971) complains
that

> ... it has become an important part of the veterans'
> pensions mythology to deny that a pension is relief and
> to insist that it represents deferred compensation for
> wartime service. In agriculture there is a myth that the
> food relief programmes are not really welfare programmes
> but are designed to benefit the farmer by removing
> surpluses from the free market. Public housers like to
> play down the idea of a decent shelter for the poor ...
> (pp.3-4.)

But veterans' pensions **are** deferred compensation for wartime
service; that is why their pension is accepted as a legitimate
form of dependency when others are not. Food relief
programmes **do** help the farmer - the destruction of food by the
Common Agricultural Policy is proof of that. And a decent
shelter for the poor is **not** accepted as an adequate reason for
dependency.

> If the payments are connected to the operation of the
> production system ... or to the future production of
> workers ... or to previous work status, then stigma does
> not attach to the support. (Miller, Roby, 1968, 75.)

This is most of the truth. Contribution is measured largely
by work status. Pensioners are respectable; they have paid
their dues, by working most of their lives. Students are
accepted, perhaps with some reservations, because they are
going to contribute in the future. Disabled people are not
generally accepted, although their dependency may be made
temporarily legitimate through the sick role, which assumes
that they will eventually be able to work again. People
disabled through industrial injury have a special status. But
it is not all the truth, because contribution can be measured
in other ways - as the status of war pensioners, or widows,
testifies. Pinker, in a small and unpublished survey (1973),
found that most people saw the different social services
either as exchange or as residual systems to be used only if
an individual was unable to help himself - more than half as
an exchange system. Very few saw the main function of the
social services as an altruistic one involving a transfer to
help people in need.

Titmuss himself recognised the importance of the norm of
reciprocity. In **The Gift Relationship**, he found that the
apparently altruistic gift of blood was usually governed by
other considerations.

> There is in all these transactions, he wrote, an
> unspoken assumption of some form of gift-reciprocity:
> that those who give as members of society to strangers
> will themselves (or their families) eventually benefit as
> members of that society. (Titmuss, 1970, 248.)

But he saw this as evidence that altruism could work; a moral
society could be developed on the basis of enlightened self-
interest. Pinker argued, by contrast, that the norm of

reciprocity undermined the principle of altruism, and Titmuss, who believed passionately in the altruistic society, criticised Pinker's arguments for their vagueness, and the conception of stigma in them as a parochial view based on the experience of one or two countries. He claimed that there was a great deal of evidence to show that the experience of being a claimant was different in different countries (Titmuss, 1974, 45). Unfortunately, he did not say where this evidence could be found, and being limited in my linguistic capacity, I have not come across it. There is, however, evidence to suggest that the problem of stigma is not confined to Britain and the United States. It appears in France (Stevens, 1973), Denmark (Westergaard, 1979), Ireland (Clifford, 1974), and Canada (Wadel, 1973). In Australia, welfare departments
> tend to be highly stigmatised, with a negative 'welfare' image. (Rodgers et al., 1979, 176.)

In Israel,
> the right to assistance ... is seen as carrying strong elements of stigma and shame. (Rodgers et al., 1979, 124.)

Even in the Soviet Union,
> public assistance, financed from local funds, keeps its clients substantially below the poverty line; by requiring them to prove destitution, as well as age or disability, it also humiliates them. (Madison, 1968, 207.)

The sole exception I have found is a statement by Dorothy Wilson that there are no problems with the takeup of benefits in Sweden (Wilson, 1979, 546). If this observation is correct, it could be taken to support the view that the rejection of financial dependency is based in the norm of reciprocity. Gergen (1969) reports a survey examining attitudes to gifts in Sweden, Japan and the US. Only in Sweden was a gift accepted with an attitude more favourable than to someone who had offered an exchange (pp.77-80.) The different attitude to reciprocity implies a different attitude to the social services.

Titmuss was inconsistent in recognising the importance of reciprocity and denying its relevance to the problems of stigma. I suspect he realised that, if Pinker was right, his own ideal would be impossible of achievement; and the accusation of 'parochialism' was a reaction to a theory which excluded his conception of the Good Society.

EXCHANGE AND STATUS

A lack of reciprocity, of which dependent poverty is a clear example, has important implications for the status of the dependent person. Simmel (1908) argued that
> what makes a person poor is not the lack of means. The

poor person, sociologically speaking, is the individual
who receives assistance because of the lack of means.
(p.140.)

Simmel's description of the process by which this happens
relied on the idea of 'gratitude'. When a person was unable
to reciprocate, he was bound to feel grateful for what he had
received - a feeling which put him at a disadvantage in
relation to the giver. Gratitude is difficult to redeem; it
has 'a taste of bondage' (Simmel, 1950, 393). The esteem the
recipient is required to feel for others is a form of homage;
they gain in status, and he loses.

This form of argument was taken further by Homans (1961).
Esteem was given to people as a reward for the things they
have done that are of value to others (p.149). As the value of
the person to the group increases, so does the esteem he gets
from them. This leaves less esteem for other people (p.163).
Esteem is the basis of status. Because an esteemed person has
a higher standing than other people, they defer to him, and he
gains 'authority' (which I would call 'influence') over them
(p.288). So, in cases where exchange is unequal, the donor
gains both status and power, and, conversely, the recipient
loses them. Homans seems to suggest that there is a limited
stock of esteem; and Blau (1964), who develops Homans' work
further, argues that status, like capital, can be drawn on,
accumulated, or invested (pp.132ff). This is an unusual
concept of status, but it is not untenable; status is a form
of relationship, but it is also a social fact.

There are two main flaws in these arguments. Firstly, status
is seen, especially by Homans, as something which is achieved
by contribution. This is not true: much status is ascribed,
by heredity, occupational status, or economic circumstances.
It can be argued that there is an assumption of some
contribution, but this is not a necessary feature of ascribed
status. Secondly, as Ekeh (1974) points out, they tend to
concentrate on social exchange as an extension of a dyadic
interaction. The pattern of exchange in a whole society is
different from that in a small group.

Levi-Strauss (1949) contrasts **restricted** exchange, which is
directly reciprocal, with **generalised** exchange, by which he
seems to mean any condition in which a circle of exchange
could be completed (p.146). That much is true of any
transaction which is not a direct exchange; it seems that any
exchange or gift which is not restricted is generalised. The
point of the idea of generalised exchange is that it entails
generalised obligations toward society. Once a circle of
exchange is complete, things come into balance, and there are
no outstanding obligations. but while it is incomplete, it
acts to create obligations and bind a society together.

Generalised exchange establishes a system of operations conducted 'on credit'. (Levi-Strauss, 1949, 265.)

Social relations in a whole society are not equivalent to those of a small group. It is possible to ignore in a large society people who cannot be ignored when contact with them is more immediate, and people who are unable to reciprocate, Gouldner (1960) suggests, are likely to be neglected because they cannot fully participate in society (p.178). Furthermore, social rejection tends to be stronger when dependency is impersonal. Berkowitz and Daniels (1963) found, in a psychological experiment, that someone who was told that his effort was being made known to a dependent person was less likely to blame him than he was when the efforts were not known. (This casts even stronger doubts on Titmuss's hopes for anonymous altruism.) It seems that exchange binds more strongly in a small group, which might have been expected, and that one effect of generalised exchange, because it is more remote, is to increase the rejection of dependent people.

The relationship between exchange and status can be described directly in terms of the norm of reciprocity. Linton (1936) defines a status as 'a collection of rights and duties' (p.113). A person who receives something has a duty to reciprocate. If he fails to do so, an obligation is outstanding - which, by definition, implies a relative loss of status. Someone who is absolutely dependent on others, and unable to contribute anything in return, has in consequence a very low status. I have argued before that Linton's definition is a limited interpretation of the idea of status, which extends beyond rights and duties into social honour, life-style, economic circumstances and social expectations. The relationship described between exchange and status can still be made out if a wider definition of status is used; a person whose behaviour or life style does not correspond to the expectations attached to his role is degraded.

There is an apparent contradiction in the assimilation of reciprocity with stigma. Stigma divides people; reciprocity binds them together. A person who is dependent is not rejected; he is bound up with the social organisation. If exchange theory is correct, this should bring him closer to society, not drive him away from it. In a brilliant essay, Marshall Sahlins (1972) resolves the paradox. He distinguishes three kinds of reciprocity: generalised, balanced and negative. Generalised exchange occurs when people give without expecting something directly in return, in the belief that the others would, or will, do the same for them. It is most often found in intimate relationships or families. Balanced exchange is strictly reciprocal: it is the reciprocity of more distant friends or business partners.

Negative exchange is self-seeking: the harshly competitive
relationship of commercial trade. Almost by definition,
generalised exchange implies a closer relationship than
balanced exchange, which is in turn closer than negative
exchange. If our exchange is generalised, we **assume** - or
conclude - that we are close. Exchange is, therefore, the
main determinant of social distance. (Sahlins, 1972, ch.5.)

If this is taken to its logical conclusion, a gulf opens
between those people who are engaged in exchange, and those
who cannot be involved because they have little or nothing to
offer. Some redistribution is necessary to bring the poor
into society, and to hold society together.

> The greater the wealth gap ... the greater the
> demonstrable assistance that is necessary to maintain a
> given degree of sociability. (p.211.)

The rich must give to the poor; and, Sahlins shows in an
appendix that is a tour de force, the obligations of high
status are common to a wide variety of cultures and societies.
However, the governing principle is not the altruism that
Titmuss hoped would emerge, but negative exchange.

> The collectivity, of which the poor person is a part,
> enters into a relationship with him, confronting him,
> treating him as an object. (Simmel, 1908, 31.)

'Noblesse oblige' is a duty that the donors would gladly avoid
but which they nevertheless recognise. As a result, people
continue to support others who they despise.

Sahlins' argument provides an explanation for stigmatisation
which is elegant, orderly and persuasive. But some
reservations should be made. Dependency is not always
dishonourable; and some conditions, including poverty itself,
are rejected although they are not dependent. The argument is
not a comprehensive explanation of social rejection; it is at
best a contribution, albeit an important one, to a complex and
difficult problem.

IMPLICATIONS FOR POLICY.

The reduction of dependency.

I have argued, in the introduction, that dependency is the
defining characteristic distinguishing social services from
other forms of public provision. If dependency is
stigmatising, the association of stigma with the social
services is unavoidable; dependency is inherent in their
nature. At the same time, it becomes desirable to limit the
degree of dependency as far as possible. The degree of
stigmatisation varies with dependency, because greater
dependency implies an increased limitation of roles, and
limited roles lead to stigma through lowered status, the

imputation of failure, or lack of reciprocity. Secondly, dependency leads to restrictions on individual freedom; a person who is dependent on others to do things for him loses autonomy, because he can only act with the aid or acquiescence of others, and because their actions may limit the choices available to him. Dependency limits an individual's power of self-determination - a power which, Downie and Telfer (1969) argue, is fundamental to respect for persons.

The administration of social services has sometimes failed to take these problems into account. Lipman and Slater (1978) cite a White Paper issued by the Ministry of Health in 1950, shortly after the abolition of the Poor Law:
  'The workhouse is doomed. Instead, local authorities are
  busy planning and opening small, comfortable homes where
  old people ... can live pleasantly and with dignity. The
  old "master and inmate" relationship is being replaced by
  one more nearly that of an hotel manager and his guests.'
They argue against this that the idea of a hotel forces inmates to rely unnecessarily on staff:
  dependency is inherent in the notion. (p.199.)
The guest in a hotel does not choose the decoration or furniture in his room, cannot use the room as he wishes, and cannot decide when to have meals. He is relieved of certain responsibilities. Although this does imply a loss of independence, I do not think it is so great as altogether to invalidate the concept of a Home as a Hotel, which some people may find desirable. A far greater loss of independence has resulted from the confusion of residential care with medical treatment. The sick role is, I have argued, an inappropriate model for chronic incapacity, because it rests on the assumption that the object of treatment is a return to normality. Treatment in hospital is regimented in a way which facilitates physical repair, but is rather less desirable as a way of living. The training of nurses has been inadequate for positions in residential care - and there is some doubt as to whether nursing is appropriate at all for many of the people they deal with. They are taught to do everything for their patients, and the lives of patients are shaped around the organisation of the ward. Institutional neurosis flourishes.
  'We do treat them like children,' the nurse admits.
  'That's what they are really, isn't it?' (Harrison, 1978,
  122.)

If dependency is to be avoided, however, it requires more than the reduction of physical dependency. Payne (1980) suggests that social workers can help their clients to reduce their sense of dependency by emphasising, wherever possible, the contribution they have made to society, and by limiting the period for which they are dependent. This approach is essentially negative; ideally, we should be trying to create

opportunities for the recipient of social services to
contribute.   One way of enabling more responsibility for
recipients is to allow for some form of participation, a
policy which I have already discussed.   The Seebohm committee
suggested that participation

> should reduce the rigid distinction between the givers
> and takers of social services, and the stigma which being
> a client has often involved in the past (Cmnd.3703, 1968,
> 151)

but it was magnificently vague as to how this could be
achieved.

The norm of reciprocity implies that a recipient must be able
to contribute something to society in return for a service.
The emphasis in programmes of rehabilitation for disabled
people has been on the reduction of dependency by filling a
job.   In some cases, this approach is entirely appropriate.
Olshansky (1970) describes one experiment in which mentally
retarded people were given work driving fork lift trucks: he
reports that this was wholly successful.

> Work enfranchises them as human beings. (p.45.)

But there are problems in taking this for general policy. The
first is that it assumes that stigmatised people are capable
of work, which is not always true. Many are old and retired;
others are simply incapacitated.   A policy concentrating on
rehabilitation through work simply does not touch them.
Secondly, those who can work are often given jobs which are
boring and petty.   Baldwin (1979) objects to the idea that
this is worse than not working: the pious hope that they
should be exempted from the need to work

> singles out a stigmatised group to spearhead the assault
> on one of the central values of a society which already
> assigns them low status.

Work, even petty work, brings with it a certain self-respect -
not a lot, but it is better that unemployment and dependency.
The third objection is that the emphasis on work gives to some
disabled people the status of the deserving poor.   The idea of
'self-determination' is a strong theme in social work, and
Soyer (1975) argues that there is a 'right to fail'. This is
all very well for the people who succeed; but, necessarily, it
must leave others behind who do not.   This objection applies
equally to any attempt to make it possible to contribute to
society.

The principle of insurance.

By contributions, a person can acquire a right to benefit. It
is received wisdom that

> People do not want to be **given** rights to pensions and
> benefit; they want to earn them by their contributions.
> (Cmnd. 3883, 1969, 12.)

This is the main justification of the principle of insurance.
While there is something humiliating in receiving
assistance without giving something in return, insurance,
which requires an effort on the part of the insured,
gives him a feeling of dignity. (Laroque, in ICSW, 1969,
86.)

The claims made for insurance are considerable. Mauss (1925),
reflecting a contemporary debate in France, saw the
introduction of insurance as a return to 'group morality', and
a foundation of 'social solidarity' (pp.65-66). This is a
strange argument; I should have thought that the principle of
insurance was more closely linked with ideas of individual
responsibility. And yet the rhetoric of the Beveridge report
(Cmd. 6404, 1942) reflects this euphoric opinion. Insurance
would be given, "not as a charity but as a right" (para.296).
It would be comprehensive (para.303) and social (para.303),
redistributive (paras. 445-7), and would ensure a "national
minimum" (para.66). In practice, insurance has fallen far
short of these ideals. This is not because it has not been
properly applied; the failings are part of any scheme of
insurance. Stevenson (1973) records how

We cling to the idea of individual insurance against
poverty and related problems, thus, by implication,
stigmatising those who have not been able to make such
provision. (p.19.)

National insurance does not help those who have not worked -
groups such as the congenitally sick and disabled, school-
leavers who are unemployed, young unmarried mothers, and
married women who have kept house or left the labour market to
raise children. Provision can be made for some of these
groups, but, as Abel-Smith (1976) argues,

If some categories are not excluded from the rights
purchased by paying the insurance contributions, it
ceases to be insurance in any normal use of the term. ...
Normally separate provision for these groups is made
through a public assistance scheme. And usually this
creates a stigma of some kind. The credibility of social
insurance is normally secured by penalising in some way
those outside the scheme. (p.43.)

This is the first objection to the idea that insurance creates
'social solidarity'. It is not comprehensive; it does not
ensure a national minimum. On the contrary, it makes it
necessary for some other provision to be made which does not
carry the same 'rights'.

A second, even more basic objection is that people do not
necessarily look on insurance as a right. Social security in
the US is less stigmatised than other benefits (Williamson,
1974c, 220), but the bald statement that unemployment
insurance is not stigmatised is questionable. Schiltz (1970)
reports that in the US

archival survey evidence neither confirms nor denies the
assumption that social insurance is more acceptable as a
remedy for the ravages of unemployment than are need-
based programmes. (p.118.)

This can be put more strongly. The attitude to Unemployment
Benefit in the UK is negative despite its being an insurance
programme. This does not mean that insurance is no better
than relief; the contributory element helps, by reducing the
feeling of degradation associated with a lack of reciprocity.
But this is only a part of the problem associated with
dependency on welfare benefits. There is a stigma attached to
the conditions, like poverty, disability, or unemployment,
which cause people to become dependent in the first place. If
the norm of reciprocity was all that mattered, an unemployed
person should be more 'entitled' to unemployment benefit than
a disabled person to non-contributory invalidity pension. But
it is unemployment which carries a greater stigma. There are
two reasons for this. Firstly, the reason for dependency is
important. Dependency because of illness is legitimated
through the sick role; dependency through unemployment is not.
This is a substantial qualification to the application of a
general theory of reciprocity. Secondly, health services are,
perhaps perversely, seen as reciprocal. Many people still
believe, mistakenly, that the NHS is paid for largely from
Insurance contributions. Pinker (1973) found that the NHS is
often thought of as a system of exchange (p.67).

In a similar vein, Briggs and Rees (1980) found a number of
recipients of Supplementary Benefit justifying their
dependency by asserting they has paid for their benefit
through taxation or even (remarkably) through insurance
contributions (p.147). This is less a tribute to the power of
insurance to legitimate dependency than an attempt to
establish reciprocity by any convenient means. It suggests
that the norm of reciprocity can be, if not overcome, at least
circumvented by a convenient myth. But it still falls a long
way short of the model of an altruistic society favoured by
Titmuss.

Means-testing.

The main alternative to insurance is means-testing; but means
tests are commonly believed to be more stigmatising than
insurance payments. The practice of means testing in the past
was oppressive and much resented (see Orwell, 1937); a legacy
has been left of mistrust and hostility. TenBroek and Matson
(1966) point out the continued opportunities for harassment,
the denial of choice, bureaucratic control and the abuse of
administrative discretion (p.499).

A part of the problem has been that means tests are of their

very nature intrusive.   It can be argued against this that
assessments for   income tax are also intrusive, but there are
important differences in practice.   Means tests are not an
automatic process applying to all, as the payment of tax is;
Briggs and Rees (1980) found a number of claimants who
suggested that the reason Supplementary Benefit seemed like
charity was that one had to claim it (p.148).   (This attitude
does not extend to claims for tax allowances – perhaps because
this is seen as reclaiming one's own money, rather than as a
form of dependency.)   Tax forms are generally dealt with in
correspondence; many means tests – notably Supplementary
Benefit – require a person to appear at the office. and be
interviewed.   Tax forms require only income to be declared,
whereas means tests may also require information about wealth,
expenditure on housing, personal spending, special needs and,
most important, personal relationships.

A second difficulty is that means tests identify the claimant
as a poor person; qualification for benefit is proof of
poverty.   This is fundamental to any system of residual
welfare.   The reluctance of people to state their income may
simply be a reluctance to admit they are poor – a problem
which does not occur with tax forms, because poverty is not an
essential prerequisite of paying tax.

I think however that Handler (1972) identifies the real
problem when he points out that there is, in the practical
administration of means tests, a presupposition that the
claimant is likely to be dishonest (p.29).   Harvey (1979)
describes the case of a couple who, in order to qualify for a
rent allowance, were asked to produce evidence of their
receipt of sickness benefit, documentation of the payment of
rent, bank statements, details of their debts, their previous
address, their reasons for moving and an outline of their
daily budget. "They had not", she notes drily, "thought to be
so mistrusted" (p.29).   The reaction of claimants to this
treatment is probably made worse by a feeling that there is
something dishonest about claiming – a consequence of their
own attitudes towards dependency.

It seems desirable that if we must have means tests, they
should not be unnecessarily offensive.   A system begun in
Alabama reformed the method of verifying entitlement to
benefit (Alabama Social Welfare, 1965).   Instead of asking
people to produce documents, verification of statements and
signatures from all concerned, an experimental group of people
were asked simply to state their position in a 'declaration'.
Out of 228 cases, only 4 were discovered, on a later check, to
be in error.   Encouraged by this result, the administrators
extended the procedure of declaration across the state.   In
the first year, 9677 cases were checked by a more thorough

examination. 156 errors were discovered. 55 of these did not involve any change of payment, and in 21 of the remaining 101 cases, the payment was increased. The administrators concluded that the extensive documentation required in the past has been unnecessary. Other states subsequently took up the procedure. Requirements such as proof of age, registration for work, verification of residence, documentation of employment record, and the signature of every adult in the household were dropped. Phillips (1972) reports that these states found no difference in the validity of declarations for benefit when compared to the previous tests, and faster administration of claims. Not only this, but the attitudes of claimants to the service, and to the benefits, changed very favourably.

Means tests in Britain usually require less information than used to be required in these states, but possibly more than is necessary. The evidence suggests strongly that people who are treated as honest do behave honestly; too many current procedures assume they will not. As the administrators in Alabama stated,
>the public assistance programme must plead guilty to charges of creating and preserving a climate that is more conducive to the harassment of clients than to the preservation of human values. (Alabama Social Welfare, 1965, 14.)

Rights and discretion.

The rejection of dependency also reflects on the attempt to overcome stigma by giving stigmatised people a right to welfare. Donative rights are not compatible with the idea of reciprocity. Entitlements cannot be given, because there will always be a residual obligation which comes from the failure to make a return. There is a curious optimism about the importance of legal rights which it is difficult to justify rationally. Raynsford (1979), for example, writes about
>the prejudices and stigma attaching to the homeless which the 1977 Act is overcoming. (p.133.)

The 1977 Act may have changed the practice of the responsible authorities, but that is not the same as overcoming prejudice.

Rights are important for three reasons. Firstly, they are a means of protection against the disadvantages which follow stigmatisation. Rights for mental patients in the US have helped to curb abuses. Rights for unemployed people under the National Insurance scheme have at least mitigated the harshness of the treatment of the unemployed between the wars (see Deacon, 1976). Secondly, rights help to guarantee minimum standards of material welfare. Rights for homeless people have helped in cases where local authorities would have turned families away. Rights are not a complete protection in themselves, but they certainly contribute towards a standard. Thirdly, rights are important because they are a mark of a universal system of social welfare. Julia Parker (1975) argues that a person's rights are the proof of his status as a citizen; where social welfare is determined by right, there is no stigma (pp.146-147). Marsden (1973) sees this as the way to overcome the traditional aversion to social welfare:

> Only by giving the families as far as possible benefits as of right, can they be allowed to escape from the stigma of the Poor Laws. (p.308.)

However, as I have already argued, the creation of rights does not in fact remove stigma. Stigmatised people lack rights because they lack status and power; legal rights can help to improve status and power, but there is a limit to their scope. Jones (1980) argues that the creation of rights may even have the effect of increasing stigma. Rights are clearly distinguished from charity; the creation of rights only emphasises the distinction, and therefore the lack of entitlement felt in other ways (p.142). This seems to me correct in theory, and in practice it has this effect in the cases of rehabilitation and insurance.

The alternative to the establishment of rights in the provision of services is a reliance on administrative discretion. Discretion is not an 'anonymous gift'. The person who wants a service must ask for it, and must ask an official who has the power to admit or refuse the request. To some extent, this is true of all services: the staff decide which claims fall into which categories. Hall (1974) found that the reception staff who did this rarely even recognised it as discretion; they thought of it as 'common sense'. The same may be true of the feelings of claimants about it. But the fact of having to ask in itself brings home an acute sense of dependency; it can make a claimant feel like a beggar. In addition, discretion gives scope for individual prejudice, and discretionary procedures therefore put at a disadvantage a person who is stigmatised.

On the other hand, discretion is necessary to guarantee flexibility. Jordan (1974) states that in the case of social security,

> flexibility and responsiveness to need have been sacrificed in an attempt to reduce stigma and make the administration of benefits more impersonal. (p.181.)

But, he argues, the necessity of some flexibility has led to demands being placed on the financial powers of local authority Social Services departments, who are not always equipped to deal with problems of this sort adequately. This is representative of a constant dilemma. There is always an element of discretion in the administration of social services; the question is not whether it should happen, but how much there should be. Benefits established by 'right' are still stigmatised for dependency; discretionary benefits may be more stigmatising, but it is a matter of degree. Responsiveness to need is not inconsistent with personal dignity. And although the use of discretion may involve a humiliating dependency, the consequences of not being provided for may be worse.

CHAPTER 6: SUMMARY.

Dependency may be physical, psychological or financial. Each form is stigmatised and confused with the others. People who are dependent are in breach of a general norm of reciprocity. A lack of reciprocity implies lowered status, and social isolation or rejection.

Dependency is inherent in the nature of the social services. A reduction of dependency is important if stigmatisation is to be reduced. This has been attempted through insurance, but the argument that insurance is not stigmatising, and that means tests, which imply dependency and poverty, are stigmatising, is questionable as a generalisation. The attempt to give 'rights' to claimants may assist as a protection against disadvantage, but rights do not remove the stigma of dependency.

Chapter 7

Moral stigmas

MORALITY AND DEVIANCE.

Morality is uncompromising. Where there are social norms, there is a social division; those groups which are within the moral code are distinguished strictly from those which are not. The distinction is made between **normal** groups and **deviant** ones. Deviance is not simply abnormality; nor is a person deviant simply because he is discredited (Cohen, 1966, 36; Goffman, 1963, ch.5). It involves a breaking of the rules which govern civil society. When mentally ill people are described as deviant (e.g. in Simmons, 1965), or women are condemned as unmarried mothers, they are being accused of immorality.

There is a substantial literature on deviance, which has grown out of criminology. It attempts to identify the process by which deviants are marked off from the rest of society. There are many different explanations for this process. One rests on the assumption that people are pathologically immoral. Another depends on the rejection of social values, either as an individual or jointly with others. Thirdly, there is the concept of 'drift' described by Matza (1964) in relation to juvenile delinquency; people become deviant, he suggests, because there is no reason not to. Fourthly, there is the view that deviants are forced into deviance by society. The object of this section is not to give a comprehensive review of the sociology of deviance, but rather to look at the relevance of these ideas to social welfare.

Pathological immorality.

The idea of pathological immorality involves the assumption that immoral conduct requires explanation; it presumes that a state of observance to morality is the natural condition of humanity. It has been regarded at certain times to be evidence of a personality disorder if an unmarried girl became

pregnant.   At the turn of the century, social problems - like
crime,   social immorality and drunkenness - were considered to
be the consequence of mental handicap.   These characteristics
were called the 'degeneracies'.   Boies (1893), writing in the
US, proclaimed:

> We believe it is established beyond controversy that
> criminals and paupers both, are degenerate;   the
> imperfect, knotty, knurly, worm-eaten, half-rotten fruit
> of the race. (p.266.)

According to Cooley (1902), better known for his concept of
the 'looking glass self',

> A degenerate might be defined as one whose personality
> - personality, note, and not behaviour -
> falls distinctly short of a standard set by the dominant
> moral thought of the whole. (p.372.)

He wrote:

> This truth that all forms of deficient humanity have a
> common philosophical aspect is one reason for giving them
> some common name, like degeneracy.   Another is that the
> detailed study of fact more and more forces the
> conclusion that such things as crime, pauperism, idiocy,
> insanity and drunkenness have, in great measure, a common
> causation, and so form, practically, parts of a whole.
> (p.375.)

Cooley advocated social isolation for degenerates. The school
of thought which this represents led eventually to the
advocacy of eugenics as a longer-term policy to deal with
social problems. Promiscuity was evidence of mental disorder,
and unmarried mothers were committed to institutions and
sometimes sterilised.

The modern descendant of the degenerate is the 'problem
family'.   'Problem families' are not the same thing as
'families with problems' - the term 'multi-problem family'
tends to confuse the issue.   They are families that **are**
problems for social agencies.   The definitions of the term
tend to vary.   Spencer (1963) notes some of their features:
they are often large, mobile, socially isolated, and organised
around the mother.   There are likely to be chronically
dependent on social services, exploitative, and fail to
respond to the help they receive - by definition, as they
would not be a problem if they did respond to help.   Their
social relations are inadequate or destructive (p.12).

Blacker (1952), an advocate of eugenics, remarks on five
'commonly recognised' features: mental subnormality,
temperamental instability, ineducability, a squalid home, and
the presence of numerous children (pp.16-28).   This is more
the language of genteel insult than informed observation.
Philp and Timms (1957), reviewing the literature, pick out
some of the most persistent characteristics.   The emphasis

tends to fall on the family's way of life, neglect of their children, and their personal defects, in health, mental capacity, or sanity. Holman (1974), it may be remembered, argued by contrast that problem families were distinguished by being designated a problem family by a social agency (pp.609-610). This is too simplistic a view. Mental handicap, criminality, chronic dependency, ill health and mental illness all have a profound capacity to stigmatise. The combination of several of these characteristics may be rare - as Rutter and Madge (1976) believe it is (ch.9) - but it can only be devastating when it occurs.

It would be going too far to say that there was no substance in the pathological view. At the same time, it is difficult to see how, when moral codes are socially defined, immorality can be defined in personal terms. It is necessarily the result of a relationship between the individual and society. It is this relationship which needs to be explained.

Deviant attitudes.

A second view of deviance attributes it to the attitudes of deviant people to society. Merton (1968) classifies the forms of deviation according to the acceptance or rejection of social values and the structure of society. If a person accepts both structure and values, he conforms. If he accepts structure and rejects values, he involves himself in ritual - the form, but not the spirit, of morality. If he accepts social values and rejects structure, he acts as an innovator in society. If he rejects both values and structure, he 'retreats'. Retreatists include
    psychotics, autists, pariahs, outcasts, vagrants, vagabonds, tramps, chronic drunkards and drug addicts. (p.194.)
They call values into question by ignoring them. Finally, there are rebels - people who reject both values and structure, but accept others which they wish to substitute. The combinations can be represented in a table, as follows: '+' signifies agreement, and '-' disagreement.

Table 7.1: Attitudes to society.
(Merton, 1968, 207.)

	Social values	Social structure
Conformity	+	+
Ritualism	-	+
Innovation	+	-
Retreatism	-	-
Rebellion	+/-	+/-

The category which is most relevant to stigmatised people is the 'retreatist' group.

The classification has two main weaknesses. Firstly, it is difficult to attribute any uniform attitudes to pariahs or outcasts. An outcast is defined by what is done to him, not by his attitudes; and a stigmatised person can share the values and opinions of others in society. Secondly, a person's attitudes are not to be assumed from one aspect of his behaviour. It does not follow that, because a person is a drunkard or a vagrant, that he rejects social values in their entirety, even if he rejects them in respect of his own condition.

Shoham (1970) uses a similar method to classify deviant behaviour and attitudes. He takes three essential factors - value deviation, deviant behaviour, and stigma - and examines each of the possible combinations. In a table, the classification looks like this:

Table 7.2: Forms of deviance.
(Shoham, 1970, ch.4.)

Description of condition:	Value deviation	Deviant behaviour	Stigma
'Solidarist' (non-deviant)	No	No	No
'Levantine' (Ritualism)	Yes	No	No
'Privileged'	No	Yes	No
'Successful sanction orientation' (primary deviant)	Yes	Yes	No
'Victimised'	No	No	Yes
'Defiant'	Yes	No	Yes
'Inner conflict'	No	Yes	Yes
'True deviant'	Yes	Yes	Yes

These categories are related, in his argument, to the deviance of criminals rather than the particular problems of the stigmatised people who rely on social services. These can be very different. Not all stigmatised people are deviant, either in values or behaviour. A person who is not deviant may be stigmatised because he has discrediting personal characteristics. His values may or may not correspond with society's. A person whose behaviour is deviant - who breaches moral norms - may have deviant values, but he may not if he is not responsible for his behaviour (for example because of mental illness), if the deviant act is not representative of all that person's values (like becoming an unmarried mother), or if society itself is ambivalent towards the behaviour (as in the case of claiming welfare benefits).

This last point highlights the common flaw of Merton's and Shoham's approaches. They assume that social values are consistent; they are not. Attitudes to old people, for example, include contempt, pity, the expectation of dependency, affection, and exaggerated respect. Mentally ill people are seen as being in need of help at the same time as they are condemned if they seek it. Everyone - or almost everyone - agrees on the necessity of some form of social security, but people are rejected if they actually take it. So it is difficult to establish whether behaviour really is deviant, or attitudes are in opposition to social norms. These classifications are useful in so far as they create a set of ideal types of deviation, but in practice they may be difficult to apply.

Drift.

Another weakness of this approach is that there is no sense of process in it; the opinions of the deviant spring ready formed into being. In real life, people do not begin as deviants or conformists; their attitudes and behaviour develop in accordance with their social circumstances. The theory of drift - sometimes called the 'anomie theory of deviance' - suggests that people become deviant, not through a deliberate choice of deviant values, but through a process of gradual separation from the main culture. It is related to anomie, because there is an absence of social norms to guide the individual and prevent him from becoming deviant; he is under-regulated. "Being pushed around", Matza (1964) writes,

>   puts the delinquent in a mood of fatalism. He experiences himself as effect. In that condition, he is rendered irresponsible. The sense of irresponsibility puts him into drift. Drift makes him available for delinquent acts. (p.89.)

This theory is, once more, formed primarily in respect of criminal activity. It is tempting to extend it to the recipients of social services. They also are 'pushed around', and a mentally ill person, or a person who has to claim social security, may be 'channelled' into a degraded status. The difference is, I think, that although a decision to claim a service may be the result of a a process, the recipient does not wander into dependency. There is no primary deviation, no gradual stage of initiation into deviance. The act of claiming benefit is, in itself, a major step defining a social role. As Marshall (1963) wrote of the Poor Law,

>   The stigma which clung to poor relief expressed the deep feelings of people who understood that those who accepted

relief must cross the road that separated the community of citizens from the outcast company of the destitute. (p.83.)

The theory of drift relies on the effect of a lack of regulation on responsible behaviour. The moral careers of stigmatised people are diverse, but there are no indications that, where moral issues are at stake, the conditions of the anomie theory are relevant to the problems of the people who use social welfare.

Labelling theory.

A different account of the process of becoming deviant is given by labelling theory, which concentrates on the attitudes of society to the deviant individual, rather than on his views of society. Lemert's (1951) distinction between primary and secondary deviation is an attempt to explain this process. The primary deviant - the person who has done something bad - becomes a secondary deviant, a 'bad person', because of labelling. This separates him from the community, reinforces his deviant conduct, and pushes him to adjust to a deviant status (ch.4).

Lemert's emphasis on labelling has been followed by many writers, in an attempt to explain the effect that the social definition of an individual's condition has on that individual. This has led to the perspective known as 'labelling theory'. Labelling theory argues, essentially, that people are deviant because they labelled as deviants. Becker (1963) has written that
    Social groups create deviance by making the rules whose
    infraction constitutes deviance. (p.9)
He is arguing that the label which society puts on the deviant person is more important as a feature of deviance than the behaviour of the deviant person. I have already looked at evidence about the rejection of people who are mentally ill; all the indications are that people are labelled because they are deviant, not deviant because they are labelled.

Labelling theory is not without value. Its scope in the field of social welfare is limited, because so much of it is concerned with formal processes of stigmatisation - particularly by the courts - which have limited relevance to most of the forms of stigma discussed in this study. But the labelling perspective has led to a healthy scepticism of many of the labels we do use, particularly in the field of psychiatry. It has led to an appreciation of the role that social agencies play in marking off deviants from the rest of society. It also helps to explain the reluctance of many people to put themselves in a position where they will be identified as deviant.

The conditions under which a label is accepted depend, however, on the nature of the stigma. Gove (1976) argues that a formal label makes little difference to disabled people, but in some cases it may have a positive advantage, because of the services which follow labelling (pp.68-69). This is true to some extent - although it is worth remembering that there is substantial resistance among physically disabled people to registration as disabled (New Society, 1978, 3). The balance which has to be struck is the choice between costs and benefits described by Weisbrod (1970). It is true that in certain cases the benefits may outweigh the costs, but there is a cost attached to the acceptance of a label which should not be denied.

IMPLICATIONS FOR POLICY.

Labelling and welfare.

The history of social administration is littered with futile attempts to achieve overnight reform by changing the names of services. 'Public assistance' was introduced in 1930 as a reform to dissociate welfare from the stigma of out-relief under the Poor Law; it soon acquired a stigma of its own. 'Transitional payments' were introduced for the unemployed, later renamed, in 1934, 'Unemployment Assistance'. As part of the abolition of the Poor Law, in 1948, Unemployment Assistance became the basis of National Assistance. (A similar change was made in France in 1954, when public assistance was renamed as 'social aid': Stevens, 1973, 10.) And when National Assistance was discovered to be disliked, after Richard Crossman had announced,
    I will change the name only when I have changed the
    system (cited Kincaid, 1973, 36),
the name was changed to Supplementary Benefit. It is not that, throughout this time, the services did not change; but in practice, the most significant changes, like the abolition of the household means test in 1941, had little or nothing to do with the new beginnings trumpeted abroad by a change of name.

It is not only the services that go under different names. Mentally handicapped people in the UK are called 'subnormal' or 'severely subnormal'; in the US, they are 'mentally retarded'; in Australia, they are 'intellectually handicapped'. 'Degenerates' have become the undeserving poor, multiproblem families, hard to reach, or problem families (a term which, Matza (1967, 290) points out, conveys the point that they are a pain in the neck). Poor people have been

called the poor, the lumpenproletariat, the submerged tenth,
the abyss. Unemployed people used to be 'idle'. A recent
letter to the Guardian suggested,
>   Sir, - The word 'unemployed' has developed unfortunate
>   connotations. Would not the use of the description
>   'unproductive' be preferable in present circumstances?
>   (Guardian, 1980.)

I was charmed by the silliness of this proposal; it is not
only that 'unproductive' means something quite different from
'unemployed', but that besides it seems to me to have no
advantage in the images it evokes.

Disreputable poverty, Matza (1967) writes,
>   has gone under many names in the past two centuries. The
>   major thrust and purpose of word substitution has been to
>   reduce and remove the stigma, and perhaps one reason for
>   its obsessiveness is that the effort is fruitless. The
>   stigma adheres in the referent and not the concept.
>   (p.289.)

This is, I think, the crucial point. The services acquire a
bad reputation because of the people they deal with, the way
they deal with them, and the dependency they entail; the
change in name makes little difference.

At the same time, names are important. They serve to identify
a stigmatised group. Blaxter (1975) distinguishes the stigma
of the general label from the specific label. She notes that
disabled people choose the label with less negative
connotations. They may, for example, say that they are
'diabetic' rather than 'disabled', but prefer the term
'disabled' to 'epileptic'. (I have noticed a tendency among
some people I have worked with to prefer the term 'registered
disabled' to 'disabled', but I do not know whether this is
representative of a wider feeling.) Similarly, it could be
argued that it is better to be thought of as a 'widow' than a
'single parent', and 'single parent' is better than 'unmarried
mother'.

Names also convey ideas about people. Nunally (1961) found
that the words describing mentally ill people - words like
'mad' or 'insane' - were not only misleading, but had strong
negative connotations. Mentally handicapped people used to be
called idiots, morons, imbeciles or feeble-minded, under the
1913 Mental Deficiency Act. These words are still insulting
now, in a way that 'subnormal' is not. The Royal Commission
on Mental Illness and Mental Deficiency (Cmnd. 169, 1957)
remarked:
>   We consider that the public attitude towards mental
>   disorder has outgrown the terms 'idiot', imbecile', and
>   'person of unsound mind', and that new terminology is
>   needed to make a step forward from ancient prejudices and

fears and to be an outward sign of real advance in public
sympathy. (p.59.)
There is some justice in this.   'Subnormality' was a   step
forward from 'idiocy' - it could hardly have been worse.

There are two things which distinguish the importance of names
in the fields of public assistance and mental handicap.
Firstly, public assistance is a system; mental handicap is a
problem.   If systems are stigmatised largely through the
people they serve, it does not help to change their name
without at the same time changing references to the people
they serve.   Changes of this kind have been made, in the
history of the Poor Law, with large groups of people ceasing
to be 'paupers': in 1885, when an exception was made for
hospital treatment; in 1908, for those who received old age
pensions; in 1930, for people on 'public assistance'; and in
1948, when pauperism was abolished.   It seems, in general, to
have helped - although avoidance of the workhouse and the
material disadvantages of pauperism may be enough to explain
the improvement in status.   Secondly,   the names imply
different things about the people involved.   There is, in the
sense   of   'handicap',   no   sense   of blameworthiness or
responsibility.   The idea of 'assistance', on the other hand,
conveys only dependency, and 'Supplementary Benefit' is a
piece of gobbledegook that conveys nothing at all.   Nunally
(1961) offers a technique, the 'semantic differential', which
makes it possible to assess the impact on attitudes of
different names. It is important that, before any further
change is made, some investigation is undertaken to see
whether it would help.

Morality and social control.

The social services are sometimes organised in a way that will
penalise moral turpitude.   Elman (1966), for example, records
how applicants for public housing in New York could be evicted
if they had illegitimate children (a similar policy was
declared illegal in Arkansas in 1967: Mandelker, 1973, 64); if
the husband and wife had beeen separated twice in the past
five years; if their work history was irregular; if they had
ever been evicted from public housing; and, strangely, if they
were mentally retarded (p.22).   The Cullingworth report on the
allocation of council housing in England expressed surprise
    to find some housing authorities who took up a moralistic
    attitudes towards applicants: the underlying philosophy
    seemed to be that council tenancies were to be given only
    to those who 'deserved' them and the 'most deserving'
    should get the best houses.   Thus unmarried mothers,
    cohabitees, 'dirty' families, and 'transients' tended to
    be grouped together as 'undesirable'.   (Central Housing
    Advisory Committee, 1969, 32-33.)

The suspension of unemployment benefit for industrial misconduct, the loss of rights by people who are judged to be 'intentionally' homeless, or the steps taken to curb 'abuse', are symptomatic of the prevailing moral framework. "Where morality is at issue", Handler argues, "welfare is conditioned, regardless of any notional entitlement" (1972, 24).

Moral stigmas, and the policies based on them, serve a purpose. They control the undesirable behaviour of individuals, in cases where that behaviour is itself detrimental to other people (as it may be, for example, in the case of some mental illnesses) or where the behaviour is inconsistent with the maintenance of the social structure, which it could be argued to be where work or family relationships are abnormal. Mary Douglas (1966) argues that morality itself serves a function by defining a society within common boundaries. So is it desirable that moral stigmas should be overcome?

I believe it is. Social welfare should seek to benefit individuals as well as society as a whole; it emphasises the need to integrate people into society. It is true that a moral norm can itself be an integrative force for the people who are not cast out, but this can only work at the expense of those who are. The material effects of moral stigmas on illegitimate children are difficult to defend. The stigma of mental illness, which is in part a moral stigma, may cause people to deny their problem and avoid seeking treatment. The stigma of venereal disease, which is largely moral, may have a similar effect, as well as causing people to conceal the sources of contagion. The moral condemnation of welfare recipients leads to harassment and humiliation. This is not to say that moral stigmas are not, in some cases, justified on other grounds. But, from the point of view of welfare, censure and confinement are not constructive. The object of the social services must be to improve the condition of the recipient, rather than to control his behaviour.

CHAPTER 7: SUMMARY.

Moral stigmas are occasioned by the breach of a moral rule. They imply a separation between normal and deviant groups. Deviance has been attributed to pathological immorality, the rejection of social values, 'drift', or because deviants are forced into deviance by society through the process of labelling. Each of these has limited relevance to social welfare. Moral stigmas may be used in social policy for the purpose of social control; this approach may be inconsistent with an intention to improve the condition of the recipient of social services.

Part 2: conclusion

This part has covered a wide range of material, and because it has dealt with diffuse and different problems, it has perhaps not seemed to form a cohesive whole. This is more a reflection on the concept of 'stigma' than on the construction of the argument. In practical terms, there are important distinctions to draw between people who are epileptic, old, alcoholic, unemployed, slum dwellers, or single parents. No one policy is appropriate to deal with all these forms of stigmatisation. Physical and mental stigmas call for enablement and normalisation; poverty needs rights, power or the redistribution of resources; dependency requires the opportunity to contribute to society; moral stigmas should lead to the re-integration of the offender. There are conflicts between these different kinds of policy, and contradictions in the policies that are followed for any particular stigmatised group. Many of the policies advocated at present are inappropriate; they may work for some groups of stigmatised people, but not for others. Participation is useless for people who have no interest in it. Donative rights are not very helpful to people who are stigmatised for dependency, although they may be valuable as a protection against disadvantage and a guarantee against deprivation. Collective action may have advantages for poor people which it does not have for those who need individual rehabilitation; rehabilitation, conversely, may not be satisfactory for poor people.

A further problem is that a policy aimed at reducing stigma in one way may increase it in others. Increased redistribution entails increased dependency. The establishment of rights, self-help or participation by a group fosters the idea that they are respectable, which may be a deviant attitude; it may serve only to make them more identifiable. An emphasis on individual rehabilitation may lead to a distinction between deserving and undeserving people. Different solutions may conflict with each other. It is contradictory to encourage participation and attempt to conceal a stigmatised group. It is contradictory to assert that both a minimum standard of living and a 'right to fail' are necessary for respect. And, although it happens throughout the social services, it is contradictory to give a person rights and status and then tell him that his condition is not legitimate and that he must be rehabilitated.

To what extent, then, can stigma be considered a unified concept? Goffman argues that, despite the apparent differences between stigmas, stigmatised people do have enough in common to merit classsification together for the purposes of analysis (1963, 174). This argument is examined in the subsequent part.

Part 3

The social relationships of the stigmatised person

Introduction to part 3

At the beginning of the second part, I argued that stigma cannot be seen solely in terms of the characteristics of the stigmatised person, but must also take into account the feelings of stigmatised people and others. In this part, I intend to discuss whether these feelings can be said to create a common experience of stigma. Firstly, the attitudes of other people may be influenced by factors which have little to do with the stigmatised person. In chapter 8, I consider whether prejudice towards stigmatised people is directed in the same way towards different kinds of stigma. Secondly, Goffman argues that there are fundamental similarities between the attitudes and reactions of stigmatised people in a variety of circumstances. These arguments are considered in Chapter 9.

Chapter 8

Stigma and prejudice

THE NATURE OF PREJUDICE.

There are many types of negative attitude. They include
disapproval, dislike, contempt, aversion, repulsion, fear and
mistrust; and they occasion discomfort, strain, pity, censure,
hostility, isolation and superstition. This is commonly
summed up as 'prejudice'. Prejudice is a portmanteau term,
which covers not only the attitudes and feelings of one person
towards another, but also his behaviour. Lyketsos and
Panayotakopoulos (1970), for example, include in 'prejudice'
against the mentally ill the likelihood that a person will
avoid, deprecate, disfavour, deny employment to, delay the
treatment of or physically attack someone who is mentally
ill. This collection of attitudes and actions is sometimes
taken as directly equivalent to 'stigma' (e.g. by Mulford,
1968). Allport (1954) defines prejudice as
> an avertive or hostile attitude toward a person who
> belongs to ... (a) group, and is therefore assumed to
> have the objectionable qualities ascribed to the group.
> (p.7.)

Prejudiced attitudes are stereotyped; they are based on the
group, not the individual. Katz and Braly (1961) show that
people respond to certain words with irrational
preconceptions: people were prepared to say things about
Turks, for example, although they had never met one (p.43).

Berger and Luckman (1967) argue that stereotypes –
"typifications of social action" – are essential means of
organising our knowledge of the world (p.31). Without them,
the information we receive would be unmanageable. Stereotypes
lose definition when their objects are distant. The
difference between generalisation and prejudice is, they
argue, a matter of degree. Allport, by contrast, believes
that stereotypy is a distortion of the natural process of
categorisation. "Prejudgments", he writes,
> become prejudices only if they are not reversible when

exposed to new knowledge. (1954, 9.)
The distinction is an important one. In the European study of
poverty, 45% of those in the UK who had seen people in poverty
thought that the cause of poverty was laziness, compared with
43% of the total (Riffault, Rabier, 1977, pp.69,71). In other
words, the experience of seeing poverty makes little
difference to expressed opinions. This is almost certainly
the result of stereotypes, formed without reference to
experience and maintained after it.

It does not follow, from the fact that a negative attitude is
held about a group, that we know what a person's reaction will
be. It could, for example, be fearful, contemptuous, or
hostile. Moreover, stigmatised people are not regarded as an
undifferentiated mass; different stigmas evoke different
reactions. Although there are similarities, which I hope to
elaborate, the stereotypes of mental illness are not the same
as the reactions to physical disability, or to dependence on
social security. Stereotypes are created by an interaction
between the people who come to form prejudices and others who
are the objects of them.

The origins of prejudice are complex. Allport (1954)
identifies six different categories of causation. These are
historical, socio-cultural, situational (that is, deriving
from a social environment), psychodynamic, phenomenological
(deriving from contact between people), and an emphasis on a
reputation which a person or group may have earned (ch.13).
The point comes, however, when it is difficult to distinguish
these factors from each other; historical factors merge into
socio-cultural ones, socio-cultural into situational, and so
on. Although the first two categories apparently describe
continuities in prejudice rather than its origins, this
distinction cannot be reinforced in practice. I have tried,
in consequence, to merge the categories into a broad
classification, distinguishing only the social roots of
prejudice - the bases of commonly held prejudices - from the
influence of individual characteristics which may help to
explain why some people accept stereotyped views when others
do not.

THE PREJUDICE OF INDIVIDUALS

Blaming the victim.

"It is a principle of human nature", Tacitus wrote, "to hate
those whom you have injured"; and negative reactions to the
victims of society have been explained in similar terms. Katz
et al. (1977) argue that there is a concealed hostility
towards the physically disabled, because they are not normal;
there is guilt, because the hostility is unfair; and the

combination of the two creates a tension (or 'dissonance') which is lessened by denigrating the person. This lessens the feeling of guilt (pp.419-420). I have doubts about the general validity of Katz et al.'s study; the findings do not substantiate the view that people feel guilty about their hostility, although they do not contradict them either; and I am not sure that the supposed expression of hostility - inflicting a painful noise on a stigmatised person - is not simply a sign of insensitivity, which would follow from a rejection of the person. Glass (1964) came to a similar conclusion in a more convincing style. He found that people who agreed, despite their expressed principles, to administer electric shocks to others, would either blame themselves if they had low self-esteem, or come to dislike the victim. He also explains this in terms of 'dissonance'.

The theory of dissonance posits that people need to reconcile inconsistencies in their behaviour or their view of the world. Festinger and Carlsmith (1959) found, for example, that people who were paid $1 for doing a monotonous task liked it more than those who were paid $20. They explain this as a result of 'dissonance': the people who said they liked the work were reconciling themselves to the fact that they had spent time doing something that was boring for little reward. Dissonance theory has been substantially criticised, because the experiments on which it is based can be interpreted in different ways (see Chapanis, Chapanis, 1964). Bem (1967) argues that Festinger's experiments can be better explained as the consequence of self-judgments. We judge ourselves, he argues, in just the same way that other people judge us. The people who did the boring work said they enjoyed it because anyone else doing it for little reward would be assumed to enjoy it. Either of these explanations is compatible with Glass's experimental results. The subjects saw themselves as good, principled people; the only way to reconcile their action with their self-concept was to blame the victim.

It is questionable, though, whether people really see stigmatised persons as their victims. Frenkel-Brunswick argues that charity is motivated by aggression. Charity is
> a possible manifestation of atonement which, in turn, is
> known to be a reaction to aggression. (in Adorno et al.,
> 1950, 307.)
Charity is, in consequence, marked by a peculiar ambivalence to its objects. Adorno argues that prejudiced people have been raised in an environment where compassion is forbidden and emotional displays lead to punishment. Their reaction, when faced with people who provoke compassion, is to punish them as they were punished (in Adorno et al., 1950, 700). This theory is intriguing, but I do not find it convincing. Factors such as 'compassion' are not measurable and the

theory is, I suspect, impossible to falsify.

An idea I find more persuasive, because of the empirical work that has been done to verify it, is the concept of the 'just world'. Lerner (1970) argues that people want to believe that the world is fair, and that people get what they deserve (p.203). The theory explains why people of high status should be looked up to; they are supposed to deserve their advantages. On the other hand, the misfortunes of repectable people may precipitate condemnation of their actions. Jones and Aronson (1973) found that a married woman or a virgin who were victims of rape were more likely to be condemned than a divorcee. The injustice in their case was thought to be greater, and this could only be reconciled with a belief in a just world if they were found to be more at fault. Conversely, people with low status are believed to deserve their disadvantages. If they suffer, they are blamed not for their actions, but their character (Lerner, Miller, 1978, 1041). The theory explains why, for example, people should be blamed for unemployment at a time when it is obvious that unemployment is caused principally by economic factors. It also explains why people should feel ashamed of their problems; they feel, in part, responsible for them. This sort of reasoning is pervasive. Herrick (1976) remarks on the survival of the primitive belief that people become ill because they have done something wrong. Their belief causes them stress, guilt, fear and anxiety, and creates a further possibility of illness (p.331). Bulman and Wortman (1977) interviewed twenty-nine people paralysed in accidents. All but one of them had asked themselves, 'Why me?'; and all of these had found some reason. Ten, for example, said that 'God had a reason'; two, that they had deserved it (pp.358ff).

The idea of the 'just world' has noble antecedents. In the Hindu idea of Kharma, there is the belief that everyone's station in life has been the result of their previous conduct, and that anyone not receiving his present deserts will have them in a future incarnation. Gore (1958) uses this to explain the condemnation of beggars in India.

> Begging itself is a misfortune ... But then - in the context of the Kharma philosophy - no person can disclaim total responsibility even for his misfortunes. And therefore, there is a sense of shame attached to begging. The beggar experiences a loss of social status even if his begging is due to factors entirely beyond his control. (p.29.)

There is something of the same reasoning in the traditional Christian concept of Heaven and Hell.

Zuckerman (1975), in a fascinating experiment, found that people who believed in a just world were more likely at a time

of personal stress to help others. Students were asked to
read to a blind student. Those who believed in a just world
volunteered more help as their own exams got nearer. This
reaction was not, however, purely altruistic. They behaved as
though they stood to gain something by becoming more
deserving. Those who believe in a just world are also more
likely to condemn those who have bad luck. So, paradoxically,
  both rejection of victims and compassionate reactions
  toward them derive from the same underlying psychological
  processes. (Lerner, 1970, 207.)
Because a stigma may represent a conflict with belief in a
just world, its presence leads to anxiety, and sometimes, as a
defence against the discomfort it causes, it may occasion
hostility. The theory helps to explain many of the problems
associated with stigma - the relationship of stigmatising
attributes to the attitudes of others, to their feelings, and
the feelings of stigmatised people. Above all, it offers an
explanation for the curious linking of low status and
misfortune with immorality, and this is important to an
understanding of the problem.

THE PREJUDICED PERSONALITY.

Negative attitudes to different kinds of stigma tend to be
assocated with each other. The coincidence of prejudices
suggests that the origins of prejudice lie, not in the objects
of the prejudices - stigmatised groups - but in the people
who hold them. Yuker et al. (1966) found correlations of
attitudes to disabled people with attitudes to mental illness
(r =.19 to .34) and attitudes to old people (r =.26 to .44)
(pp.146-7). Szuhay (1961) discovered that a moderate
association in the attitudes of young children to disabled
people and Negroes (r =.25) became much stronger in older
children (r =.52) (pp.56-7) - suggesting that a process of
socialisation is at work which either leads to generalised
prejudice, or which reduces prejudices in cases where they are
not part of a general framework. And Katz et al. (1977) found
a similar rejection of Negroes and physically disabled people:
  the successful replication suggests that despite obvious
  differences in the status of blacks and the
  orthopaedically disabled in American society, the
  assumption that they are both regarded ambivalently is
  useful for predicting certain types of behaviour towards
  them. (p.427.)

Kogan (1961) found striking correlations of attitudes to old
people with attitudes to mental illness (r =.46), Negroes
(.46), minorities (.43), blindness (.52), deafness (.48) and
cripples (.53). The association was, however, substantially
lower when, instead of agreeing with an unfavourable opinion
about old people, the subjects would have had to disagree with

a favourable one (p.50). This could be interpreted in two
ways. One is that the association is a mark, not of
generalised prejudice, but of a willingness to take
suggestion. This would not mean that the attitudes are
unimportant, because unthinking cliches can still be hurtful
to stigmatised people; but there is no reason to suppose that
these opinions are likely to be reflected in any adverse
behaviour. The second possibility is that it is simply more
difficult, given the ambivalence that we feel towards old
people, to disagree with favourable statements made about them
than it is to agree when they are denigrated. The indications
of an association between different negative attitudes are, I
think, too consistent to be ignored.

It is not possible to maintain that all prejudice is the
outcome of a prejudiced personality. But certain personal
characteristics may dispose people to prejudiced reactions.
Siller (1962) found no distinctive pattern related to the
acceptance or rejection of disabled people, but suggested that
    a negative self-image and disturbed object relationships
    are conducive to an aversive reaction.
Eisenman (1970) also found that people with low self-esteem
were likely to rate disabled people as inferior, and concluded
that
    low self-esteem may be associated with prejudice.
    (p.153.)

This research is mainly related to physical stigmas, and it
may be that this is the only area in which psychological
factors are relevant. There is one major study which goes
further: **The Authoritarian Personality**, written in 1950. The
study was intended to discover the causes of anti-semitism.
The authors rapidly discovered that anti-semitism was not an
isolated problem; a person who was anti-semitic was also
likely to oppose other minority groups, and to condemn
outsiders. This led to a theory of **ethnocentrism**, which
    is based on a pervasive and rigid ingroup-outgroup
    distinction; it involves stereotyped negative imagery and
    hostile attitudes regarding outgroups, stereotyped
    positive imagery, and submissive attitudes regarding
    ingroups, and a hierarchical, authoritarian view of group
    interaction in which ingroups are rightly dominant,
    outgroups subordinate. (Adorno et al., 1950, 150.)
These attitudes form the kernel of the prejudiced personality.
The individuals with the strongest prejudices were examined in
detail, and a composite picture of the 'authoritarian
personality' was formed. In this personality,
    a basically hierarchical, authoritarian, exploitive
    parent-child relationship is apt to carry over into a
    power-oriented, exploitively dependent attitude toward
    one's sex partner and one's God and may well culminate in

a political philosophy and social outlook which has no room for anything but a desperate clinging to what appears to be strong and a disdainful rejection of whatever is relegated to the bottom. (Adorno et al., 1950, 971.)

The signs of this attitude are prevalent in status distinctions. Williams (1956), in a study of an English village, found a remarkably clear division made in people's attitudes to other status groups in relation to their own. The attitudes of the different 'classes' to the lower class are a graphic example. To the 'upper upper' class, the lower class were

the immoral element in the village ... the worst of the lower orders. (p.107.)

To the 'lower upper' and 'intermediate' classes, they were "dirty people". The 'upper medial' class said they were

People who don't try to lift themselves. (p.108.)

The 'medial' and 'lower medial' groups thought they were

Folk who don't care what they look like. (p.108.)

To the lower classes themselves, they were "decent folks", and everyone else was a snob of some degree (p.109). The study generally shows a rigid, hierarchical division of a small rural society, a strong identification with the ingroup, and antipathy towards the outgroups (which in attitudes to higher classes seems to be stronger than deference).

The Authoritarian Personality is a study of a psychological as well as a social phenomenon. The strict divisions that are drawn between groups are an indication of deeper distinctions.

The inherent dramatisation ... extends from the parent-child dichotomy to the dichotomous conception of sex-roles and of moral values, as well as to a dichotomous handling of social relations as manifested especially in the formation of stereotypes and of ingroup–outgroup cleavages. (Adorno et al., 1950, 971.)

In other words, there is a psychological basis for the division between what is good and bad, acceptable and unacceptable, stigmatised and unstigmatised. The lines of battle are drawn up by a society, but the strength of the rejection and its divisiveness is the result of the prejudiced personality. Attitudes to the poor are an example of this.

Abolition of the dole ... the spirit of the adage, 'who does not work, shall not eat', belong to the traditional wisdom of economic rugged individualism ... the ideas involved have a tinge of punitiveness and authoritarian aggression which makes them ideal receptacles of some typical psychological urges of the prejudiced character. (p.699.)

There are other feelings involved: the cynicism of the authoritarian, in believing that people respond only to

material incentives; his projectivity, blaming the poor for
his own passivity and greed; and his adverse reaction to
feelings of compassion, which are apparently linked to the
punishments he received as a child.

The Authoritarian Personality has been heavily criticised on
methodological grounds. Hyman and Shatsley (1954) have
accused it of over-generalisation and discarding contradictory
evidence. The selection of the sample by membership of
groups, rather than randomly, implied that the subjects had a
previous commitment to group values; certain topics in the
scales have been duplicated, and correlations between the
scales are then taken as supporting evidence. These points
are well taken. Adorno et al. set out to prove a hypothesis
rather than to disprove it - which is, from the point of view
of scientific inquiry, a cardinal sin. But criticisms of
methodology do not necessarily invalidate the findings. There
is much in the work that remains challenging and important.

The 'F'-scale, the measure of authoritarianism which is used
in the study, correlates well with negative attitudes to
stigmatised people. Rosenberg (1974) found a correlation of
.86 between the F-scale and authoritarian attitudes to the
mentally ill (pp.30-31). Mayo and Havelock (1970) found that
it accounted for 13% of the variance in the rejection of
mentally ill people by staff in institutions (p.292). Canter
(1963) found a correlation of .43 with the attitudes of
student nurses to mental patients. This affected their
behaviour: there was an inverse correlation of .57 between the
F-scale and an assessment of their relationships with their
patients. Mulford and Murphy (1968) record a correlation of
-.48 between the F-scale and acceptance of mentally ill people
(p.106), and Mulford (1968) found -.50 (p.109). Jabin (1965)
measured various factors against attitudes to the physically
disabled. He found that authoritarianism - including
authoritarian aggression and submission - was associated with
feelings of pity, hostility and repulsion, but most strongly
with feelings of pity (p.55). Noonan et al. (1970) found the
F-scale was inversely related to favourable opinions about
disabled people (r = -.33) (p.6). And Cowen et al. (1958)
found that there was a low but reliable relationship between
prejudice against minorities, authoritarianism, and negative
attitudes to the blind (pp.302-3). The blind are not strongly
stigmatised in comparison to other groups, and a more
pronounced relationship could not really be looked for.

Kogan (1961) found that the correlation of authoritarianism
with attitudes to old people was positive when the sentiments
were negative - but negative when people were asked to agree
with positive statements (p.49). One explanation for this is
that authoritarianism leads to conformity in responses;

Triandis and Triandis (1965) suggest that the F-scale in fact measures conformity to dominant social values, and certainly it contains a ferocious response bias. This would reinforce the idea that stereotypy and socialisation are at the root of prejudice.

Another view is that authoritarians have, more than other people, a peculiar ambivalence - an exaggerated respect for old age coupled with an exaggerated contempt for its weaknesses. This would be consistent with the analysis in **The Authoritarian Personality.** Old people may be low in a hierarchy of physical appearance and financial status, but they are high in a structure that demands respect for seniority.

The F-scale is also associated with a belief in a just world (Rubin and Peplau, 1975, 76-77). The reason for the connection is uncertain; it may be that authoritarianism disposes people to an outlook which facilitates the rejection of others, or simply that both reflect dominant social values. It is clear, though, that authoritarianism is related both to negative attitudes to stigmatised people, and to a general outlook that favours stereotypy and prejudice. The evidence is, however, limited to physical and mental stigmas, and the hypothesis that it can be extended further has yet to be substantiated.

THE SOCIAL DETERMINANTS OF PREJUDICE.

Stereotypes are fostered by a process of socialisation. People learn their attitudes from others - from their families, from social contacts, from written and spoken information; the absorption of generalisations is a part of this process. The formal instruments of socialisation - such as the Press - can have only a limited effect. The Press has been blamed for creating an atmosphere around the claiming of social security benefits which deters or humiliates respectable claimants. But, as Golding and Middleton argue, the role of the Press has been not so much to create an issue - the image of claimants as social parasites was evident long before the Press became a major factor influencing opinions - as to define it, to create certainty in areas where there may have been doubt (1982, ch.3). The majority of their respondents who condemned 'scroungers' claimed that their belief was based on personal experience (ibid, p.172). Socialisation involves a gathering of views from a variety of sources, of which the Press is only one.

Social factors, such as class or culture, are not primary instruments of socialisation, but there is an association of these factors with the formation of stereotypes, because they stand for the environment within which socialisation takes place. There is, notably, a relation of prejudice with social class - that is, 'socioeconomic status'. Some writers present the lower classes as tolerant, permissive and forgiving of other people's misfortunes. Goldthorpe and Lockwood (1963), for example, suggest that a typical 'working class' attitude to the poor is that poverty is the result of bad luck :

    'They have been unlucky'
    'They never had a chance', or
    'It could happen to any of us'. (p.317.)

The middle classes, by contrast, supposedly believe that the poor are idle and could be as rich as anybody else if only they worked.

    'Many of them had the same opportunities as others who have managed well enough.'
    'They are a burden on those who are trying to help themselves' (Ibid, 317.)

This view is questionable. Williamson (1974b) shows that 'many of the poor share the view of the rest of the population' about social security (p.645). Ransford (1972) found that 74% of lower class workers in the US agreed

    There's more concern today for the 'welfare bum' who doesn't want to work than for the hard working person struggling to make a living. (p.338.)

Davidson and Gaitz (1974) found no significant difference in the attitudes to work of the lower class: if there is any difference, the poor are possibly more committed to 'dominant' values than the middle class are. This conclusion is borne out by Cohen and Hedges' study of 'lower-lower class' males. These men valued,

    more than anybody else, the routine, the familiar, the predictable. (1963, 316.)

Their way of thinking is entirely compatible with a strict and conventional morality - as well as stereotyped responses to social problems. It is true that this class is less likely to 'blame the victim' for his poverty, and that they are less likely to demand that welfare recipients should sell their home or car; but the emphasis on dominant values about work and social security means that, in practice, attitudes are less than sympathetic. People in the lowest class are also likely to think that a person's morals should be taken into account in determining whether they should get poor relief (Northcutt, 1959, 52ff).

The lower classes also tend to reject people who are physically different more than the middle class do. Westie and Westie (1957) found, in an important review of evidence about racial prejudice, that there was more social distance between whites and blacks of low status than there was between the races at higher statuses. Negative attitudes to physically disabled people are also more common in the lower

social classes (English, 1977, 165).   Attitudes to mental
defects   are   more complex.   Rootman (1972) found people in
social class IV - mainly semi-skilled manual workers - were
most likely to favour the isolation of mentally ill people
(pp.26-7). Bord (1971) distinguished types of mental illness,
and found that people in low-status jobs were more likely to
reject someone who was paranoid or a depressed neurotic, but
less likely to reject someone suffering from a phobia or
simple schizophrenia (pp.504-5).   Hudzinski (1975) discovered
that people in the highest social class were most likely to
reject epileptics (pp.97-102). The differences in reaction to
different stigmas argue for quite specific differences in
socialisation between the social classes.

This may be because the education of the classes is different
- largely because education determines, in part, a person's
occupational status.   Education has the general effect of
increasing tolerance, and people with higher education tend to
be more accepting (English, 1977, 166).   Tringo (1968) found
that females tended to be less accepting than males; but
       An increase in educational level was invariably
       associated with a decrease in social distance for males.
       The direct relationship was reversed on eight disability
       variables for females. (p.33.)
This is difficult to explain. Gender has been a significant
factor in many studies (English, 1977, 164-5) but it is
difficult to see why education should have opposite effects on
the different sexes.

One explanation is that educated people are less likely to
attach importance to physical characteristics, and more to
other standards of achievement.   This explanation has certain
disadvantages.   One might suppose that someone who puts more
emphasis on mental ability would feel a greater threat, and so
a stronger aversion, than others, when faced with mental
defects; this is not the case. Further, the attitude of
females should, one might have thought, reflect their
socialisation into an exaggerated emphasis on physical
appearance.   But females are generally more accepting of
physical disability, not less; and females who are more
educated, and might therefore be expected to put less emphasis
on physical attributes than other females, are less accepting
than other females.   A second view is that education
encourages patterns of thought that are less rigid and
stereotyped than uneducated views.   This is not, however,
consistent with the fact that educated females reject disabled
people more than other females.

A third explanation is that the responses reflect differences
in the culture of the social classes.   True cultural
variations are important: there are clear differences in

attitudes to stigmas between countries and ethnic groups. Jenkins (1966) found, for example, that Negroes were more likely to stigmatise tuberculosis patients than American whites or Hispanics were (pp.420-1). Sanua (1970) found a wide range of attitudes to cerebral palsy in seven countries, and different determinants of attitudes. Triandis and Triandis (1965) note substantial differences in social distance from physically disabled people in different countries. Tseng (1972) compared the attitudes of US and Asian students to disabled people, and found not only that US students were more favourable, but that those Asians who had been in the US longest were more favourable than other Asian students. Jacques et al. (1970) compared the reactions to disability of males and females in different countries. In the US, there was no significant difference between the attitudes of the sexes; in Denmark, the males were more favourable to the disabled, but in Greece, the females were. This is a strong indication that these attitudes are socially determined.

However, there are also similarities of attitude between countries. Richardson et al. (1961) argue that, although there are differences in the strength of reaction, the ranking of physical disability is constant between cultures (p.244). This implies that there is either a common psychological basis, or a functional one, for the rejection of physical disability. There are exceptions to Richardson et al.'s proposition - like the case of the Kuba - which make reference to a fixed psychological reaction unconvincing. An argument based on the effect of disability on social functioning is stronger. Jackson (1977), for example, makes out a case to look at mental handicap in this way; in any society, he argues, there is a minimum standard of competence below which a person cannot fall. This case can be extended: every society demands standards of appearance, physical capacity, mental capacity and behaviour. In the case of physical disability, the disability itself is the most significant determinant of capacity, and although incapacity may have different implications in the context of different societies, the hierarchy of disabilities remains fairly constant.

The question remains whether there is an equivalent process at work between social classes. Most work suggests that the classes share the same basic culture, but it could be argued that the lower social classes reject physical disability more because physical disability is a greater handicap to people who rely on manual skills or physical appearance. The stigmas rejected by middle-class people - notably epilepsy - are, in turn, the characteristics which might threaten their livelihood if they were found to possess them. Females in general are socialised to put less emphasis on a career in employment, so that they are less threatened by people who are incapacitated; but educated females emphasise work and career more, and consequently reject stigmatised people more.

This interpretation puts a great stress on economic factors, expressed through general social norms which are related to the capacity to work and contribute to society. If it is correct, then the association of prejudice with factors such as class, sex, education and culture reflects the relation of these factors to the norms.

IMPLICATIONS FOR POLICY: THE EFFECTS OF FAMILIARITY AND EDUCATION.

It would seem to follow, from the view that stereotypes are unjustified generalisations about people, that a process which contradicted those generalisations, through education and familiarity with the objects of the stereotype, would break down the prejudice. Moseley (1973), for example, found that children who had contact with disabled children in their classes at school became more favourable to disabled people in general - suggesting that a positive stereotype had replaced a negative one. But this can cut both ways. Gottlieb and Budoff (1973) made a study in an experimental school built without internal walls, and discovered that retarded children were rejected more there than in other schools. Increased contact seems to have led to a negative reaction.

The same problem occurs with educational programmes. Safilios-Rothschild (1970) writes,
> Educational campaigns informing a population about the nature of an illness or a disability and describing specific symptoms may unintentionally bring about a greater intolerance of mildly disabled persons who might have 'passed' as normal. (p.10.)

Cumming and Cumming (1957) found that a project to reform the attitudes of the public towards mental illness because the public's view was more permissive than professional attitudes. This is not to be interpreted as a liberal attitude. It is rather that ignorance allows mentally ill people to pass. If a person is discovered to be mentally ill, rejection follows. Phillips (1967) found that
> the ability to correctly identify ... behaviours as mental illness is not associated with acceptance, but rather with rejection. (p.266.)

Physical and mental stigmas are not particularly attractive. People who come into contact with them may feel threatened; the knowledge that, for example, mental illness can happen to anyone may increase the sense of threat. Sorensen (1972) found that attempts to familiarise people with the nature of epilepsy, by showing a film of an epileptic having a fit,

increased their rejection of the condition (pp.19-20).
Familiarity or education do not necessarily lead to sympathy
or understanding.

It may seem strange, in the circumstances, to talk about
'stereotypy' as the root of the problem. The term seems to
suggest that stigmatisation is based in ignorance, and this is
not necessarily the case. But the term is appropriate,
because there is a process of generalisation about stigmatised
people. It does not follow, because a person has an
unattractive disability, that he is an unattractive person.
The stigma obliterates the other features of an individual
personality, and this is a reaction based on stereotype rather
than mature observation.

Education which concentrates on the stigmatising
characteristic must fail. It only increases the tendency of
the stigma to obscure the characteristics of the person who
has it. It is necessary to encourage people to look at the
person, not at the category he belongs to. Familiarity can
contribute to education only if it is more than superficial;
education is meaningless if it teaches only recognition.
Familiarity and education together can achieve an effect that
neither can have independently, by making people aware of the
stigmatised person as an individual. But the conditioning of
reactions by material circumstances suggests that stereotypes
may prove resistant to change if there is no change in the
circumstances which fostered them.

CONCLUSION.

The concept of prejudice adds a further dimension to the
understanding of stigma. It helps to explain the tenacity of
common misconceptions, and something of the basis of social
rejection. But it is not, I think, helpful to argue that
stigmatisation is directly the result of prejudice, because
the idea of 'prejudice' is itself so vague. The attitudes and
reactions the term refers to, and the reasons for them, are
diverse; none of the accounts given can be considered a full
explanation of the problems, and none excludes others. In the
next chapter, I hope to broaden the scope of the argument by
considering the feelings of the stigmatised person, his
relationship to others, and the consequent effects on his
social identity.

CHAPTER 8: SUMMARY.

Negative attitudes are characterised as 'prejudice'. Some
people tend to 'blame the victim'; this may be attributable to
a belief that the world is just, or to certain traits of
personality. But the effect of socialisation in the creation

of stereotypes suggests that material circumstances may condition the response of social groups to people with certain attributes, and this may vitiate attempts to alter stereotypes through educational programmes.

Chapter 9

The social position of the stigmatised person

THE MORAL CAREER.

Goffman (1963) describes the process by which a person comes to be stigmatised as a 'moral career'. His life style is changed by a series of events, both formal and informal, which channel him into a new status (pp.45ff). A stigmatised person has to adjust, to learn to live with his stigma. The moral career takes into account the process of stigmatisation - the things which are done to him - and the experience of stigma, which depends on his reaction to the process.

Pinker (1971) defines the dimensions of the moral career as **depth, time,** and **distance. Depth** refers to the extent to which a person is made aware of his stigma, and accepts stigmatisation as legitimate. Stigma has a tendency to obliterate any other characteristics a person has; the deeper a stigma is, the more it becomes the outstanding feature of his social identity. **Time** is the duration of the stigma; a stigma that is permanent and inescapable, such as a deformity, creates problems of adjustment that are different from one that is temporary, like unemployment. The longer a stigma lasts, the more likely it is that the person who has it will come "to redefine his total social life in terms of the stigma" (p.170). **Distance** may be social or spatial; it is the distance between a person who is stigmatised and another who holds a negative attitude towards him. As distance increases, it becomes more difficult to distinguish individuals; their characteristics recede and grey until they are no different from the mass of others. A stigma is usually more noticeable than other features, and it tends to be the last thing that fades from view.

These are general dimensions, but they have a personal and individualistic flavour. Depth, in particular, is a source of differentiation, not only between stigmatised groups, but within them; there is no reason why any two people who are ill, or poor, or unmarried mothers, should feel rejected and accept a stigma all to the same extent. The classification describes differences rather than similarities between stigmatised people. Goffman, by contrast, is describing patterns of behaviour which he thinks are common to all stigmatised people in some degree. The stigmatised person has difficulties with his self-concept, in interaction with others, his personal relationships, and his social identity. These elements define the **social position** of the stigmatised person.

THE EFFECTS ON THE PERSON.

The prejudices of stigmatised people.

"The stigmatised individual", Goffman writes, "tends to hold the same beliefs about identity that we do" (1963, 17). Stigmatised people are not necessarily 'wise'; they judge themselves in much the same way, and by much the same standards, as other people do. Orwell (1937) describes how,
> When I first saw unemployed men at close quarters, the thing that horrified and amazed me was to find that many of them were **ashamed** of being unemployed. ...The middle classes were still talking about 'lazy idle loafers on the dole' and saying that 'these men could all find work if they wanted to', and naturally these opinions percolated through to the working classes themselves. I remember the shock of astonishment it gave me, when I first mingled with tramps and beggars, to find that a fair proportion, perhaps a quarter, of these beings whom I had been taught to regard as cynical parasites, were decent young miners and cotton workers gazing at their destiny with the same sort of amazement as an animal in a trap. (Orwell, 1937, 86.)

Dixon (1973) reviewed evidence on the prejudices of disabled people, and concluded that
> By and large, these studies tend to report that disabled persons bear a large amount of prejudice toward disabled people. (pp.53-54.)

But this does not follow a regular pattern. Deaf adolescents were found by Blanton and Nunally (1964) to rate others who were deaf and blind lower than normal people did. Brookfield (1969) found (in a sample that was possibly unrepresentative) that, although the attitudes of disabled people to other disabled people were negative, they were more favourable than the attitudes of those who were not disabled. Dixon (1973) found the same, with the exceptions of amputees and persons suffering from stroke - both groups of people who had become disabled after a period without disability - but noted that they were more favourable to others with the same handicaps as themselves. With that difference, they ranked disabilities in roughly the same order as those who were not handicapped did (pp.98-117). Lastly, Bell (1967), working with a small sample, produced the understandable result that disabled people who accepted their own handicaps were also less likely to think of disabled people in general as different from others.

These results suggest that some people may be sympathetic to their own, but they are not conclusive. In other areas, the reverse is probably true. Crumpton et al. (1967) found that normal people tended to see mental patients as 'sick' or 'dangerous'; the patients themselves were more likely to think of a mental patient as a 'criminal' or 'sinner'. The mental patient seems to judge himself in moral terms, and not in the most favourable way. Similarly, social security claimants, and potential claimants, are likely to condemn other welfare recipients. Wyers (1975), for example, found little difference between the attitudes of users and non-users to statements that claimants were 'lazy', 'chiselers' or that they should be made to work (p.158). And a similar view emerges from other studies:
> 'I felt very bad; I understood it was for people who don't want to work or are lazy. I'd worked all my life.'
> 'I felt like a social parasite.'
> 'I felt as if I was scrounging.' (Richardson, Naidoo, 1978, 25.)

Kerbo (1976) mentions a study he took part in, in which a third of the claimants interviewed agreed with two out of three propositions: that people are poor because they are lazy; that poverty is self-induced; and that people in the suburbs work harder, and if everyone did the same there would be no poverty (pp.173-4).

The condemnation is perhaps more than agreement with common prejudice. As Velho (1978) points out,
> When people accuse others of deviance they are classifying themselves as normal, nice, good people ... Stigmatised by the place they live in, they develop a militantly moralistic attitude, emphasising their position as good and decent people. (p.530.)

This explains in part why blacks reject mental illness more:
> blacks already feel stigmatised as a minority and cannot tolerate the additional stigmatisation of mental illness. (Jalali et al., 1978, 699.)

This intolerance serves to separate them from the deviant group. Ritchie and Wilson (1979) found that Supplementary Benefit claimants aged between 25 and 60
> disliked calling at the office or felt degraded or embarrassed, partly because of the procedure they had to go through, but also because they disapproved of the

other people with whom they felt forced to associate.
(p.7.)
Cooper (1965), in much the same terms, remarks that
those who are unhappy living (in public housing) are
generally far more concerned about the types of people
with whom they have to associate, than they are about
being 'charity cases' living in Housing. (p.181.)

Stigmatised people may share common beliefs about stigmas, but
they do not necessarily have the same degree of prejudice.
Victimisation, Allport wrote (1954),
can scarcely leave an individual with a merely normal
amount of prejudice. (p.155.)
A person can react by sympathy for his own group, as a defence
of his condition; prejudice against the out-group, as a way of
devaluing their opinions; or aggression towards his own group,
in an attempt to separate himself from it.   Any of these is
likely to distort his views in comparison to other stigmatised
people, and consequently to affect his opinion of himself.

The self-concept of stigmatised people.

The concept a person has of himself is a complex thing. It is
important, not only what he believes himself to be, but how he
evaluates his position, and whether he accepts it. The ideas
of self-concept, self esteem and self-acceptance (or
'adjustment') are difficult to separate; self concept has
elements of self-evaluation, and self-evaluation tends to
determine adjustment.

It is easy to make the broad assumption that stigma leads to
low self-esteem. A person who is rejected by other people can
be expected to feel inferior.   Edgerton (1968), for example,
argues that
The label of mental retardation ... not only serves as a
humiliating, frustrating and discrediting stigma in the
conduct of their live, it also threatens to lower their
self-esteem to such a nadir of worthlessness that the
life of a person so labelled is scarcely worth living.
(p.80.)
Ziller et al. (1964) found that neuropsychiatric patients had
a lower social construct of themselves than normal people did
- a form of low self-esteem (pp.61-62) - although it could
also be seen as a realistic assessment of their social
position.   Cohn (1977) found that unemployment caused a loss
of self-esteem.   And Ward (1977) discovered that those people
who identified themselves as old were more likely to accept
negative images of old age - a problem of self-concept,
esteem, and adjustment. Their self esteem was strongly
associated with their attitudes to old age and their
satisfaction in life (pp.144-146), but attitudes were not

directly related to satisfaction (p.172).

On the other hand, there is some evidence that is difficult
to reconcile with this assumption.   The association between
low self-esteem and perception of stigma in welfare benefits
is apparently low - Goodman et al. (1969), in a survey of
several thousand recipients, calculate the correlation at -.06
(pp.60-61).   And the incidence of low self-esteem in
stigmatised people is uncertain.   Blind adolescents did not
have a significantly different self-concept from normal
adolescents (Cowen et al., 1961).   Poor blacks did not have a
lower self-concept than those who were not poor (Coward et
al., 1974, 626).   Disabled people did not have a lower self-
concept than non-disabled people (Brookfield, 1969), and
disabled people who were labelled as disabled did not have
lower self-esteem than those who were not (Christensen, 1977,
108).   A number of studies have shown, on the contrary, that
stigmatised people have a higher self concept than others.
Soares and Soares (1969) discovered that culturally
disadvantaged children have higher self-perceptions than
others (pp.39-40).   Arluck (1941) found that epileptics had a
higher self-concept than others, although they believed that
their behaviour was inferior and they fell further short of
their ideal (pp.50-57).   And Epstein (1955) found that
schizophrenics were likely to rate themselves lowly when a
conscious evaluation was made, but a test of unconscious
evaluation - what they really thought - indicated that they
had a higher view of themselves than others.   This could be
dismissed as a quirk of schizophrenia, but for the fact that
the same higher self-concepts can be found elsewhere.   The
confusion which exists in this field is well summed up by
Wright (1960).   Reviewing studies of the adjustment of
disabled people, she noted that three showed they had adjusted
badly to disability, three more showed no relation, and two
actually showed a better adjustment than people who were not
disabled.   "Psychological processes", she notes, "do not add
up in a simple way" (p.53).   Dixon (1973) found that different
types of disability would lead to different self-evaluations
(ch.5), but it is not clear from the study why this should be.

The high self-concept of certain stigmatised people needs to
be explained.   One possible reason is that people are not
telling the truth - that they are overcompensating for their
damage to their self-esteem.   This is difficult to falsify,
but Epstein's study apparently contradicts it.   Another view
is that the self-concept depends on a comparison with a
reference group.   Culturally disadvantaged children do not
have culturally advantaged people to compare themselves with.
This is not borne out by Arluck's findings: epileptics were
prepared to accept that other people's behaviour was better,
but this did not lead to a low self-concept.   A third view is

that the prejudiced person who is stigmatised will not admit
to a lower self-concept. According to Adorno et al. (1950),
    the   prejudiced   tend   towards self-glorification,
    conventionality of ego-ideal, and lack of insight; and at
    the same time, they exhibit self-contempt which is not
    faced as such and which they try to deny. (p.443.)
This, again, is difficult to apply; there is no clear reason
why the effect should be different for different stigmas.

Goffman (1963) presents the problem as a paradox.
    The stigmatised individual defines himself as being no
    different from any other human being, while at the same
    time he and those around him define him as someone set
    apart. (pp.132-3.)
The stigmatised person sees himself, at one and the same time,
as someone who is inferior and a normal person, as something
bad and something good.   The image which is most important to
him depends on the nature of his stigma, the reactions of
other people, and his own attitudes.

INTERACTION.

Strained interaction.

Blaxter (1976) records that the perception of stigma by
disabled people is strongest
    in all those conditions which threatened the taken-for-
    granted world of everyday interaction ... (e.g.) ataxias,
    spasticity,   severe   multiple sclerosis,   deafness,
    blindness to a lesser extent, and epilepsy. (p.198.)
Physical stigmas intrude on contact with other people, making
conversation awkward, tense and constrained.   Goffman (1963)
extends this to all forms of stigma.   He distinguishes four
features of stigma which affect the pattern of interaction.
One is visibility.   The second is given the clumsy title of
'known-about-ness', which describes the extent to which other
people might know about a stigma beforehand.   Thirdly, there
is obtrusiveness: a wheelchair, he points out, is less
obtrusive than a stammer, because a stammer continually gets
in the way during a conversation. Lastly, there is 'perceived
focus' - the opinions other people already have about a stigma
(pp.64-68).

Although Goffman's essays on 'Stigma' are concerned with wider
issues, the focus is very much on the interaction between
stigmatised people and others.   Goffman's work has been
influential, and many of the studies which have been made of
the effect of stigma have looked specifically at its effects
on the mechanics of interaction. A stigma may affect personal
distance, the time of an interaction, or the behaviour of the
parties during their contact.

Several studies have shown that people stand further away from a disabled person than they do from a normal person (e.g. Worthing, 1974; Kleck, 1968a; Comer, Piliavin, 1972). Kleck et al. (1968) tried to assess relative acceptance or rejection by measuring this distance.   The results are a little eccentric: the subjects placed themselves nearest to a professor they liked, furthest from a professor they disliked, nearer to a Negro than to a stranger, and nearer to a stranger than to an amputee (p.114).   But it does seem that there is some relationship in this between acceptance and physical distance.   Kleck (1968a) found that people had more eye-contact when they were listening to a disabled person than they would in conversation with someone who was normal.   He suggests that, because disabled people move less, people who talk to them are unable to rely on the visual cues that they would normally take in conversation, and find it necessary to concentrate harder on what the disabled person is doing (pp.23-26).   Langer et al. (1976) take a less charitable view of the process.   People want to stare at the disabled, they argue, because they are different. Unfortunately, it is rude to stare.   This could be a reason for the distance they keep from stigmatised people.   The amount of eye-contact a person is permitted is a function of the distance he is placed from someone he is talking to (Argyle, 1967, 88).   Standing at a further distance makes it easier to stare; it also makes interaction more formal.

A second possible effect on interaction is the effect on the time that someone takes with a stigmatised person.   Kleck et al. (1966) argue that a disabled person was given more time; Worthing (1974) that there was no significant difference. Thirdly, the behaviour of others towards stigmatised people is often different to their behaviour towards those who are not disabled.   Kleck (1968a) judged that conversation with disabled people tended to be stereotyped and lacking in variety, and that people would distort their opinions into something they supposed was more acceptable to the disabled (pp.25-26).   Katz et al. (1978) found that people were less likely to offer help to a disabled person who was thought pleasant than to someone who was pleasant and not disabled - but more likely to offer help to an unpleasant disabled person than to someone who was unpleasant and not disabled. It seems that people are prepared to make allowances, but are not prepared to treat a disabled person on the same basis as others.

The importance of this material lies in the effect that small indignities can have on stigmatised people.   A stigmatised person, especially one who is ashamed of his stigma, is likely to be sensitive to the subtle differences with which he is treated.   The ways people act in conversation towards him are

likely to reinforce his feelings of stigma, and the effect a
stigma has on him.

Tension management.

When a person's stigma is known about, he has to learn how to
take the tension it causes out of a conversation. This is the
problem Goffman (1963) calls 'tension management' (ch.2).
There is no reason to expect that people will be equally able
to do this, or, for that matter, that they will be very good
at it. Comer and Piliavin (1972) found that disabled people
tended to feel more inhibited, smile more, and have less eye-
contact with normals than they did with other disabled people.
Farina et al. (1971) suggest that ex-mental patients did not
adjust their behaviour, but they **felt** some tension because
they believed that other people were unfavourably inclined
towards them.

Sullivan (1971) attempted to test the relevance of this
concept to social security claimants. He asked a welfare
rights group what problems the claimants - mothers on AFDC -
experienced, and then asked the mothers about them. There is
some confusion, in his study, between tension management and
acceptance of stigma, but there were items which were directly
relevant to tension management. These included questions
whether recipients were self-conscious and concerned about the
impression they made; if they suspected other people of being
two-faced; if they avoided people who were not on welfare; and
if they 'alternated between cringing and bravado'. In each
case the welfare rights group had said that the recipients
did. The means of answers given by the mothers, on a five-
point scale where 1 indicates the most negative answer and 5
the most positive, ranged from 1.62 to 2.64 (pp.108-111). So,
although some individuals may have agreed, the overall picture
suggests that tension management was not important. It may
be, of course, that the welfare rights group simply had a
romantic but wrong idea of what people did and how they felt;
but the results suggest a stronger conclusion - that the idea
of tension management may have little application in cases
where a stigma does not affect the appearance or behaviour of
the stigmatised person. The validity of Goffman's statements
may be limited to physical and mental stigmas.

Information management.

People whose stigmas are not known about are in a different
position. They are, in Goffman's words, 'discreditable' but
not 'discredited' (Goffman, 1963, 57). They have to decide
whether they should let other people know about their stigma,
and, if they do, how it should be done. This problem is
called 'information management'. It is, for the stigmatised

person, a crucial decision.   If he is open about his stigma,
he risks rejection; if he hides it and is them discovered, or
if his stigma is already known about, he may be rejected more
(Jones, Archer, 1976).   Even if he does not reveal it, he may
be inhibited by his own knowledge:

> Concealing the disability does not eradicate it; it still
> remains in the eyes of the person as the barrier to his
> acceptance by the sought-for group. The stigma of
> disability that prompts his efforts to cover up at the
> same time negates his effort. (Wright, 1960, 40.)

Fishbein and Laird (1979) argue that concealment may lead a
person to think of an attribute negatively, and disclosure,
conversely, to think of it positively - which would imply that
disclosure is to be encouraged as a form of stigma management.
A person may prefer to disclose his stigma for other reasons.
It may be a way of looking for sympathy, or a means of
forestalling criticism.   Handler and Hollingsworth (1969)
found that AFDC recipients who are more embarrassed about
being on AFDC than others are more likely to discuss it with
their friends or relatives (pp.6-7).   It may be a way of
asserting that there is nothing really wrong.   Wadel (1973)
writes that

> for many unemployed, their 'aggressive' arguing is an
> effort to maintain their dignity. (p.112.)

The disclosure may be done defensively. It may be accompanied
by some mitigating factor: Clark and Anderson (1967) give the
example of mentally ill old people who compensate for their
loss of status by emphasising their supposedly noble descent
(p.182). It may be done persistently. Erikson (1973) remarks
on a pattern of behaviour by mental patients:

> All children are taught in this culture that it is
> impolite to stare at or make reference to the infirmities
> of cripples ...

(this is an important point; if a person wants to avoid
embarrassing references to his stigma, it is likely the other
person will assist);

> ... So it is interesting to note that the generous
> impulse of outsiders to overlook a patient's less visible
> infirmities is likely to put the patient in an instant
> state of alarm, and to bring urgent assurances that he is
> severely sick and in serious need of treatment. Patients
> often bring this topic into conversation on scant
> provocation and continue to talk about it even when
> fairly vigorous attempts are made by visitors to change
> the subject. (p.388.)

Erikson suggests that this may be an attempt to justify their
condition to the world; a person who is sick is not
responsible for his state. But it could be many other things:
a form of self-abasement, made to expiate guilt (Turner,
1972); an attempt to elicit sympathy; a type of covering up,
claiming sickness to avoid the accusation of madness; or a

consequence of self-absorption that convinces people that
their disorder is of enormous interest to others.

The alternative to disclosure is concealment. Concealment
takes three main forms, for which Goffman (1963) uses the
general term 'passing'. Firstly, people may not tell others
about their stigma, and hope it never emerges. This is
passive concealment. Walsma (1970) quotes claimants of Old
Age Security in the US:
> '...I don't advertise it. I came down in status.'
> 'I wouldn't tell about being on OAS. I would rather
> work.' (p.149).
> 'I don't like to tell anyone as I don't want them to know
> my age.' (p.147.)
Secondly, some people will go out of their way to cover up
their stigma. This is **active concealment.** Concealment shades
into misrepresentation.
> 'I never say I live in Knowle West', one person told
> Tucker (1966). 'I always tell people it's Novers Park or
> Knowle. That clears you of stigma.' (p.64.)
Misrepresentation shades into falsehood. Naturally enough,
not everyone who lies will admit to it, and this makes it
difficult to tell how widespread it is; but Jones (1972)
found, in a small study of boys in special classes for slow
learners, that most said they lied about what they did at
school (p.560).

Petty subterfuge is possible. Schafer and Olexa (1971) give
one example. (Translations from the American are in
brackets.)
> A non-college prep girl (a girl who was not being given
> an academic education in preparation for entry to
> college) told one of the authors that she always carried
> her general-track books (the books used for the lower
> stream) upside-down to make them less identifiable,
> because of the humiliation she felt when other students
> saw them ... (Schafer, Olexa, 1971, 62.)
Many subterfuges are more elaborate. Westergaard (1979) gives
an example of unemployed people in Denmark who may go out
during the day so that people will not know they are not
working; I have come across a similar case in Newcastle.
Fabrega (1971) writes about beggars in San Cristobal, Mexico:
> Most **limosneros** beg only away from their home town or
> city for fear of being seen by people they know. (p.284.)
And Scarfe (1974) describes the embarrassment of someone who
was illiterate:
> on occasions he's walked off the job without being paid
> rather than admit it. (p. 65.)

A third form of concealment can be described as **masking:** a
stigmatised person tries to disguise his stigma as something

else.   Cole and Lejeune (1972) discovered that, among welfare recipients,

> women who   accept the dominant view   of   welfare are more
> likely to view their health as poor than those who reject
> that view. (p.351.)

This may be because they have to be more ill to claim welfare
in the first place; but it may also be that sickness is a more
acceptable reason for dependency than unemployment. (This
leads to the intriguing possibility that the stigma of welfare
may increase the demand for health services: Lejeune (1968,
201) found that people who accepted their dependency less were
likely to see their doctor more.)   Goffman (1963), similarly,
gives the example of mentally retarded people in a mental
institution who pretended that they were mentally ill, because
it was less stigmatising than mental handicap (p.117).

The reaction of stigmatised people to their stigma varies, and
it   is   difficult   to   generalise   about   concealment and
disclosure.   The reaction does not seem to be determined by
the form the stigma takes: Kleck (1968b), for example, found
that epileptics made different decisions about disclosure.
There is some evidence, though, that the importance of
'passing' has been overestimated.   Sullivan (1971) tested
several assumptions made about welfare recipients: that they
delayed making essential payments with their welfare cheques;
they avoided other welfare recipients; and they hesitated to
mention at job interviews that they were on welfare.   There
is no evidence in the material he presents to indicate that
these assumptions were justified.

PERSONAL RELATIONSHIPS.

The attitudes of significant others.

The social environment of the stigmatised person is crucially
determined by 'significant others', the people who are closest
to the stigmatised person.   The most significant others tend
to be the family, and they are affected by the stigma as much
as they help to create it. Scott suggests (1969) that

> high social status is in part contingent upon the ability
> of children to improve, or at least maintain, the social
> status of their parents. (p.127.)

Romano (1968) elaborates this view: the parent regards the
child, in many ways, as an extension of himself. Parents see
in the child a means of transcending death; they derive a
vicarious satisfaction from his achievements.   When people
have a child who is mentally handicapped, it reflects on them.
The child is difficult and demanding to bring up: they may be
able to derive a feeling of worth from meeting the child's
needs, but their reaction cannot be the same as it would be to
a 'normal' child (p.59).   It is significant, I think, that

deaf children who have deaf parents have higher self-concepts
than those with parents who can hear (Meadow, 1969, 432-4).
This may be because children judge themselves against their
parents, but I suspect it has more to do with the reactions of
the parents to the child.

Watson and Midlarsky (1979) found that mothers of retarded
children had in general a more favourable attitude to retarded
children than other mothers did, and that they were more
inclined to think that other people's views were unfavourable.
This may be true; their experience of prejudice may lead them
to the overprotectiveness that is common with parents of
handicapped children. On the other hand, it may be that the
mothers project their own negative feelings onto other people.
Redner (1980) tried to assess from reactions to taped
interviews with mothers of mentally handicapped children
something of the stigma they experienced by association. He
found that there were differences in his subjects' reactions
to these mothers and reactions to mothers of children who were
not handicapped, but that these differences did not depend on
the information that a mother had a handicapped child. The
difference is probably, then, rooted in differences in the
mothers' behaviour - although this will not always be
recognised by the mothers themselves. Dow (1965) found 8 out
of 97 adults, in 58 families, who would not take their
disabled child out to shop, to the beach, or on a visit in the
neighbourhood (p.49). (11 families failed to respond - which
may conceal further embarrassment.) Pehrsson (1972) asked
similar questions about blind children, and found that 60% of
his sample (86 couples) were embarrassed by their children.
This correlated perfectly with their willingness to allow
their child to do household chores, go shopping, or visit
friends with them (p.87).

Schmid (1977), taking this line further, found that the
decision to place a mentally handicapped child in a
residential institution was associated, amongst other things,
with their embarrassment about the child (p.125), their
reluctance to reveal that he was handicapped (p.128), the
visibility of the handicap (p.165), and the sorrow,
disappointment and depression they felt (pp.238-240) - but not
with the severity of the handicap. This represents another
way in which stigma can affect the demand for services.
Alivisatos and Lyketsos (1968) found, in Greece, that a large
proportion - 255 out of 291 relatives - did not want a mental
patient to come home. Nine said that they considered the
patient dead. Four, out of the 36 who wanted the patient to
return, wanted it because they were ashamed to have a relative
in a mental institution (p.363). This could represent a
rejection of the undesirable behaviour of a person who is
mentally ill, but it seems more to be due to his social

position.   In general, rejection leads to the separation of
the stigmatised person from   the community.   Moroney (1976)
notes that
    Families who did seek institutionalisation were not
    stigmatised.   In fact, the evidence seems to suggest the
    opposite.   Families who decided to care for the mentally
    handicapped felt isolated from the rest of the community.
    (pp.71-2.)
This helps to explain something of the social isolation of
residential institutions.   Families are encouraged to remove
handicapped children from   their lives; it is unsurprising
that, once they do, so many fail to visit.

Parents are unusually important, because they control and
shape the social position of the child.   Husbands and wives
also have a special relationship: the husband's status tends
to determine the wife's.   A wife who is in a stigmatised
position is therefore less affected than a husband would be;
the stigma does not obliterate her personality as much as her
husband does.   Edgerton (1967) remarks on how some husbands
enjoy dominating their mentally retarded wives: it is a
'benevolent conspiracy' in which the handicap becomes
irrelevant (p.204).   On the other hand, when the husband is
affected, problems are likely.   Some of these difficulties,
like the fear of financial insecurity recorded by Cappeller
(1972), follow from the handicap rather than the stigma it
carries; but he also found that the wives of mental patients
were concerned about identification with their husbands
(p.105).   Schwartz (1956) found wives afraid they would be
demoted to a lower 'caste' because of their husband's mental
illness.

This sort of fear is not so true of other relatives, although
there is still a fear of stigma by association.   Stigma is
treated as though it were infectious.   Nearly a quarter of the
relatives of ex-mental patients interviewed by Freeman and
Simmons (1961) took this view - mainly on the grounds that
they thought they would lose the respect of their fellow
workers, or suffer embarrassment when inviting people to the
house (p.315).   Gove and Fain (1973) found no support for this
view, because relationships seemed if anything better than
they were before hospitalisation (p.498).   But this does not
mean that they felt no stigma; it is rather, I suspect, that a
person who has been discharged from mental hospital is easier
to live with than someone who ought to go into one, and this
outweighs the disadvantages of stigma by association.

Isolation.

Friends can be expected to react in a similar fashion.   A
friend is not linked as intimately to a stigmatised person as

a member of the family is, and friendship does not convey the
same stigma of association; but, by the same token, it does
not imply the same commitment to a relationship. The
stigmatised person is likely to become isolated. There is, as
Scheff (1966) remarks,

> a vicious circle begun by stigmatisation, withdrawal to
> avoid more stigma, stigmatisation because of withdrawal
> or its effects, and so on around the circle. (Scheff,
> 1966, 98.)

Stigmatisation leads initially to rejection. Bogardus's
social distance scale (1925) gives an indication of this
problem: if, for example, a person says he will not work with
someone who is stigmatised, some coldness can be expected if
they are employed together even though the threat of rejection
is not carried out. But rejection is not the only reason why
someone should become isolated. Firstly, a stigmatised person
may be oversensitive to any slight, and feel rejection where
none was intended. Cappeller (1972) notes that mental
patients

> expressed overtly the over-sensitivity to stigma that
> made it difficult for them, in many instances, to
> differentiate between ordinary behaviour and prejudicial
> reactions. (p.103.)

Secondly, if stigma leads to a lowered self-esteem, a person
may be less likely to make contact with others. Rosenberg
(1965) found, in a study of adolescents,

> a striking relationship between self-esteem and club
> membership. (pp.192ff.)

On the other hand, I have already noted that stigma does not
necessarily imply lowered self-esteem. Moriarty (1974)
records that stigma (by which he means the knowledge that one
is different)

> decreases the attractiveness of the fellow minority
> member. (p.854.)

This is probably because the high self-concept of many
stigmatised people is a compensation for their stigma. The
stigmatised person does not want to be reminded of his
disadvantage; an association with others who have similar
problems would be inconsistent with his self-concept. At the
same time, it cuts him off from others who might best
understand his position.

Isolation is not necessarily the result of stigma. Many
stigmatised people are in a low social class, and members of
the lower social classes are less likely than others to
participate - as the administrators of the American 'War on
Poverty' discovered (Curtis, Zurcher, 1971, 347ff). This may
be the result of cultural differences, of education, or simply
of low income. The last is most likely. Social activities
are expensive; people on Supplementary Benefit are less likely
than others to take part in them for that reason (Clark, 1978,

401). And there are other reasons why stigmatised people may
be isolated. Old people may find that their circle of friends
narrows as they grow older. Disabled people may have problems
getting out and about.

It is difficult to know which factors are most important.
Chaiklin and Warfield (1973) interviewed amputees, who were
isolated to a disturbing degree.
   'I guess ... I can't do anything. I don't participate.'
   'I have trouble getting around. I don't see them so
   often.'
   'I haven't seen my old friends. One is all I've seen
   since I had my leg off. I just stay home. I never go
   out.' (pp.165-166.)
These statements are richly ambiguous. It is not clear
whether the people are rejected by friends, isolated by their
disability, or have simply withdrawn from the world. Rogler
and Hollingshead (1965) write, of the mentally ill person in
Puerto Rico:
   He withdraws from society out of fear that he will be
   stigmatised as a loco; in turn, the rejection of his
   friends and associates pushes him to withdraw. The
   stigma attached to this role is so strong that the
   withdrawal of the sick person from participation in all
   types of social groups appears to be a natural sequel to
   the condemnation he suffers. (p.245.)
Withdrawal can be a reaction to rejection, or an anticipation
of it.

SOCIAL RELATIONSHIPS.

The attitudes of stigmatised people to society.

The stigmatised person is rejected by society, and this could
be expected to colour his attitude to society in turn.
Handler and Hollingsworth (1969) found that the people who
felt embarrassed by receiving benefits were more likely to be
those who had experienced difficulties, and were more likely
to feel that the community was hostile (p.5). Theorists of
deviance have argued that the experience of becoming an
outcast encourages the stigmatised person to behave like one.
Becker (1963) writes:
   Treating a person as though he was generally rather than
   specifically deviant produces a self-fulfilling prophecy.
   (p.34.)
The secondary deviant explores his role, and takes full
advantage of it. This can be extended to people stigmatised
for reasons other than crime. Blind people, Lemert argues,
are forced to make a profession of dependency - they are
expected to be dependent, and consequently exploit their
situation (1951, ch.5).

However, this is only one possible reaction. Levinson (1964)
classifies the attitudes of the stigmatised person to society
in three categories: moral, calculative, and alienative
reactions.   **Moral** reactions are those which accept the
dominant social norms - and therefore stigmas - as legitimate.
Calculative reactions are exploitative; the stigmatised person
tries to make the best of his position.   This corresponds to
the position of the secondary deviant.   **Alienative** reactions
are of three kinds: feelings of powerlessness, normlessness
and meaninglessness. A person feels **powerless** when there is a
probability or expectation that he cannot control his own
fate.   **Meaninglessness** is suffered when he cannot make sense
of what is happening, or predict what will happen in any way.
Normlessness occurs when he believes that he can only gain
control by a breach of norms.

This classification is taken from Seeman's (1959) decription
of alienation, which includes two further categories omitted
by Levinson: isolation and self-estrangement. **Isolation** is a
feeling of distance from society: a low value is placed on
social goals and values.   **Self-estrangement** is distance from
one's self, experienced when a person's actions are not
rewarding in themselves.   This concept of 'alienation' is not
the same as the Marxist idea. Marx's concept of alienation is
most closely linked to powerlessness and, to a certain extent,
self-estrangement.   Meaninglessness has more to do with
Durkheim's classic conception of 'anomie'.   The alienated
person rejects conventional values; the anomic person wants to
conform, but has nothing to conform to. "Social constraint",
Lukes (1977) writes,
      is for Marx a denial and for Durkheim a condition of
      human freedom and self-realisation. (Lukes, 1977, 81.)
I do not think these views are really exclusive, because the
person who is alienated may find he has no values to put in
the place of the ones he has rejected; but they are not alike.

Are stigmatised people alienated?   It is a difficult question
to answer.   Sommer and Hall (1958) found, using a scale which
measured conformity to common values and aspirations, that
newly admitted mental patients were not alienated, but long-
term patients were.   This is hardly surprising: a long spell
in a closed institution may lead people to lose the
aspirations that are common in the world outside, like the
wish to have a car.   Rodgers (1977) found, in a sample of
welfare recipients, that they were more alienated and felt
more powerless and helpless than the group of welfare
officials, teachers and students with whom they were compared
(ch.4).   And Handler and Hollingsworth (1971) found that
welfare recipients who felt stigma were also more likely to
complain about the services - a reaction which the researchers
thought healthy. "The more worrisome cases", they comment,

... are the recipients who do not feel stigma. They seem
to be passive, accepting, satisfied and unable to take
advantage of the few things that the AFDC programme has
to offer. (p.177.)
By contrast, Sullivan (1971), who took his measure directly
from Levinson's work, found a very low correlation of the
attitudes to society with a perception of stigma (p.199);
Goodman et al. (1969), in a large study, record a correlation
of only .01 of alienation with the perception of stigma
(pp.60-61); Joyce (1973) found no significant relationship
between feelings of powerlessness and the extent of dependency
on social services (p.194); and Kerbo (1976) found that those
people with a high sense of stigma were less likely to blame
the system (p.178) - which suggests they were less alienated
than others. It is possible that the relationship of
alienation to stigma would be clearer if 'alienation' were
assessed by other criteria - in particular, isolation or self-
estrangement - but this must wait for further research.

The relation of stigma to anomie is also difficult to assess.
An individual scale of 'anomia' has been devised (Srole,
1956), and Rodgers (1977) found using this that welfare
recipients were more likely to be 'anomic' (ch.4); Sullivan
(1971), on the other hand, found no real association of
'meaninglessness' and stigma (p.199). There is some
indication that anomie, in the traditional sense, is not
related to stigma. Durkheim (1952) found that poor people
were less likely than others to commit suicide. Suicide, he
argues, is an indicator of anomie; it follows that poor people
are less likely to be anomic, possibly because they are more
constrained by society (ch.5). Sainsbury (1955), similarly,
found that
    in distribution, poverty and suicide are mutually
    exclusive. (p.251.)
But poverty is a stigmatised condition. It could be argued,
therefore, that stigma is not related to anomie. But this
approach is questionable. Firstly, suicide is higher in
'degraded' areas (HL Smith 1955, cited Sainsbury, 1955, p.50),
where stigmatised people live. Secondly, Sainsbury found that
    among the suicides were many who had lost status, either
    through unemployment, illness, business failure or the
    poverty of old age. (1955,72.)
This was not statistically significant, but it squares with
the view that stigma can lead to anomie. A person who loses
status has, for a certain time, a spoiled identity; a
discrepancy between status and self-concept is forced on him.
At the same time, he loses his place, and his role, in
society; he loses the security that his acceptance of social
values had given him. Stigmatisation and anomie, in this
event, are results of the same process.

Clifford (1975) argues, after Goffman, that a stigmatised
person accepts the values of society. He feels stigmatised
precisely because his acceptance of those values leads him to
condemn himself, and makes him aware of how others feel – or
makes him feel that they are condemning him (p.53). This
would suggest that stigma is the reverse of alienation and
anomie: that it stems, not from the rejection of social
values, nor from the lack of them, but from their acceptance.
It is unwise, I think, to assume that one explanation excludes
the others. Stigmatisation is complex, and the careers of
stigmatised people differ. Some may be alienated, some
anomic, while others accept the norms that condemn them.
Those who accept dominant values are the most likely to feel
stigma; but they are not the only people affected by it.

Spoiled identity.

Goffman (1963) describes stigmatisation as the spoiling of
social identity. Stigma, he writes,
> constitutes a special discrepancy between virtual and
> actual social identity (pp.12–13);

that is, between those characteristics attributed to the
stigmatised person, and those which he can be proved to
possess. This formulation is unsatisfactory. Firstly, social
identity is defined by society, and it is unclear how someone
can be 'proved' to be different from that definition.
Secondly, there is no reason why a person who is discredited
because of an attribute or characteristic he actually
possesses should not be said to be stigmatised. Watson (1980)
argues that people who are responsible for their condition
> should be stigmatised – they deserve it. (p.56.)

It should be clear, he writes, that
> an individual responsible for his dependence on social
> services to provide what would otherwise be found through
> his fulfilment of the work role or maintenance of
> supportive family relationships, on the principle of
> respect for person, is unduly reliant, and the individual
> is justly a victim of stigma. (pp.56–57.)

Goffman's conception of stigma does not leave room for this
interpretation. As Lemert writes (1972),
> The definition of stigmatisation as a collective process
> which necessarily misrepresents what (the stigmatised
> person) has done and attacks his integrity permits the
> deduction that it 'naturally' arouses feelings of
> injustice. (Lemert, 1972, 67.)

The idea that someone is only stigmatised when there is a
discrepancy implies that he is being dealt with unfairly.
This is not necessarily true.

Thirdly, as Goffman himself says, it is important to
understand what a man believes himself to be, rather than what

he actually is.   The feelings of a stigmatised person are
inseparable from the idea of stigma.   It is true that in some
cases, there is a discrepancy between self-concept and social
identity, and if the idea of spoiled identity has any meaning,
it must be within this context.   Blaxter (1976) gives an
example from her study of physically disabled people.

> They defined themselves as normal except for a handicap
> that was purely physical, but it seemed to them that they
> were being defined   as   abnormal in character,   or
> intelligence, or mental condition.   They were being
> labelled in ways which they felt to be entirely wrong and
> unfair. (p.203.)

Spoiled identity is a   form of maladjustment - Lemert (1951)
calls a person in this position a 'maladjusted deviant' (p.91)
- because a person does not accept a social definition of
himself.

If a person has a high self-concept and low status, he is
going to feel resentful if he is treated in a way that is less
than he thinks it should be.   Goffman's proposition seems too
obvious to disagree with.   But the dimension of time changes
this simple pattern.   Bem (1967) argues that people's opinions
of themselves are determined by other people's opinions:

> Self-perception ... is a   product of social interaction.
> (p.75.)

This suggests that there should be a reformulation of a
person's self-concept as time goes on,   leading him to accept
the social definition of his identity.   This does not always
happen.   Carson (1967), for example, found in a survey of
welfare recipients and   others using Vocational Rehabilitation
Offices that

> The group that scored highest on self-concept and self-
> acceptance was the group that had received welfare for
> three years or more. (p.427.)

This is paradoxical.   Brehm and Cohen (1962) try to explain a
similar problem in terms of cognitive dissonance:

> where the behaviour cannot be changed or misinterpreted,
> that is, where the cognition of behaviour is also highly
> resistant to change, then the dissonance may well be
> reduced by a reaffirmation of that aspect of the self-
> concept with which the behaviour is discrepant.   In other
> words, the discrepant behaviour may only strengthen the
> dissonant aspects of the self-concept. (p.59.)

A stigmatised person compensates for the discrepancy between
ego- and social- identity by shoring up his self-concept.   A
simpler way of putting it might be that he denies there is
anything wrong with him, and therefore he does not have to
feel uncomfortable about it.   An illustration of this process
is the way in which unemployed people deny that other people's
opinions are important to them.   Cohn (1977) asked both
employed and unemployed people whether it mattered to the

unemployed what other people thought.   Unemployed people were
more likely to say it did not.   In effect, a person with
spoiled identity tries to preserve an image of himself which
is only defended by ignoring the opinions of others.   If he
fails to do this, his self-esteem will plummet.

The idea of 'spoiled identity' introduced by Goffman can be
presented in another way: as a discrepancy between features of
a social identity.   A stigma is a characteristic which forces
someone into a position that is lower than the one he would
otherwise occupy.   In this form, the idea of 'spoiled
identity' bears a striking resemblance to that of **status
inconsistency**.   Lenski (1954) introduced the concept as
'status crystallisation'.   A person's social position was
determined by his position in a number of hierarchies - in
particular, hierarchies of income, education, occupation and
ethnic group (p.406).   A person who is high in all the
hierarchies, or low in all of them, has a high degree of
status crystallization.   People who were high in some and low
in others - like a black doctor, or an unemployed graduate -
had a low status crystallization.   The person with low
crystallization was in a position similar to Stonequist's idea
of the 'marginal man' (1935).   Placed between two cultures,
the marginal man is a part of neither.   The result, Lenski
suggests, is that the person with incongruent statuses has
problems in dealing with others that cause him to avoid
contact and limit his participation in society.   Lenski's
findings can be explained as an example of spoiled identity.
A person may formulate an image of himself by referring to a
higher status; but there is then a discrepancy between this
image and his lower statuses.   The unemployed graduate is an
instance of this.   His education leads him to think highly of
himself; his unemployment causes others to look down on him.

However, the idea of status inconsistency has been knocked
firmly on the head by empirical research.   Bauman (1968) found
that status inconsistency had no significant effect on the
behaviour of working-class people, and an opposite effect to
that predicted on middle-class people.   Segal et al. (1970)
found that inconsistency didn't matter; people simply averaged
their statuses.   Blocker and Riedesel (1978) comment on a
        near-total absence of positive findings ... (pp.285-6)
and find that, even when an attempt is made to use a
subjective test of inconsistency, there is no effect:
        In day-to-day life, the average person is not really
        bothered by the inconsistencies in status which somehow
        do bother sociologists. (p.287.)
Where does this leave the idea of 'spoiled identity'?   The
adjustment of people to their incongruent statuses is, I
think, to be expected; discrepancies in social identities
become irrelevant.   Spoiled identity may be a part of the

moral career, but it is not a permanent feature of it.

STIGMA AS A SOCIAL RELATIONSHIP.

The moral career has a dimension of structured social relationships as well as the personal problems which arise from immediate contact. The process of stigmatisation is determined by the behaviour of others toward the stigmatised person, and it is possible to represent this process in terms of its effect on social relationships. Three main aspects may be distinguished. The first is the lowering of the status of the stigmatised person; the second is the denial of status; and the third is the denial of humanity.

Status is directly related to esteem. Weber called status
>   a quality of social honour or a lack of it ...
and asserted that status groups are
>   determined by a specific, positive or negative, social
>   estimation of honour. (Gerth, Mills, 1948, 186-187.)
There are, clearly, close connections between status and stigma: Watson (1980) suggests that they are two sides of the same coin (p.48). People who are stigmatised may lose position, either because a stigmatising characteristic may limit their capacity to adopt certain social roles, or because some stigmas - like unemployment, or financial dependency - define inferior roles for them. Stigmatised people are also likely to be poor, because they are unable to earn or are in a position where they are not earning; their life style is therefore restricted. Brown (1966) writes:
>   There must be few situations more degrading to the
>   dignity of man than the realisation that his disability,
>   which has already deprived him of his independence, will
>   eventually demote him to a socially inferior class.
>   (p.135.)

Most important, stigma is a quality of social dishonour: a mark of degradation, loss of esteem, or loss of reputation. Low status implies inferiority, and the imputation of inferiority is an aspect of stigmatisation. People with low status may have problems which are similar to those of stigmatised people: Newby (1977), for example, records a comment from an agricultural labourer who told him,
>   I hide it I'm a farm worker if I go out - I won't tell
>   anybody. (p.346.)
And it can be argued that it is stigmatising to treat somebody as a social inferior. Fabrega (1971) describes how
>   Residents of San Cristobal usually refer to **limosneros**
>   (beggars) regardless of their age, sex or background by
>   means of the informal personal pronoun 'tu' and overtly
>   describe their status as a socially inferior and
>   reprehensible one. (p.284.)

Stigma and low status become difficult to distinguish. Titmuss (1974) wrote,

> If men and women come to think of (and feel) themselves as inferior persons, subordinated persons, then in part they stigmatise themselves, and in part they are reflecting what other people say about them. (p.44.)

This is not completely adequate as a description of stigma, which goes beyond a sense of inferiority. When Griffiths (1975) writes that

> the system of providing accommodation for the majority of lower income people carries a stigma of inferiority (p.9),

or Goffman argues that we are all stigmatised to some degree (1963, 154), I think they understate the force of the idea, and to some extent devalue it. A person who has an inferior status is expected to defer to others; his life style is restricted; he is held in low esteem. The implications of 'stigma' are complementary, but they are not the same. Stigma is a more extreme and, I think a more restricted, idea than low status; it contains elements, not only of degradation, but of rejection and humiliation.

The second form of stigma is the destruction of social identity - the denial of status, of rights, of a social existence. Goffman remarks, at the beginning of his study, that the origin of the word 'stigma' lies in the brand that was put on a criminal in ancient Greece (1963, 11). But the Greeks also had another concept -   , literally 'dishonour' - which meant both social disgrace and the loss of civil rights. (Aristotle uses this word in relation to suicide : 1871, 105.) The Romans also denied social rights to stigmatised people: the codes of Justinian, formed in 530 A.D., denied legal status to persons who were deaf and dumb from birth. They had no rights, could not marry, and had guardians appointed for them (Meadow, 1969, 430). In more modern societies, legal status has been denied to mentally ill people, epileptics (Gudmundsson, 1966, 100), and paupers. The loss of citizenship is a mark of their social as well as their legal standing; they are less than other people. There is a sense, then, in which the loss of rights is a stigma.

Thirdly, the stigmatised person loses his claim to common humanity. Goffman (1963) writes that

> we believe that the person with a stigma is not quite human. (p.15.)

Stigmatised people are held in contempt. They are often compared with animals, for example, by the public health inspector who told Damer (1974),

> Animals, that's what they are ... (p.227)

or the clerk of the hostel for homeless men, who complained about bedwetters,

they're worse than animals, some of them.   You can't do
anything for them. (cited Turner, 1960, 34.)
A television programme about Rampton, a special hospital for
mentally ill and handicapped offenders, asked a former inmate:
- What was the most frightening thing to you about it?
- Being treated like an animal. (Cutler, Willis, 1979.)
Fabrega (1971) notes that beggars in Mexico who are offered a
place for the night are put in the kitchen, corridor or patio,
like dogs (p.284).

Much of the problem of stigma arises from the fact than people
who are thought of   as animals are treated like them.
Wolfensberger (1969)   argues that the provision made in
institutions for mentally handicapped people reflects the
assumptions we make about them.   We believe that their
behaviour is likely to be primitive and uncontrolled, and so
institutions are designed to be 'abuse resistant' - things are
not left around which they might break.   Because mentally
handicapped people are supposed to be destructive and violent,
they are given what is euphemistically called 'custodial care'
rather than help.   They are supposed to be incapable of
choice, and so there are no light switches or thermostats
accessible to them.   They are dirty, and so there are mass
cleaning facilities.   They are like animals, so they have to
be 'kept' in asylums designed for supervision.   They have no
aesthetic sense,   so the institutions are drab.   Their
inability to learn means that they are given no stimulation.
And because 'animals have no rights', they are not allowed
privacy, property, communication, relationships with each
other, or individuality (pp.70-77).

Each of these aspects of stigma - the loss of status, of
society, and of humanity - is a description of the social
position of the stigmatised person. ' They define his social
identity, his roles, his relationships with others.   But these
relationships are determined principally by the feelings and
reactions of other people besides himself.   The stigmatised
person is treated as an object; and his own feelings are
reactions to a situation which is largely outside his control.
If stigma is seen as a social relationship, these feelings may
best be understood as a reaction to stigma rather than a part
of the stigma in themselves.

CHAPTER 9: SUMMARY.

The stigmatised person has difficulties with his self-concept,
in interaction with others, his personal relationships, and
his social identity.   This reflects his position in the social
structure, which may mean lowered status, a denial of social
status, or even a denial of humanity.

Part 3: conclusion

The diversity of the experience of stigma seems to emerge from
this study more strongly than any unifying factors. Goffman's
belief that stigmatised people share a common experience in
their interaction with others is at best questionable.
'Stigmatisation' refers to a variety of experiences, attitudes
and feelings, which depend on a wide range of personal
circumstances. But this lack of cohesion does not imply that
the use of the term is irrational, or that the idea is
inappropriate. The underlying coherence of a concept rests,
not in an attempt to confine its use to a specific or
unambiguous use, but in a pattern of 'family resemblance'
which defines similarities between related clusters of
factors. The idea of 'family resemblance' recognises that two
members of the same family may be quite unalike, but they are
linked to the family by their similarity to other members.
The experiences of a person with a physical handicap and a low
paid worker may be fundamentally dissimilar, but there are
elements which connect them with other people stigmatised in
different ways. If there is a unifying thread, it rests, not
in the moral careers of individuals, but in the pattern of
structured social relationships which mark stigmatised people
out from the other members of society. In the final part, I
intend to examine these relationships in more detail and
consider their implications for social welfare.

Part 4

Stigma, society and social welfare

Chapter 10

The moral division of society

MORALITY AND PREJUDICE.

Edmund Burke argued that prejudice was equivalent to morality.
It reflected the wisdom and experience of previous
generations. Prejudice, he wrote,
> is of ready application in the emergency; it previously
> engages the mind in a steady course of wisdom and virtue,
> and does not leave the man hesitating of decision,
> sceptical, puzzled and unresolved. Prejudice renders a
> man's virtue his habit; and not a series of unconnected
> acts. Through just prejudice, his duty becomes a part of
> his nature. (1790, 105-106.)

The meaning of prejudice has changed since Burke's time, but
its identification with morality deserves emphasis. Both
prejudice and morality are based on social norms. People are
condemned for a breach of a moral principle; a prejudice is
itself a condemnation. In this, they are clearly comparable.

Gibbs (1972) distinguishes social **expectations** from
evaluations. It is a logical distinction, but in practice, it
is difficult to maintain. People value their concept of
normality, and a person who falls outside the boundaries of
that conception will be valued negatively. As Goffman says,
> We lean on those anticipations that we have, transforming
> them into normative expectations, into righteously
> presented demands. (1963, 12.)

Moral norms are not essentially different from other
expectations, although they are distinguished by the elements
I have described before - responsibility, gravity, and a
social sanction. A moral norm is an idealised standard of
approved behaviour; a prejudice is a generalisation which
assumes a set of negative characteristics. The connection
between them is strong enough to mean that a person who
breaches a moral rule may become the object of prejudice; the
breach invites, not only contempt and rejection, but a
generalisation based on stereotype. Conversely, the person

who is the object of prejudice is likely to be condemned morally.

This depends, of course, on the attitudes of the prejudiced person.   Although many expectations are shared, it is not by any means true that everyone in society thinks in the same way.   Zavalloni (1973) criticises Goffman for presenting a set of middle-class values as a social consensus (pp.72-74).   I think the epithet 'middle-class' is unfair, because working-class people are just as likely to be prejudiced against stigmatised people; but the substance of the criticism is reasonable.   There is not a consensus about these values.   However, there is enough agreement about them to make it a problem when someone falls foul of the norms.   A person who has breached a moral rule, or who is the object of prejudice, becomes the object of a stigma.

A stigmatised person is someone whose characteristics or behaviour go so far beyond the norm as to be unacceptable.   "The general principle at work", Lemert (1972) asserts,
> is a simple one: when others decide that a person is persona non grata, dangerous, untrustworthy, or morally repugnant, they do something to him, often unpleasant, which is not done to other people.   This may take shape in hurtful rejections and humiliations in personal contacts, or it may be formal action to bring him under controls which curtail his freedom. (p.68.)

But it is not quite so simple.   A social division may be caused by extreme social distance rather than positive rejection; it may reflect a relationship between a dependent person and the community, rather than a rule breaker and those who create the rules.   There is, nevertheless, an ultimate division between those who are accepted and those who are not.   The division is dichotomous, because the norms which bring it about are dichotomous.
> Stigma involves categorical societal definitions which depict polarized moral opposites (Lemert, 1972, 63),

and the stigmatised person is an outcast.

DIVISION AND CASTE.

In this respect, the stigmatised person is directly comparable to the deviant.   Scott (1972) argues that the function of deviance is to preserve the social order.   The separation of deviants from the rest of society is to enforce standards within society.   The deviant is
> demarcated off from the rest of society, and moved to its margins. (p.30.)

The deviant is excluded, not so that he will be reformed — little emphasis is put on this — but in order to impress a code on the rest of society.   This extends beyond the moral

issues, although the deviant is generally seen as someone who
is morally inferior.   It includes abnormalities of behaviour,
appearance and social circumstances.   The deviant, or the
stigmatised person, is cast out to uphold the values of a
society.

Nadel (1953) suggests that the outcast is a feature of the
advanced society.   In primitive societies,
        there is no intentional discrimination against the
        offenders **qua** offenders; nor is there any thought of a
        stigma imposed on them.   Rather ... stigmatisation is on
        the whole alien to primitive society. (pp.269-270.)
I find it difficult to accept this as it stands.   The
accusation of witchcraft, which makes outcasts of the accused
and may lead to their deaths, is an extreme form of
stigmatisation (see M.Douglas, 1970, ch.8).   What is true is
that those who break lesser rules in small-scale societies may
be reintegrated rather than cut off from the normal social
structure.
        In principle, the **deviant** act is not considered immoral.
        ... The social attitude to the **deviant person or group**
        corresponds to the attitude to the deviant act.   The
        deviant is not stigmatised, and there is **no secondary
        deviance.**   Instead of alienating the deviant, he is
        reintegrated and rehabilitated. (Seibel, 1972, 255.)

This does not mean that these societies have no position
analogous to stigmatisation.   In traditional Indian society,
there are no outcasts, but there are pariahs. It is a feature
of the caste system that, at all levels, it carries
traditional privileges as well as disadvantages.   The
untouchables have exclusive rights to occupations which only
they can do.
        In a class society the 'people at the bottom' are those
        who have been forced there by the ruthless forces of
        economic competition; their counterparts in a caste
        society are members of some closely organised kinship
        group who regard it as their privileged right to carry
        out a task from which all other members of society are
        rigorously excluded. (Leach, 1976, 183.)
At the same time, the integration of untouchables into Indian
society is not 'integration' as it is understood in the West.
Niesewand (1980) cites a survey of 141 villages in Madhya
Pradesh, where there had been a series of unpleasant physical
attacks on Harijans, the untouchable caste.   Only one
washerman in 82 - washermen themselves belonging to an
inferior caste (Barth, 1960, 140) - was prepared to wash for a
Harijan; 107 out of 124 barbers, also in low castes, would not
cut a Harijan's hair; 56 temples refused them access; 29
village councils made them squat on the floor as a sign of
their low status. This shows a degree of hostility and

rejection far in excess of the reaction that I have described to stigmatised people. The Harijans are treated in a way that is if anything worse than an 'outcast' would be treated in the West.

The system of caste has no direct equivalent in Western society. Barth (1960) describes it as

a pattern of social stratification - that is, a conceptual scheme for ordering the individuals of a community, each occupying multiple statuses, in terms of a limited set of hierarchical categories. (p.129.)

But hierarchical organisation is only one aspect of a distinctive social structure. A further aspect is hereditary specialisation. Caste is more accurately defined as

a hereditary, endogamous, usually localised group, having a traditional association with an occupation and a particular position in the local hierarchy of castes. (Srinivas, 1962, 3.)

It is this feature which sets caste apart from other forms of social stratification. Thirdly, caste depends for the maintenance of social distinctions on the idea of pollution.

Relations between castes are governed, among other things, by the concepts of pollution and purity, and generally, maximum commensality occurs within the caste. (Ibid, 3.)

Castes are separated by social boundaries, and pollution occurs when boundaries are crossed. Dirt is matter out of place; when there is a confusion between those things which ought to be kept separate, there is disorder, and where there is disorder, there is pollution.

The object of the code of pollution, like the object of the exclusion of deviants, is to preserve social order. Pollution disturbs the social order, and disrupts social norms. It is therefore a fundamental sign of immorality - 'therefore' not in the sense of a logical progression, but because immorality and disruption are taken to be synonymous. The borders of society are maintained by 'pollution powers', which are designed to preserve order. Pollution powers, Douglas (1966) writes,

punish a symbolic breaking of that which should be joined or joining of that which should be separate. (p.113.)

A person who tries to cross a boundary is a polluting agent. he is a disruptive force; a source of fear as well as contempt because he threatens to disturb the natural order of things. Douglas argues that "a polluting person is always in the wrong" (p.113); but the polluting person can be a symbol of power as well as an object of rejection, because only a person of power can join things which should be separate. A disabled person is a pollutant; he does not conform to the norms of the body image. So it is that the disabled person is treated, in some societies, as a person with mystical powers: blind people can be taken for seers, handicapped people for sorcerers (Jaques et al., 1960, 10-12).

Paradoxically, the pariah is considered to be a polluting person. It is paradoxical because it is the position of the pariah to be in a fixed place in the lowest caste, which is in keeping with order rather than disorder. But the pariah is also at the bottom of society; he is expected to do the dirtiest jobs, and to work with polluted articles, which do not affect him because he is already polluted. As pollutants, pariahs are also treated as immoral people. They are considered

> innately polluted, manifestly or latently, first by some form of inherited intellectual inferiority resulting in potentially defective mental processes; second, by irremovable forms of ugliness, uncleanliness, or communicable disease; and third, by forms of innate moral depravity which lead pariahs to commit reprehensible, forbidden acts ... Whereas individual members of a pariah group may be overtly free of any of these stigmata, by nature of their genetic identity they are inescapably carriers ... (de Vos, 1967, 297.)

This is strongly reminiscent of the position of stigmatised people in general, and of the 'degeneracies' in particular, which suggests that there is at least a parallel to be drawn between stigma and low caste. Stigma is not the same thing as low caste; there is no element of endogamy, or of hereditary specialisation. But it shares with caste a concept of a divided society, and the importance of repulsion in maintaining social boundaries. Stigma is a form of pollution, a mark of disorder, and the stigmatised person is a polluting person.

STIGMA AND IMMORALITY.

As polluting people, stigmatised people are treated as immoral. This may be fair in some cases. As Watson (1980) says,

> Those who neglect their capacity and opportunity for self-help ... fail to display those abilities which make a human being worthy of respect ... Stigmatisation in such cases is a demand of our social morality. (p.57.)

This may explain, in part, why poverty is considered as an immoral state. A poor person has neglected his capacity for self-help. A substantial proportion of British people are ready to attribute poverty to laziness, drink or having too many children (Riffault, Rabier, 1977, 69); people in the US are likely to blame it on loose morals and drunkeness (Feagin found 48% who agreed this was the case: 1975, 97). At a time when poverty is mainly the result of old age and unemployment,

this opinion indicates an irrational concern with a limited
section of the poor. In general,
    welfare recipients are viewed as being more idle, more
    dissolute, more dishonest and more fertile than they
    actually are. (Williamson, 1974a, 172.)
Free and Cantril (1967) found that two thirds of their sample
agreed
    the relief rolls are loaded with chiselers and people who
    don't want to work (p.27)
at a time when few of the claimants could be considered
employable.

Poverty and dependency are believed to be inherently immoral.
An example of this is the attitude to begging. Begging, in
Britain, is a criminal act.   A beggar is, under the Vagrancy
Act of 1824, classed as a person with a 'disreputable mode of
life'. An ordinary beggar would, when the Act was introduced,
be charged as an 'idle and disorderly person' - an interesting
use of the word 'disorderly' ; one who exposed wounds and
deformities, as a 'rogue and vagabond', and on a second
offence as an 'incorrigible rogue'.   The offence beggars
commit, vagrancy, was the same offence committed by people who
abused the Poor Law, or who possessed implements for
housebreaking (Cd. 2852, 1906, 8). The classification is
revealing: beggars and thieves were clearly linked in the
minds of the legislators.

Dependency is linked with dishonesty.   'Scrounging'   -
'chiseling' in the US, 'bludging' in Australia - is a
dishonest activity, although its precise meaning is unclear:
it sometimes means that people take advantage of the services
available, and at other times implies that they are cheating
the system. However, as Deacon (1978) says,
    whilst scrounging exists, the degree of popular concern
    is out of all proportion to its extent. (p.122.)
Smigel (1953) points out that 'chiseling' is a criminal
offence, but that it does not have the stigma of criminality
(p.60) - perhaps because of the ambiguity in the term I have
noted. Even so, a large minority of people believe that
welfare recipients are dishonest. Kallen and Miller (1971)
found, out of 300 black and 300 white subjects, that 20% and
28% respectively disagreed that most claimants are honest
(pp.86-87).   Similarly, Feagin (1972) found 71% agreeing that
most claimants are not honest (p.926).   Williamson (1974a),
asking people what proportion of claimants they thought were
dishonest, found an average of 41% (p.165). Recently, in the
UK, 30% of respondents to a survey estimated that over a
quarter of claimants were scroungers (Golding, Middleton,
1982, 172) - which is perhaps evidence of a more liberal
attidue.   The belief that claimants are dishonest is
associated with the view that poverty is the result of lack of

effort (Alston, Dean, 1972). 'Dishonesty' which takes the form of working while claiming benefit does not suggest 'lack of effort', and it is strange to see them confused.   Marsden and Duff (1975) suggest that people 'fiddle' by working because it is more acceptable than doing nothing (p.249), although clearly it is also affected by a desire to supplement a limited income.

The East London Claimants' Union (1974) attributes accusations of abuse to a deliberate attempt to control or deter the recipients of welfare; they argue that the members of the Fisher Committee, a body set up to investigate the problem of abuse,

> failed to see that its prime function was that of stigmatising claimants and reducing their self-esteem in the community. (p.88.)

This is, I think, a misinterpretation; the concern of successive governments with abuse reflects a deep public suspicion rather than a specific policy of repression.   The effect, however, has been to create attitudes and an atmosphere in the offices which is detrimental to a service intended to help the individual.   The current policy of the Department of Health and Social Security is to clamp down on abuse as a way of improving the position of claimants.

> 'If we can clean up the image of the unemployed there will be less stigma about people on the dole being scroungers' (a spokesman said).
>
> And perhaps the people who DON'T claim the £300m a year they are entitled to will come forward without feeling they are being branded with the scrounger stigma. (Blair, 1980.)

It is difficult to see how the reputation of a service could be improved by a clampdown on abuse.   If the clampdown fails, it leaves a service with a tarnished reputation; if it succeeds, the reputation is tarnished just as badly because of the adverse publicity which accompanies the clampdown. Poverty and dependency become associated with abuse in the minds of the claimants and of the public.   This may not actually deter people from claiming, but it may be a source of humiliation, and it runs a risk of creating a self-fulfilling prophecy, by making people feel they are doing something dishonest when they claim.   Moreover, the measures which are necessary to deal with abuse involve a rigorous investigation of circumstances which is likely in itself to be the cause of resentment and distress. The concern with abuse is excessive, and the steps taken to deal with it are offensive.   From the evidence of the 'declaration' procedure in the US, they are also wasteful and unnecessary.

Poverty aand dependency are associated, not only with dishonesty, but with sexual immorality.   It is true, as Day

(1977) remarks, that
       part of the stigma toward welfare recipients arises from
       the fact that they are sex-role deviants. (p.872.)
A limited proportion of recipients are female single parents –
about twelve per cent of Supplementary Benefit claimants.
Large families, the other main dependent group which is blamed
for lack of sexual restraint, may contribute to the numbers of
those in poverty – 98% of families with five or more children
have an income less than 140% of the Supplementary Benefit
level (Layard et al., 1978, 15) – but only 8% of the
households in poverty in the UK are families with **three** or
more children, where the man is not disabled (p.30). The
emphasis on having 'too many children' in the European study
of attitudes to poverty is not justified.

Nevertheless, accusations of sexual misconduct are frequent.
Velho (1978) remarks of a building in Copacabana that it was
       notorious as a place of sexual encounters (p.527)
– apparently on the basis that it was overcrowded, and that
overcrowding is an indication of promiscuity. Benington
(1972) describes in Hillfields, Coventry, how
       the process of stigmatisation had begun to label the area
       as a source of vice, drugs and crime. (p.5.)
Berg (1968) describes how a school's reputation was tarnished
by sexual innuendo about the libertarian headmaster (pp.126-
127). Cook and Braithwaite (1979) give the example of
attitudes to vagrants:
       the intensity and frequency with which allegations of
       sexual misconduct are made against vagrants is always
       alarming and invariably at considerable variance from the
       knowledge and experience of workers in the field. (p.8.)
I have already remarked on attitudes to divorced women.
Fecundity is one of the 'problems' of problem families. And
it is interesting to note that criticisms based on sexual
morality may be raised against other stigmatised people, as in
the association of mental handicap (Romano, 1968) or leprosy
(Richards, 1977, xvi) with venereal disease.

POVERTY, IMMORALITY AND DIRT.

Stigmatised people are not only believed to be immoral.
Orwell once wrote,
       It may not greatly matter if the average middle class
       person is brought up to believe that the working classes
       are ignorant, lazy, drunken, boorish and dishonest; it is
       when he is brought up to believe he is dirty that the
       harm is done. (1937, 130.)
And it is the case that the lower classes are believed to be
dirty as well as immoral. Rodman (1965) notes that
       Members of the lower class are often thought to be
       'immoral', 'uncivilised', 'promiscuous', 'lazy', 'dirty'

and 'loud'. (p.220.)
Williams' study of Gosforth, with its descriptions of the
lowest class as "the immoral element of the village", "dirty
people who have no self respect", or "folk who don't care what
they look like", bears this out (1956, 107-108). And poor
people are still accused, partly in jest, of keeping coals in
the bath because they don't know what baths are for (Damer,
1974, 227). Of course, some poor people are dirty. Vagrants
may have nowhere to wash, and no clothes to change into.
Beggars in Ireland, Gmelch and Gmelch (1978) suggest, choose
to be dirty because of the prejudice that someone who is not
dirty cannot be in need (pp.444-6). But as a generalisation,
the accusation of dirtiness is difficult to maintain. Rokeach
and Parker (1970) asked people to rank the values they
considered important to their daily life. Poor people were
more likely to think cleanliness important than richer people
did (pp.102-103); low-educated people ranked it higher than
the higher-educated; Negroes ranked it higher than Whites
(p.109). Their explanation is, simply, that these are the
people who have to worry more about cleanliness; it is more
difficult to keep clean when there is a shortage of hot water,
amenities, or washing facilities, and it therefore takes more
attention. But this does not square with the view that the
poor are dirty. On the contrary, although there may be
practical difficulties in keeping clean, the emphasis on
cleanliness generally compensates for this.

Similarly, the idea that the poor are immoral is very
questionable. There is some indication that some poor people
do not share a conventional moral attitude to the family.
Rodman (1971) argues that this stems from the marginal
importance of the male in the family as breadwinner, which
necessitates a reduction in the stability of marital
relationships. But tests of moral values have indicated that
there is a more rigid adherence to traditional moral
standards among the lowest classes (Cohen, Hedges, 1963, 316).
The association of poverty and dependency with immorality and
dirt seems to be ill-founded.

Stigma, and the stigma of poverty in particular, seems to be
linked irrationally with these ideas. The same association
can be found in the idea of pollution. A stigmatised person
is, I have said, a polluting person. Dirt is matter in the
wrong place; disorder is the root of immorality. Poverty,
immorality and dirt are bound up together in an image of
society based on a primitive and powerful conception. This
reinforces the identification of stigma with caste. Like the
pariah, the stigmatised person is held at a distance; he is
assumed to be immoral and dirty. He is kept outside the
boundaries of society. This gives the impression of a group
of outcasts, of deviant groups; but the process is more

complex than many theories of deviance suggest.   The creation
of pariahs is   a   basic mechanism of social organisation,   and
stigmatised people are the pariahs of our society.

THE IDEA OF STIGMA

Stigmatised people do not have an identical social position;
like the members of low castes, there are important
distinctions made between them, not least the distinctions
they make themselves. Old and disabled people have in general
a higher status than unemployed men or unmarried mothers.   At
the same time, they share an inferior position in relation to
the rest of society.   A boundary separates them from other
people.   This boundary can be represented as a division, a
barrier,   or as a social distance - a gulf - between
stigmatised people and others. They have a place in society -
which is, in relation to the social services, a dependent one
- but their very dependency only serves to remove them from
the normal pattern of social relationships.   The distance
between us makes it difficult to see them as individuals; and,
because we like to believe that people are responsible for
their fates, they tend to be rejected and isolated further,
and, in the lowest castes, stereotyped as dishonest, dirty and
immoral.

The status of stigmatised people is determined by a number of
factors - by their dependency, their poverty, and their lack
of power. We reject them because they have low status, but we
also reject them for other reasons - because of our prejudices
against them,   or because they have violated our expectations,
our ordered view of society.   And this degrades their status
further, because rejection limits a person's roles in society,
and social honour also depends on the roles he plays.   Stigma
perpetuates itself.   It denies people access to roles, status
or influence; it increases social distance; it isolates people
from the main body of society.   By doing this, it bars access
to the advantages offered by normal social contact.

Figure 10.1: The causes of social rejection.

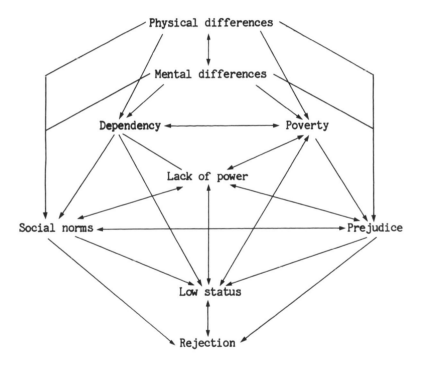

This diagram is a representation of the principal relationships between the clusters of factors associated with stigma. (The arrows in the diagram represent sequential links rather than direct causation.) Physical and mental stigmas, which are related, are associated, sometimes irrationally, with dependency and poverty, which are also related. All four imply breaches of social norms - norms of behaviour and appearance - and prejudice, which is founded in the same process of socialisation which structures social norms. In turn, these lead to low status and rejection. The symmetrical pattern is determined by the affinity of poverty and dependency, and of prejudice and social norms. The interpretation of the diagram depends on the weight that is given to the different factors. It should be clear, for example, that I do not think that power is a major determinant of these relationships; but a different interpretation, which put more emphasis on power, would not be inconsistent with the basic model.

CHAPTER 10: SUMMARY.

The roots of morality lie in the same social norms as the origins of prejudice. These norms are dichotomous; stigma consequently involves polarised social categories. Stigmatised people are outcasts. Their position is analogous to that of people of low caste, or pariahs. A pariah is a polluting person, simultaneously immoral, disruptive, and at the lowest rung of society. Like pariahs, stigmatised people are believed to be dishonest and sexually immoral, and dirty.

Stigmatised people have a common social position, separated by a boundary from other members of society. Through an interaction of factors, stigmatised people become dependent, poor, powerless, low in status and socially rejected.

Chapter 11

Stigma and social policy

Stigma and social welfare are both complex concepts, and the relationship between them is multi-faceted. In the first part, I discussed some of the common explanations for stigmatisation in the social services - degrading treatment, loss of rights, attitudes to 'charity', labelling and selectivity. None of these is a sufficient explanation of stigmatisation, but each helps to explain some of the dynamics of the process by which the recipients of social services become stigmatised. The rejection of social welfare as 'charity', for example, is a rejection of the dependency inherent in the nature of the social services. The services may also stigmatise recipients through labelling, which is a mark of status; by denying rights, which is a way of defining an inferior status; or through selectivity, which sets apart a status group. However, the role of the services in creating stigma is only a part of the whole picture. The possession of other stigmatising characteristics - poverty, immorality and physical and mental stigmas - often means that people are stigmatised before they come to the services. The services are not only stigmatising in themselves, but tainted with the reputation of the people they serve.

At the conclusion of part II, I argued that the varied nature of different stigmas implied policies which are fundamentally inconsistent with each other - rehabilitation and individual rights, redistribution and the pursuit of independence, collective action and individual reform. The conception of stigma as a division in society casts a different light on these conflicts. The focus is changed: the issue is not whether a policy is appropriate to a particular stigma, but whether a coherent policy can be followed to deal with the essential problems stigma presents.

RESIDUAL AND INSTITUTIONAL WELFARE.

The concept of stigma as a social category poses a conflict

between alternative models of policy. There is a choice to be
made between normalisation and the acceptance of differences,
gifts and exchanges, dependency and self-determination, social
control and the redistribution of power, discretion and
rights.   The choice is often represented as a choice between
the residual and institutional forms of welfare.   Butterworth
and Holman (1975) write:

> Whereas the **residual** view of social welfare implies that
> those in need are relatively discrete groups which
> require a concentration of resources upon them as the
> main priority of policy, the **institutional** view implies
> that most people are likely in their lives to need help
> to meet various crises and eventualities for which it is
> difficult to plan adequately and that responsiblity for
> help rests with the state. (pp.14-15.)

The   model   of   residual welfare,   according   to   this
interpretation,   is characterised by its response to problems
as the problems of individuals. It seeks to provide for those
people who are most in need.   It is selective; it uses means
tests, or tests of need, to establish who should receive
social welfare.   It   retains discretion   to   guarantee
responsiveness to individual problems.   It works as a safety
net in society, as a supplement to the economic system
protecting those unable to compete in it.   Institutional
welfare,   by   contrast,   is   collective.   It   provides
comprehensive categorical benefits to people as a mark of
citizenship, and establishes formal rights to services.   It
replaces the economic market with the social market, and the
exchange with the gift.   These models stand in opposition to
each other.   Tests of   means or needs are opposed to
comprehensive categorical benefits, discretion to rights,
individual to collective provision, the economic market to the
social market.

The focus of the debate on policy has fallen on a discussion
of 'universality' and 'selectivity'.   It has been argued that
selective systems of welfare, which attempt to give aid to the
people who are most in need, necessarily stigmatise the
recipients.   Wilensky and Lebeaux (1958), for example, state
that

> Because   of   its   residual,   temporary,   substitute
> characteristic, social welfare ... often carries the
> stigma of 'dole' or 'charity'. (p.139.)

Equally, it is claimed that stigma can only be overcome by
means of an universal system of welfare. Titmuss (1968) wrote
of universality:

> One fundamental historical reason for the adoption of
> this principle was the aim of making services available
> and accessible to the whole population in such ways as
> would not involve users in any humiliating loss of
> status, dignity or self-respect. ... If these services

were not provided by everybody for everybody they would
either not be available at all, or only for those who
could afford them, and for others on such terms as would
involve the infliction of a sense of inferiority and
stigma. (p.129.)
These arguments are examined in the following sections.

Selectivity.

The first objection to selectivity is that it creates an
underclass - a pariah group. Titmuss argued that
     the greatest source of stigma is likely, in a competitive
     society, to derive from the continuous process of
     selection and rejection that the individual experiences
     in the private sector. (Reisman, 1977, 51-52.)
He identified this process with selectivity in the social
services. Residual welfare is intended to help people who
are least able to cope in the market society, and selectivity
is the mechanism by which this is done. Selectivity therefore
defines those who have failed in a competitive society.
Dependency on social services becomes stigmatising because it
identifies the lowest class - people who are not only
dependent, but dirty and immoral. Selectivity, Townsend
(1976) argues,
     fosters hierarchical relationships of superiority and
     inferiority in society, diminishes rather than enhances
     the status of the poor, and has the effect of widening
     rather than reducing social inequalities. Far from
     sensitively discriminating different kinds of need it
     lumps the unemployed, sick, widowed, aged and others into
     one undifferentiated and inevitably stigmatised category.
     (p.126.)

The second objection is that selectivity acts, in itself, as a
form of labelling. It announces that a person is poor and in
need, and indicates what that need is by marking the benefit
as one for the unemployed, the disabled, the sick, and so on.
To claim a service, a person must accept the label attached to
it. But residual welfare also affects the identity of these
groups in ways other than labelling. Much concern has been
expressed that groups should not be marked out as undeserving;
this emerges in many debates on policy. The Seebohm report
commented as follows on the idea of giving Social Services
departments responsibility for difficult tenants:
     To relieve (housing departments) of responsibility for
     dependent or unreliable tenants would discourage them
     from looking at the housing needs of their area as a
     whole and create or reinforce degrading stigmas and
     social distinctions. (Cmnd. 3703, 1968, 126.)
The transfer of responsibilities for homeless families to
housing departments from Social Services departments

(Department of the Environment Circular 18/74) was made for
much the same reason. The rationale was not that housing
departments are less stigmatising than social work
departments, but rather that homelessness should be treated as
a housing problem rather than a personal one. The change in
policy is a response to the belief that clients were being
misidentified.

It is more frequent, though, that the objection is made not to
misclassification but to a more precise distinction of
stigmatised groups. This is the third, and possibly the most
important, element in policy. The review of the Mental Health
Acts (Cmnd. 7320, 1978) considered the criteria for compulsory
admission to mental institutions, and noted:
>   some people have pointed out that making dangerousness a
>   criterion for admission might increase the stigma often
>   attaching to those detained under compulsory powers.
>   (p.23.)
The objection to the sale of council houses is that sales
>   take out of the council stock houses in popular areas.
>   Their loss increases the stigmatisation of the rest.
>   (Karn, 1979, 738.)
The effect of this policy, according to its critics, will be
to identify council housing as housing for the poor rather
than housing for the people. (It is noteworthy that many of
the critics of council house sales on this ground, including
myself, would nevertheless favour the allocation of housing
according to need, which implies a certain inconsistency; it
arises because of the belief that those in need should receive
the best service possible.)

The problem is not rejection alone, but a question of whether
the stigma is brought to other people's attention. The
salience of a stigma leads, collectively, to a problem
equivalent to the individual's concern with information
management. It is important enough that a person feels he
acknowledges a stigma by using a social service; this creates
reluctance to seek help and embarrassment when he does. It is
doubly important whether other people know about it, because
then the fear of rejection is translated into reality; and
whether they know about it depends on the salience of the
stigma. The provision of a service may increase salience.
English (1978) remarks how
>   The unpopularity and stigma which are suffered by many
>   slum clearance estates were exacerbated in the case of
>   Ferguslie Park by an enclave of 45 'supervised' houses
>   dating from 1942 (p.4);
and Higgins (1978) argues that
>   An already stigmatised area may become even more
>   stigmatised by being chosen to take part in a poverty
>   programme. (p.112.)

Retarded people are rejected more when they have been in
special classes; mentally ill people when they are in, or have
been in, residential institutions; public tenants, when
developments are architecturally distinctive and physically
isolated (Newman, 1972). These are all examples of physical
salience. But there are also cases where it is the
stigmatised person's social identity, rather than material
circumstances, which is salient. Stigmatised people with
common problems - like 'the disabled', 'the mentally ill',
'the poor' - become identified as a group. Unemployed people
are marked out socially by the fact that they register as
unemployed or claim benefits. They are not generally
identifiable as individuals, but the group itself is a subject
of scorn - 'lazy idle loafers on the dole' - which affects
both the attitudes of the individual to his condition, and the
attitudes of others towards him when he is discovered.

The acceptability of a service is largely influenced by the
reputation of the people it serves. In those circumstances
where a service deals with several categories of recipient,
the relative salience of stigmatised groups is crucial to the
image of the service as a whole. Nearly half the claimants of
Supplementary Benefit are pensioners, but the image of
Supplementary Benefit seems far worse than their reputation
would suggest. This is because unemployed people and single
parents attract substantially more attention. The propensity
of selective provision to stigmatise seems to depend both on
the degree of discrimination that is exercised, and the
characteristics of the group selected. It is not a simple
question of which group is in a majority, but how far the
image of that group becomes prominent in relation to the
service. In some cases, the reputation of a service may be
enhanced by the inclusion of 'respectable' recipients. In
other cases the stigma attaching to some recipients becomes
identified with the entire service, and the service passes on
the stigma to other recipients like an infection.

Universality.

The principle of universality is the distinguishing feature of
such services as the National Health Service, Child Benefit,
and comprehensive education. Properly speaking, these
services are not available to all: they are available to
everyone in a specified category, defined by age or need, but
not by means. Reddin (1977) argues that universal benefits
are distinguished from selective ones by a test of means;
Seldon, on the other hand, advocates selective benefits on the
basis that they include a test of means **or need** (Seldon, Gray,
1967, 3). This makes for a rather pointless and sterile
debate; the two sides never really come to grips with each
other.

Clearly, there must be some selection for treatment on the basis of needs; not everyone wants or needs chest surgery or psychiatric care. Titmuss thought that

> the real challenge resides in the question: what particular infrastructure of universalist services is needed in order to provide a framework of values and opportunity bases within and around which can be developed acceptable selective services provided, as social rights, on criteria of the **needs** of specific categories, groups and territorial areas and not dependent on individual tests of means? (1968, 122.)

This would be nonsense if 'selective' was taken to mean 'means tested'; Titmuss evidently thinks, like Seldon, that services based on needs are selective. (This seems to include the NHS.)

It seems to me that Titmuss, even allowing for confusions in terminology, mistakes the issue. The main problem caused by selectivity is that it identifies a dependent group. This can be avoided by a universal service, like Child Benefit, which is intended to benefit the poor, but which does not distinguish them from other people in its treatment of them. Tax forms are a means test, but most wage earners have to fill them in; again, they do not distinguish the poor, even though the tax office does treat people on an individual basis after the form has been filled in. The problem with selection is that it separates the poor from the rest of society and makes them aware of the separation, not that it asks for a statement of income. If selective services are based on need but not on means, then the problem remains - whether or not the services are given as a right. Because the group is stigmatised before it becomes dependent, the main determinant of rejection is not whether they have rights, but whether the service draws attention to them. Unemployment Benefit, which does establish rights, is stigmatised. The 'universal' health service supposedly offers a right to medical care, but mentally ill people are rejected when they take it up.

This emphasises the importance of one of Titmuss's strongest principles, the anonymous gift, where neither donor nor recipient are known to each other. He saw this as the foundation stone of social integration. But his ideal is difficult, perhaps impossible, to achieve. There is no hope of providing a service which is responsive to need without in some way identifying the recipients as a group. The best result that can be looked for is that their dependency should be accepted as legitimate - as it is in the NHS. This leads to a second problem: that in general, dependency is only legitimate where there has been a contribution, either past (as in the case of pensioners) or future (as with students), or, in the case of the sick role, dependency is accepted as a temporary aberration.   This is arguably as true of the NHS as it is of other services.

Rights are still important in the context of universalist services.   The effect of selectivity is to emphasise the division of society; where someone is stigmatised morally, an outcast or a pariah, a universal system - one which can offer benefits and services as of right - ideally can aid the process of integration by bringing them into a relationship of gift and exchange which binds society together, and by asserting the status of the stigmatised person as a citizen. However, although they are helpful to pariah groups, their potential for social change should not be overestimated.

Residual and institutional models of welfare.

In theory, at least, residual and institutional welfare are antithetical.   But they are not necessarily distinguished by aims. Selective benefits, like housing benefits, or universal ones, like Child Benefit, may both be concerned with the protection of individuals in states of dependency.   Nor are the models distinguished by their methods: the NHS, which is supposedly universal, acts in large degree as a safety net for those who fall sick.

The models of residual and institutional welfare are effectively distinguished, not by their methods or aims, but by their intentions towards the people they serve.   Residual welfare sees dependency as an exception; institutional welfare treats it as an accepted feature of social life. If stigma is seen as a division of society, its identification with residual welfare is virtually tautologous.   The difference between residual and institutional welfare is in part defined by stigma, and selectivity, which is the main distinguishing characteristic of a residual system, creates the conditions necessary for an identification of stigmatised groups. However, institutional welfare is not sufficient in itself to avoid stigma, because the problem is not confined within the field of social welfare.   Comprehensiveness and rights do not in themselves get around the problems of stigmatisation.   In so far as dependency itself is stigmatising, universal provision is preferable to selectivity only because it conceals or encourages the acceptance of certain states of dependency, and sets aside policies which are degrading because they foster a structured form of inequality.

The distinction betwen institutional and residual welfare is not entirely satisfactory.   A distinction based on intentions implies a greater concern with the moral virtues of the services than with their effects, and this merely obscures the issues. It is quite true that a general acceptance of the

the principles of universal welfare would largely dispose of stigma, but this says no more than the fact that stigma would not be a great problem for the social services if there was no social division and everyone was prepared to accept responsibility for those who were poor and dependent. The assurance that institutional welfare is morally superior to residual welfare is unenlightening as a guide to practical action.

THE SOCIAL CONTEXT OF WELFARE.

There is a fundamental incompatibility between two of the approaches to stigma which I have examined. One, represented by policies of rehabilitation and individual insurance, argues that the only way to avoid stigma is to allow a person to adopt an independent role in society. This approach emphasises the importance of individual self-determination as the source of personal dignity - the element of choice which Downie and Telfer (1969) argue is essential to any conception of social respect (pp.20-21). The second, which encourages participation and the creation of social rights as a mark of citizenship, is based in the belief that stigma may be reduced by a change in the structure of society, a reorientation of collective status. These approaches are incompatible, not because the policies cannot co-exist - they already do - but because they lead to an incongruous position. A person whose status is legitimate has no need for rehabilitation; a person who can acquire rights by an individual contribution achieves a legitimacy that is greater than he would have as a member of a dependent group.

The conflict between these two approaches reflects not only a difference in attitudes, but also different assumptions about the social context of welfare. The first approach is essentially individualistic: it aims to help the individual adjust to society, and makes it possible for him to avoid stigma by re-establishing his dignity. Its disadvantage is that some people who are unable to assume a normal role will continue to be stigmatised. The second is collectivist: it tries to change the status of dependent groups by changing their social, economic and political relationships. The disadvantage of this approach is that it institutionalises dependency in a society which does not accept it.

The social context of the policy is a vital consideration; this context determines the reaction to the policy and its beneficiaries, and therefore the potential of the policy to stigmatise. Scott (1972) argues that attributions of stigma by experts vary between cultures: in a 'capitalist' society, people are stigmatised for a lack of self-reliance, and in a 'communist' society, they are stigmatised for their failure to contribute to the community (p.272). An individualistic approach to welfare is most compatible with a view of society as a **competitive** structure, which recognises the virtues of independence and individual achievement. The collectivist view is more appropriate to a **socialist** conception of society, which emphasises the interdependence of its members and the values of collective action.

These views of society have tended to dominate the contemporary debate, but they offer only a limited appreciation of the social context. A third view is implied by the argument of chapter 10: that status divisions in society are effectively stratified, and that each person receives the treatment that is considered appropriate to his social position. Stigmatisation, under these conditions, may be an integral mechanism of the social structure, serving to define social boundaries and at the same time to bind society together.

Each of these views represents a dimension of a complex social structure. In his book on **Social Justice**, David Miller (1976) presents these three dimensions in the form of three ideal models of society, to which reality may conform in greater or lesser degree. He argues that our idea of justice depends on its social context, and identifies a different theory of justice with each of these models. A stratified or **hierarchical** society fosters a concept of justice based on "rights", or privilege. An individualistic or competitive society, the **market** society, bases its idea of justice in the idea of desert. Finally, a collectivist society (which Miller typifies as a **primitive** society, because he maintains its conditions could only exist in a primitive community) bases justice on need. Miller presents these are discrete theories of justice; I prefer to think of them as different applications of a principle of justice. "The just", as Aristotle wrote, "is the proportionate" (Thomson, 1953, 147). An action is considered just when it is appropriate to certain defined criteria. In a hierarchical society, it is 'just' to give someone an amount that is proportionate to his status; in a market society, to his desert; and in a 'primitive' society, to his need. The plea for 'social justice' is often an emotive appeal based on a moral judgement as to which kind of society is most desirable.

These models of society also correspond to different concepts of exchange. Uttley (1980) classifies three types of gift/exchange associated with the social services. The first is the seeming 'unilateral transfer', an exchange based on beneficence, made as 'gifts' or benefits to meet personal needs. This is the dominant form of exchange in a hierarchical society; it is typified in the concept of 'noblesse oblige'.   The second is reciprocal exchange, which leads, in a market society, to the demand for a contribution to be made in return for the benefit received.   Thirdly, there is exchange based on the rights of citizenship, which is the distinguishing feature of   the collectivist or socialist society.   This is the Universal Gift advocated by Titmuss, a transfer that is not a pure gift, but which helps to bind society together by the recognition of common interests.

Heath (1976) interprets Titmuss's arguments against stigma in the light of his views of society.

> If 'charity wounds', it is because we live in a society
> that emphasises ... desert, not need. (p.154.)

A society that emphasises desert distinguishes the deserving from the undeserving, and rewards people accordingly.   The idea of the 'just world', it should be noted, is strongly rooted in this conception of justice; it reasons that people **deserve** their fate, and regards them as responsible for their condition.   In other societies, the rationale for blaming the victim differs.   In a society that emphasises privilege, the condition of the lowest group is accepted fatalistically.   The world can be seen as just only if fate is just - a view which is supported by a religious interpretation of status like the doctrine of Kharma.   Kerbo (1976) found that

> those who believed their poverty is the plan of heaven
> feel less stigma (p.181)

- presumably because they have faith in the justice of their situation.   If need is stressed, the idea of a just world becomes untenable, unless the existence of need is denied altogether.   Titmuss was committed to a concept of justice based on need, a concept which precluded the possibility of blaming the   victim,   which would make irrelevant   the distinction of the deserving and the undeserving poor, and which he believed could therefore end the problems of stigma. "On this view", Heath (1976) writes,

> stigma is not a cultural universal to be found wherever
> there is unequal exchange but a   phenomenon that
> flourishes above all in the capitalist societies of the
> west. (p.154.)

This argument is tenable only in so far as modern society is thought of in terms of ideal types.   In practice, society is complex, and has elements of each model; Titmuss's desire to eliminate stigma by moving towards a socialist society is itself an ideal, dependent on a form of society which does not and which has not existed.   The objections I have raised so far to Titmuss's arguments have been based on the evidence of existing societies, societies which correspond better to the models of a hierarchical or market society than to a socialist one.   It is unclear whether the concept of a generalised exchange made in respect of social rights is feasible.

Modern industrial society is often described as 'capitalist', inviting identification of our social structure with the values of individualism, competition and the economic market. It would be consistent with this argument to settle on an individualistic model of welfare as a response to stigma - a model which, despite its deficiencies, at least offers an opportunity to minimise stigma within the constraints of a market society and reciprocal exchange.   However, social reality does not correspond to this simple model.   The social services have to work in diffuse and complex circumstances; they cannot expect to have simple, consistent effects.   On the one hand, it is possible for people to make a contribution through social insurance, which legitimates dependency when they become old, sick, disabled or unemployed; but these people are still rejected to a degree, partly because of the continued acceptance of social divisions which define these groups as lower castes, or treat them as pariahs.   On the other, services like health care and Child Benefit may be widely accepted even though they are not based on individual contributions; with reservations, they indicate that collectivist principles are also accepted in part.

It is difficult to derive any clear prescription for policy from a theoretical analysis.   Our aims, the principles on which we work, and the social context of the policies, are neither uniform nor consistent.   It may be possible to represent stigma as a single, if complex, problem, but it does not follow that it is susceptible to a single solution.   The theory defines principles, offers some explanation of the causes of stigma, and may suggest possible measures, but it can do little more.   In the end, we are driven to an incremental, pragmatic approach to social policy.   I could recommend no better method of proceeding than Edmund Burke's precept of sound government:

> By a slow but well-sustained progress, the effect of each step is watched; the good or ill success of the first, gives light to us in the second; and so, from light to light, we are conducted with safety through the whole series.   We see, that the parts of the system do not clash.   The evils latent in the most promising contrivances are provided for as they arise.   One advantage is as little possible sacrificed to another. We compensate, we reconcile, we balance. We are enabled to unite into a consistent whole the various anomalies and contending principles that are found in the minds and affairs of men.   From hence arises, not an excellence in simplicity, but one far superior, an excellence in composition. (1790, 209.)

CHAPTER 11: SUMMARY.

The social services may create or reinforce the stigmas which
attach to recipients.   Different stigmas imply different
policies to deal with the problems that result. These must be
seen in their social context. The debate about 'universality'
and 'selectivity' reflects a concern with different forms of
social organisation, but the related distinction between
'institutional' and 'residual' welfare is inadequate, because
it gives no guide to practical action.

An attempt is made to relate different approaches to welfare
to certain social contexts. An individualist approach to
welfare is most compatible with a competitive view of society,
a collectivist approach with a socialist one, and both may
lead to stigma in different circumstances.   Social structures
may also be   stratified or hierarchical,   and in these
circumstances stigma may act as an integrative force.   These
dimensions of social organisation correspond to Miller's
classification of societies with different conceptions of
social justice, based on rights, desert or need, and to
different concepts of exchange.   It is difficult to draw
concrete conclusions for policy from this analysis.   The
models represent different attitudes in modern industrial
society, and the success of a policy in any particular context
depends on their relative importance.

References

All publications are from London unless marked otherwise.

Ph.D. dissertations are published by University Microfilms, Ann Arbor, Michigan.

United Kingdom Government papers are listed separately at the end of the bibliography.

B.Abel-Smith, 1964.
   The hospitals 1800-1948: a study in social administration in England and Wales. Heinemann.
B.Abel-Smith, 1976.
   Value for money in health services: a comparative study. Heinemann Educational Books.
H.Acland, 1971.
   "What is a 'bad' school?", New Society, 9th September, 18(467), 450-452
T.W.Adorno, E.Frenkel-Brunswick, D.J.Levinson, R.N.Sanford, (1950).
   The authoritarian personality. New York: W.W.Norton and Co., 1969.
Age Concern, 1974.
   The attitudes of the retired and the elderly. Mitcham: Age Concern.
Alabama Social Welfare, 1965.
   "A simplified method of establishing continuing eligibility in the adult categories." 30(Jan-Feb), 13-14.
T.Alcock, 1752.
   Observations on the defects of the Poor Laws. R.Baldwin, R.Clements.
W.P.Alison, 1840.
   Illustrations of the practical operation of the Scottish system of management of the poor. Edinburgh: paper read before the Statistical Section of the British

Association.
G.Alivisatos, G. Lyketsos.
"A preliminary report of a research concerning the attitude of the families of hospitalized mental patients." 358-366 of Spitzer and Denzin, (eds.), 1968.
G.W.Allport, 1954.
The nature of prejudice. Cambridge, Mass.: Addison-Wesley.
J.P.Alston, K.I.Dean, 1972.
"Socioeconomic factors associated with attitudes toward welfare recipients and the causes of poverty." Social Service Review, 46(1), 13-23.
Anon, 1835.
Abolition of pauperism: a discovery in internal national polity. B.Steill.
I.Anstruther, 1973.
The scandal of the Andover workhouse. Geoffrey Bles.
M.Argyle, 1967.
The psychology of interpersonal behaviour. Harmondsworth:Penguin.
Aristotle, (1871).
Ethica Nicomachea. Oxford: James Parker.
E.W.Arluck, 1941.
"A study of some personality characteristics of epileptics." Archives of Psychology, 37(263).
G.Armstrong, 1975.
Long term unemployment in a deprived Scottish housing scheme Glasgow: University of Glasgow.
S.R.Arnstein, 1971.
"A ladder of citizen participation", Journal of the Royal Town Planning Institute, 57(4), 176-182.
A.B.Atkinson,1969.
Poverty in Britain and the reform of social security. Cambridge: University Press.

S.Baldwin, 1979.
"Redesigning work", New Society, 6th December, 50(896), 552.
R.G.Barker, 1948.
"The social psychology of physical disability", Journal of Social Issues, 4(4), 28-38.
F.Barth, 1960.
"The system of social stratification in Swat, North Pakistan", 113-146 of E.R.Leach, (ed.) 1960.
R.W.A.C.Barton, (1959).
Institutional neurosis. Bristol: Wright. (3rd edition, 1976.)
N.Bastin, J-M.Stievenard, M.Vinchon, 1977.
"Epilepsie et hemophile: la lutte contre leurs effets de stigmatisation", Revue Francais de Sociologie 18(4), 651-677.

K.E.Bauman, 1968.
"Status inconsistency, satisfactory social interaction, and community satisfaction in an area of rapid growth", Social Forces, 47(1), 45-52.

N.Beacock, 1979.
"Campaigning for the homeless and rootless", 119-139 of T.Cook (ed.), 1979.

J.T.Becher, 1828.
The antipauper system: exemplifying the positive and practical good realized by the relievers and the relieved, under the frugal, beneficial and lawful, administration of the Poor Laws, prevailing at Southwell. W.Simpkin, R.Marshall.

B.Beck, 1967.
"Welfare as a moral category", Social Problems, 14(3), 258-277.

H.Becker, 1963.
Outsiders: studies in the sociology of deviance. New York: Free Press.

R.Beerman, 1958.
"A discussion on the draft law against parasites, tramps and beggars", Soviet Studies, 9(2),214-222; and subsequent articles, Soviet Studies, 11(4), 453-455, and Soviet Studies, 13(2), 191-205.

A.H.Bell, 1967.
"Measure for adjustment of the physically disabled", Psychological Reports, 21(3), 773-778.

S.S.Bellin, L.Kriesberg, 1967.
"Relationships between attitudes, circumstances and behaviour: the case of applying for public housing", Sociology and Social Research, 51(4), 453-469.

D.J.Bem, 1967.
"Self-perception: an alternative interpretation of cognitive dissonance phenomena", Psychological Review, 74, 183-200.

R.Bendix, S.M.Lipset, 1967.
Class, status and power: social stratification in comparative perpective. Routledge and Kegan Paul. (2nd. edition.)

J. Benington (ed.), 1972.
Coventry Community Development Project: background and progress.Coventry: Home Office/Coventry C.D.P.

J. Bentham, 1831-32.
Papers: 154b, pp 602-604.
-----, 1843.
The works of Jeremy Bentham (J.Bowring, ed.): vol. 8. Edinburgh: William Tait.

L.Berg, 1968
Risinghill: death of a comprehensive school. Harmondsworth: Penguin.

P.L.Berger, (1963).

Invitation to sociology: a humanistic perspective.
Harmondsworth: Penguin, 1966.

P.L.Berger, T.Luckmann, 1967.
The social construction of reality.   New York: Anchor,
1967.

L.Berkowitz, L.R.Daniels, 1963.
"Responsibility and dependency", Journal of Abnormal and
Social Psychology, 66(5), 429-436.

M.Berry, 1977.
"Whose city? The forgotten tenant", Australian and New
Zealand Journal of Sociology, 13(1), 53-59.

E.Bisset, J.Coussins, 1982.
Badge of poverty: a new look at the stigma attached to
free school meals, Child Poverty Action Group.

C.P.Blacker (ed.), 1952.
Problem families: five inquiries. Eugenics Society.

A. Blair, 1980.
"Exposed! The dole queue spy ring", Newcastle-upon-Tyne
Evening Chronicle, 18th February, p.8.

R.L.Blanton, J.C.Nunally, 1964.
"Semantic habits and cognitive style processes in the
deaf", Journal of Abnormal and Social Psychology, 68(4),
397-402.

P.M.Blau, 1964.
Exchange and power in social life.   New York: John Wiley
and Sons.

M.Blaxter, 1974.
"Health 'on the welfare' - a case study", Journal of
Social Policy, 3(1), 39-51.

------, 1975.
"Disability and rehabilitation: some questions of
definition", 207-223 of C.Cox, A.Mead (eds.), A sociology
of medical practice, Collier-Macmillan.

------, 1976.
The meaning of disability: a sociological study of
impairment. Heinemann Educational Books.

P.J.Blizard, 1971.
"The social rejection of the alcoholic and mentally ill
in New Zealand", Social Science and Medicine, 4(5), 513-
526.

T.J.Blocker, P.L.Riedesel, 1978.
"Can sociology find true happiness with subjective status
inconsistency?", Pacific Sociological Review, 21(3), 275-
291.

S.W.Bloom, 1963.
The doctor and his patient.   New York: Russell Sage
Foundation.

E.M.Bogardus, 1925.
"Measuring social distance", Journal of Applied Sociology
9, 299-308. In K.Thomas (ed.), Attitudes and behaviour:
selected readings, Harmondsworth: Penguin, 1971.

H.M.Boies, 1893.
Prisoners and paupers. New York: Knickerbocker Press.
M.Bone, B.Spain, F.M.Martin, 1972.
Plans and provisions for the mentally handicapped.
George Allen and Unwin.
R.J.Bord, 1971.
"Rejection of the mentally ill: continuities and further
developments", Social Problems, 18(4), 496-509.
H.Bosanquet, 1902.
Excerpt from The strength of the people, 263-4 of
E.J.Evans (ed.), 1978.
J.W.Brehm, A.R.Cohen, 1962.
Explorations in cognitive dissonance. New York: John
Wiley and Sons.
E.Briggs, A.M.Rees, 1980.
Supplementary benefits and the consumer. Bell.
A.Briod, (1926).
L'assistance des pauvres au moyen age dans le Pays de
Vaud. Lausanne: Editions d'en bas, 1976.
British Association of Social Workers, Kent Branch, 1974.
Homelessness in Kent: a survey. Shelter.
K.K.Brookfield, 1969.
Attitudes of the disabled and non-disabled toward self
and toward disabled and normal persons. Ph.D.: Columbia
University. 70-6941.
H.Brown, 1966.
"Some anomalies of social welfare", 131-141 of P.Hunt
(ed.), 1966.
M.Bruce (ed.), 1973.
The rise of the welfare state: English social policy
1601-1971. Weidenfeld and Nicolson. 1976.)
M.Budoff, G.N.Siperstein, 1978.
"Low income children's attitudes toward mentally retarded
children: effects of labelling and academic behaviour",
American Journal of Mental Deficiency, 82(5), 474-479.
R.J.Bulman, C.B.Wortman, 1977.
"Attributions of blame and coping in the 'real world':
severe accident victims react to their lot", Journal of
Personality and Social Psychology, 35, 351-363.
P.Burgess, 1978.
Letter to New Society, 16th November, 46(841), p.411.
E.Burke, (1790).
Reflections on the revolution in France, and on the
proceedings in certain societies in London relative to
that event. New York: Holt, Rinehart and Winston, 1959.
R.A.Butler, (1971).
"The politics of the 1944 Education Act", 1-26 of
G.Fowler, V. Morris, J. Ozga (eds.), Decision-making in
British education, Heinemann 1973.
E.Butterworth, R.Holman (eds.), 1975.
Social welfare in modern Britain. Glasgow:

Fontana/Collins.
A.Byrne, C.Padfield, 1978.
Social services made simple. W.H.Allen.

F.M.Canter, 1963.
"The relationship between authoritarian attitudes, attitudes towards mental patients and effectiveness of clinical work with mental patients", Journal of Clinical Psychology, 19(1), 124-127.
V.J.Cappeller, 1972.
Stigma in the lives of psychiatric hospital patients and their families with special reference to their children. Ph.D.: Brandeis University (Florence Heller Graduate School for Advanced Studies in Social Work). 72-26325.
G.L.Carson, 1967.
"The self-concept of welfare recipients", Personnel and Guidance Journal, 45(5), 424-428.
A.Cartwright, 1964.
Human relations and hospital care. Routledge and Kegan Paul.
-----, 1967.
Patients and their doctors: a study of general practice. Routledge and Kegan Paul.
V.Carver, P. Liddiard (eds.), 1978.
An ageing population: a reader and sourcebook. Hodder and Stoughton.
E.K.Ceeney, 1981.
Letter to The Guardian, 18th April, p.12.
Central Advisory Council for Education (England), 1967.
Children and their primary schools. HMSO.
Central Council in Education and Training for Social Work, 1974.
Social work: people with handicaps need better trained social workers. Report of a working party on training for social work with handicapped people. CCETSW.
Central Housing Advisory Committee, 1969.
Council housing: purposes, priorities and procedures. HMSO.
E.Chadwick, 1833.
Report from E.Chadwick Esq. on London and Berkshire. Publisher unknown.
H.Chaiklin, M.Warfield, 1973.
"Stigma management and amputee rehabilitation", Rehabilitation literature, 34(6), 162-166 and 172.
W.Chambliss, 1964.
"A sociological analysis of vagrancy", Social Problems, 12(1), 67-77.
N.P.Chapanis, A.Chapanis, 1964.
"Cognitive dissonance: five years later", Psychological Bulletin, 61(1), 1-22.
S.G.Checkland, E.Checkland (eds.), 1974.

The Poor Law report of 1834. Harmondsworth: Penguin.
G.F.Christensen, 1977.
   A test of the labelling theory approach to deviance: the
   case of the disabled.   Ph.D: American University,
   Washington. 77-16815.
M.Clark, 1978.
   "The   unemployed   on   Supplementary Benefit: living
   standards and making ends meet on a low income", Journal
   of Social Policy, 7(4), 385-410.
M.Clark, B.Anderson, 1967.
   Culture and ageing: an anthropological study of older
   Americans. Springfield, Illinois: Charles C. Thomas.
J.D.Clifford, 1974.
   "The public, the client and the social services: a study
   in an Irish town", Social Studies (Irish Journal of
   Sociology), 3(5-6), 457-498.
-----, 1975.
   "Stigma and the perception of social security services",
   Policy and Politics, 3(3), 29-61.
A.K.Cohen, 1966.
   Deviance and control. Englewood Cliffs, New Jersey:
   Prentice-Hall.
-----, (1973)
   "A theory of subcultures", 233-4 of Rubington, Weinberg (
   eds) 1973.
A.K.Cohen, H.Hodges, 1963.
   "Characteristics of the lower blue-collar class", Social
   Problems, 10(4), 303-334.
W.S.Cohen, J.Berman, 1952.
   "A chapter of legislative history. Safeguarding the
   disclosure of public assistance records: the legislative
   history of the 'Jenner amendment' - s.618, Revenue Act of
   1951", Social Service Review, 26(June), 229-234.
R.M.Cohn, 1977.
   The consequences of unemployment on evaluations of self.
   Ph.D.: University of Michigan, 1977. DBJ77-17971.
S.Cole, R.Lejeune, 1972.
   "Illness and the legitimation of failure", American
   Sociological Review, 37(June), 347-356.
Wilkie Collins, (1859: 2nd. edition, 1861).
   The woman in white. JM Dent, 1910.
R.J.Comer, J.A.Piliavin, 1972.
   "The effects of physical deviance upon face-to-face
   interaction: the other side", 102-107 of D.M.Boswell,
   J.M.Wingrove, The handicapped person in the community,
   Tavistock, 1974.
T.Cook (ed.), 1979.
   Vagrancy: some new perspectives. Academic Press.
T.Cook, G.Braithwaite, 1979.
   "A problem for whom?", 1-10 in T.Cook (ed.) 1979.
C.H.Cooley, 1902.

Human nature and the social order.   New York: Charles
Scribner's Sons.
C.Cookson, 1980.
"Jensen says tests fair to minorities in face of mounting
public criticism", _Times Educational Supplement_, 1st
February, p.13.
C.G.Cooper,1965.
_Some social implications of house and site plan at Easter
Hill Village: a case study._   Berkeley: University of
California Institute of Urban and Regional Development.
L.Cooper, R.Henderson (eds.), 1973.
Something wrong? Arrow Books.
A.Corbett, 1968.
"Priority schools", _New Society_, 30th May, 11(296), 795-
787.
L.Corina, 1976.
_Housing allocation policy and its effects: a case study
from Oldham CDP._   York: University of York Department of
Social Administration and Social Work.
L.A.Coser, 1965.
"The sociology of poverty: to the memory of Georg
Simmel", _Social Problems_, 13, 140-148.
Coventry Social Services, 1973.
Looking for trouble among the elderly.
B.E.Coward, J.R.Feagin, J.A.Williams, 1974.
"The culture of poverty debate: some additional data",
Social Problems, 21(5), 621-634.
E.L.Cowen, R.P.Underberg, R.T.Verillo, 1958.
"The development and testing of an attitude to blindness
scale", _Journal of Social Psychology_, 48(2), 297-304.
E.L.Cowen, R.P.Underberg, T.Verillo, F.G.Bentham, 1961.
Adjustment to visual disability in adolescence.   New
York: American Foundation for the Blind.
G.M.Cox, 1971.
The circle of despair. Shelter.
The Cripples' Journal, 1926.
"The making of a cripple: an authentic document." 2(8),
285-293.
G.M.Crocetti, 1973.
_Identification of the mental illnesses and social
distance toward the mentally ill._   Ph.D.: Columbia
University. 70-02296.
E.Crumpton, A.D.Weinstein, C.W.Acker, A.P.Annis, 1967.
"How patients and normals see the mental patient",
Journal of Clinical Psychology, 23(1), 46-49.
E.Cumming, J.Cumming, 1957.
Closed ranks: an experiment in mental health education.
Cambridge, Mass.: Harvard University Press.
J.Cumming, E.Cumming, 1965.
"On the stigma of mental illness", _Community Mental
Health Journal_, 1(2), 135-143.

R.L.Curtis, L.A.Zurcher, 1971.
   "Voluntary associations and the social integration of the
   poor", Social Problems, 18(3), 339-357.
J.Cutler, J.Willis, 1979.
   The secret hospital. Rampton - the big house. Yorkshire
   TV broadcast.

S.Damer, 1974.
   "Wine Alley: the sociology of a dreadful enclosure",
   Sociological Review, 22(2), 221-248.
C.Davidson, C.M.Gaitz, 1974.
   "'Are the poor different?': a comparison of work
   behaviour and attitudes among the urban poor and
   nonpoor", Social Problems, 22(2), 229-245.
B.Davies, with M.Reddin, 1978.
   Universality, selectivity, and effectiveness in social
   policy. Heinemann Educational Books.
P.J.Day, 1977.
   "The scarlet 'W': public welfare as sexual stigma for
   women", Journal of Sociology and Social Welfare, 4(6),
   872-881.
A.Deacon, 1976.
   In search of the scrounger: the administration of
   unemployment insurance in Britain 1920-1931. Bell.
A.Deacon, 1978.
   "The scrounging controversy: public attitudes towards the
   unemployed in contemporary Britain", Social and Economic
   Administration, 12(2), 120-135.
N.K.Denzin, S.P.Spitzer, (1966).
   "Paths to the mental hospital and staff predictions of
   patient role behaviour", 334-343 of Spitzer and Denzin
   (eds.), 1968.
Departement of Health and Social Security, 1981.
   Social security statistics 1981. HMSO.
Department of the Environment, 1974.
   Circular 18/74: Homelessness.
A.Digby, 1978.
   Pauper palaces. Routledge and Kegan Paul.
K.Dion, E.Berscheid, E.Walster, 1977.
   "What is beautiful is good", 71-76 in J.C.Brigham,
   L.S.Wrightsman, Contemporary issues in social psychology.
   Monterey, California: Brooks/Cole Publishing.
J.K.Dixon, 1973.
   Self-evaluation and attitudes toward disability groups in
   normal and disabled populations. Ph.D.: University of
   Connecticut. 73-28516.
D.V.Donnison, 1976.
   "Supplementary Benefits: dilemmas and priorities",
   Journal of Social Policy, 5(4), 337-58.
J.W.B.Douglas, 1964.
   The home and the school: a study of ability and

the primary school. Macgibbon and Kee.
M.Douglas, 1966.
Purity and danger: an analysis of concepts of pollution and taboo. Routledge and Kegan Paul.
-----, 1970.
Natural symbols: explorations in cosmology. Barrie and Rockliff.
T.Dow, 1965.
"Social class and reaction to physical disability", Psychological Reports, 17, 39-62.
R.Downie, E.Telfer, 1969.
Respect for persons. George Allen and Unwin.
R.Duff, A.Hollingshead, 1968.
Sickness and society. New York: Harper and Row.
E.Durkheim, (1952).
Suicide: a study in sociology (trans. J.A.Spaulding, G.Simpson). Routledge and Kegan Paul.

East London Claimants' Union, 1974.
"East London Claimants' Union: the concept of self-management", 79-89 of D.Jones, M.Mayo (eds.) 1974.
R.B.Edgerton, 1967.
The cloak of competence: stigma in the lives of the mentally retarded. Berkeley, California: University of California Press.
-----, 1968.
"Anthropology and mental retardation: a plea for the comparative study of incompetence", 75-87 of H.J.Prehm, L.A.Hamerlynck, J.E.C Crosson (eds.), Behavioural Research in Mental Retardation. Eugene, Oregon: University of Oregon Rehabilitation Research and Training Centre in Mental Retardation.
R.Eisenman, 1970.
"Birth order, self-esteem, and prejudice against the physically disabled", Journal of Psychology, 75(2), 147-155.
P.Ekeh, 1974.
Social exchange theory: the two traditions. Heinemann.
R.M.Elman, 1966.
The poorhouse state: the American way of life on Public Assistance. New York: Pantheon Books.
Encylopaedica Judaica, 1971.
"Charity", 338-353 of vol. 5. Jerusalem: Kether Publishing House.
F. Engels, 1845.
The condition of the working class in England. W.O Henderson and W.H.Challoner, trans. and eds. Oxford: Basil Blackwell, 1958.
J. English, 1978.
A profile of Ferguslie Park. Paisley: Paisley CDP.
R.W.English, 1977.

"Correlates of stigma toward physically disabled persons", and "Combatting stigma toward physically disabled persons", 162-182 and 183-193 of R.P.Marinelli, A.E.DellOrto (eds.), 1977.

S.Epstein, 1955.
"Unconscious self-evaluation in a normal and schizophrenic group", Journal of Abnormal and Social Psychology, 50, 65-70.

K.T.Erikson, (1973).
"Patient role and social uncertainty", 385-391 of E.Rubington, M.S.Weinberg (eds.), 1973.

E.J.Evans (ed.), 1978.
Social policy 1830-1914: individualism, collectivism and the origins of the welfare state. Routledge and Kegan Paul.

H.Fabrega, 1971.
"Begging in a southeastern Mexican city", Human Organization, 30(3),277-287.

C.C.Fairchilds,1976.
Poverty and charity in Aix-en-Provence 1640-1789. Baltimore: Johns Hopkins University Press.

J.R.Feagin, 1972.
"America's welfare stereotypes", Social Science Quarterly, 52(4), 921-33.

-----, 1975.
Subordinating the poor: welfare and American beliefs. Englewood Cliffs, NJ: Prentice-Hall.

L.Festinger, J.M.Carlsmith, 1959.
"Cognitive consequences of forced compliance", Journal of Abnormal and Social Psychology, 58, 203-210.

S.E.Finer, 1952.
The life and times of Sir Edwin Chadwick. Methuen.

M.J.Fishbein, J.D.Laird, 1979.
"Concealment and disclosure: some effects of information control on the person who controls", Journal of Experimental Social Psychology, 15(2), 114-121.

D.Flessati, 1978.
"The new breadline", shown on Horizon, BBC2, 24th March.

R.Ford, 1966.
"Quite intelligent", 29-43 of P.Hunt (ed.) 1966.

M.Foucault, (1961).
Madness and civilisation: a history of insanity in the age of reason. Tavistock, 1965.

D.Fraser, 1973.
The evolution of the British welfare state: a history of social policy since the industrial revolution. Macmillan.

L.A.Free, H.Cantril, 1967.
The political beliefs of Americans: a study of public opinion. New Brunswick, NJ: Rutgers University Press.

H.E.Freeman, O.G.Simmons, 1961.
"Feelings of stigma among relatives of former mental patients", Social Problems, 8(4), 312-321.
R.Freeman, 1979.
"Modest but enticing", The Guardian, 20th November, p.13.
E.Fromm, 1942.
The fear of freedom. Kegan Paul.

H.B.Gascoigne, 1818.
Pauperism: its evils and burden reduced by calling into action the labours of the poor, and by the useful direction of charity... Baldwin, Cradock and Joy.
E.Gauldie, 1974.
Cruel habitations: a history of working-class housing 1780-1918. George Allen and Unwin.
K.J.Gergen, 1969.
The psychology of behaviour exchange. Reading, Mass.: Addison-Wesley.
H.H.Gerth, C.Wright Mills (trans. and eds.), 1948.
From Max Weber: essays in sociology. Routledge and Kegan Paul.
J.P.Gibbs, 1972.
"Issues in defining deviant behaviour", 39-68 of Scott, Douglas (eds.) 1972.
N.Ginsburg, 1979.
Class, capital and social policy. Macmillan.
W.E.Gladstone, (1889).
Excerpt from a speech made in Cheshire, p.133 of EJ Evans, 1978.
D.C.Glass, 1964.
"Changes in liking as a means of reducing cognitive discrepancies between self-esteem and aggression", Journal of Personality, 32(4), 531-549.
B.Glastonbury, M.Burdett, R.Austin, 1973.
"Community perceptions and the personal social services", Policy and Politics, 1(3), 191-211.
H.Glennerster, 1962.
National Assistance - service or charity? Fabian Society.
G.Gmelch, S.B.Gmelch, 1978.
"Begging in Dublin: the strategies of a marginal urban occupation", Urban Life, 6(4), 439-454.
E.Goffman, 1959.
The presentation of self in everyday life. Harmondsworth: Penguin Books, 1971.
-----, 1961.
Asylums: essays on the social situation of mental patients and other inmates. Harmondsworth: Penguin Books, 1968.
-----, 1963.
Stigma: notes on the management of spoiled identity.

Harmondsworth: Penguin Books, 1968.
-----, 1967.
     Interaction ritual: essays on face-to-face-behaviour.
     New York: Anchor.
P.Golding, S.Middleton, 1982.
     Images of welfare: press and public attitudes to poverty.
     Oxford: Martin Robertson.
J.Goldthorpe, D.Lockwood, 1963.
     "Affluence and the British class structure", 311-318 of
     E.Butterworth, D.Weir (eds.) 1976.
L.H.Goodman, S.M.Meyers, J.McIntyre, 1969.
     Welfare policy and its consequences for the recipient
     population: a study of the AFDC programme. Washington
     DC: US Department of Health, Education and Welfare
     Social and Rehabilitation Service.
M.S.Gore, 1958.
     "Society and the beggar", Psychological Bulletin, 7(1),
     23-48.
J.Gottlieb, M.Budoff, 1973.
     "Social acceptability of retarded children in schools
     differing in architecture", American Journal of Mental
     Deficiency, 78(1), 15-19.
A.Gould, J.Kenyon, 1972.
     Stories from the dole queue. Temple-Smith.
A.W.Gouldner, 1960.
     "The norm of reciprocity: a preliminary statement",
     American Sociological Review, 25(2), 161-177.
W.R.Gove, 1976.
     "Societal reaction theory and disability", 57-71 of
     G.L.Albrecht (ed.), The sociology of physical disability
     and rehabilitation, Pittsburgh: University of Pittsburgh
     Press.
W.R.Gove, T.Fain, 1973.
     "The stigma of mental hospitalisation", Archives of
     General Psychiatry, 28(Apr.), 494-500.
J.Greve, (1975).
     "Comparisons, perspectives, values", 184-193 of
     Butterworth, Holman (eds.) 1975.
Earl Grey, 1834.
     Corrected report of the speech of the Lord Chancellor in
     the House of Lords on July 21 1834, on moving the second
     reading of the bill to amend the Poor Laws. James
     Ridgway and Sons. (2nd edition.)
P.Griffiths, 1975.
     Homes fit for heroes: a SHELTER report on council
     housing. Shelter.
The Guardian, 1980
     Letter: 3rd. July.
-----, 1981.
     "New deal 'will end the stigma of the handicapped
     child'", 3rd. February, p.20.

G.Gudmundsson, 1966.
Epilepsy in Iceland: a clinical and epidemiological
investigation. Munksgaard, Copenhagen: Acta Neurologica
Scandinavica 43 supp. 25.
Z.Gussow, G.S.Tracy, 1968.
"Status, ideology and adaptation to stigmatised illness:
a study of leprosy", Human Organization, 27(4), 316-325.
L.Guttman, 1959.
"A structural theory for intergroup beliefs and action",
American Sociological Review, 24(3) 318-328.

C.Haffter, 1968.
"The changeling: history and psychodynamics of attitudes
to handicapped children in European folklore", Journal of
the History of the Behavioural Sciences, 4(1), 55-61.
W.C.Haggstrom, 1964.
"The power of the poor", 205-223 of F.Riessman, J.Cohen,
A.Pearl (eds.), Mental health of the poor, New York: Free
Press.
A.S.Hall, 1974.
The point of entry: a study of client reception in the
social services. George Allen and Unwin.
J.Handler, 1972.
Reforming the poor: welfare policy, federalism and
morality.New York: Basic Books.
-----, 1973.
The coercive social worker: British lessons for American
social services. Chicago: Markham.
J.F.Handler, E.J.Hollingsworth, 1969.
"Stigma, privacy and other attitudes of welfare
recipients", Stanford Law Review, 22(1), 1-19.
-----,-----,1971.
The 'deserving poor': a study of welfare administration.
Chicago: Markham.
J.R.Hanks, L.M.Hanks, 1948.
"The physically handicapped in certain non-occidental
societies", Journal of Social Issues, 4(4), 11-20.
P.Harrison, 1978.
"Living with old age", 121-127 of V.Carver, P.Liddiard
(eds.), 1978.
A.Harvey, 1979.
"Intrusive inquiries", New Society, 16th August, 49(880),
352-353.
D.L.Harvey, 1970.
Potter addition: stigma and community. Ph.D.: University
of Illinois at Urbana-Champaign.
A.Heath, 1976.
Rational choice and social exchange. Cambridge:
Cambridge University Press.
U.R.Q.Henriques, 1979.
Before the welfare state: social administration in early

industrial Britain. Longman.

J.W.Herrick, 1976.
"Placebos, psychosomatic and psychogenic illnesses and psychotherapy", Psychological Record, 26, 327-342.

J.Higgins, 1978.
The poverty business in Britain and America. Basil Blackwell/ Martin Robertson.

A.B.Hollingshead, F.C.Redlich, 1953.
"Social stratification and psychiatric disorders", 102-111 of Spitzer and Denzin (eds.) 1968.

R.Holman, 1970.
"Combatting social deprivation", 142-205 of Socially deprived families in Britain, National Council of Social Service.

-----, (1973).
"Poverty: consensus and alternatives", 403-419 of Butterworth, Holman (eds.) 1975.

-----, 1974.
"Social workers and the 'inadequates'", New Society, 5th September, 29(622), 608-610. G.C.Homans, 1961.
Social behaviour: its elementary forms. Routledge and Kegan Paul.

P.M.Horan, P.L.Austin, 1974.
"Social bases of welfare stigma", Social Problems, 21(5), 648-657.

E.Howe, 1978.
"Legislative outcomes in human services", Social Service Review, 52(2), 173-188.

L.G.Hudzinski, 1975.
Public rejection of the epileptic: an empirical investigation. Ph.D.: University of Pittsburgh. 75-19559.

P.Hunt (ed.), 1966.
Stigma: the experience of disability. Chapman.

E.D.Huttman, 1969.
Stigma and public housing: A comparison of British and American policies and experience. Ph.D.: University of California at Berkeley.

H.H.Hyman, P.B.Shatsley,1954.
"The authoritarian personality - a methodological critique", 50-122 of R.Christie, M.Jahoda (eds), Studies in the scope and method of 'The Authoritarian Personality': continuities in social research, Glencoe, Illinois: Free Press.

International Council on Social Welfare, 1969.
Social welfare and human rights: proceedings of the 14th international conference on social welfare, Helsinki, Finland, 18-24.8.68. New York: Columbia University Press.

N.Jabin, 1965.
Attitudes toward the physically disabled as related to selected personality variables. Ph.D.: New York University. 66-5781.

R.Jackson, 1977.
"Mild mental retardation: myth and reality", British Journal of Mental Subnormality, 23(45), 76-82.

B.Jalali, M.Jalali, F.Turner, 1978.
"Attitudes toward mental illness: its relation to contact and ethocultural background", Journal of Nervous and Mental Disease, 166(10), 692-700.

M.Jaques, 1960.
"Treatment of the disabled in primitive cultures", in C.H.Patterson (ed.), Readings in rehabilitation counselling, Champaign, Illinois: Stipes Publishing.

M.E.Jaques, D.C.Linkowski, F.L.Sieka, 1970.
"Cultural attitudes toward disability: Denmark, Greece and the United States", International Journal of Social Psychiatry, 16(1), 54-62.

C.D.Jenkins, 1966.
"Group differences in perception: a study of community beliefs and feelings about tuberculosis", American Journal of Sociology, 71(4),417-429.

C.Jones, E.Aronson, 1973.
"Attribution of fault to a rape victim as a function of respectability of the victim", Journal of Personality and Social Psychology, 26(3), 415-419.

D.Jones, M.Mayo (eds.), 1974.
Community Work One. Routledge and Kegan Paul.

E.E.Jones, R.L.Archer, 1976.
"Are there special effects of personalistic self-disclosure?", Journal of Experimental Social Psychology, 12(2), 180-193.

K.Jones (with others), 1975.
Opening the door: a study of new policies for the mentally handicapped. Routledge and Kegan Paul.

K.Jones, J.Brown, J.Bradshaw, 1978.
Issues in social policy. Routledge and Kegan Paul.

P.N.Jones, 1980.
"Rights, welfare and stigma", 123-144 of N.Timms (ed.), Social welfare: why and how?, RKP.

R.L.Jones, 1972.
"Labels and stigma in special education", Exceptional Children, 38(7),

W.Jordan, 1973.
Paupers: the making of the new claiming class. Routledge and Kegan Paul.

-----, 1974.
Poor Parents: social policy and the cycle of deprivation. RKP.

T.Joyce, 1973.

An exploratory study of the relationships between welfare dependency and the attitudinal characteristics of welfare mothers. Ph.D.: Cornell University. 74-10854.

D.J.Kallen, D.Miller, 1971.
"Public attitudes toward welfare", _Social Work_, 16(3), 83-90.
V.Karn, 1979.
"How can we liberate council tenants?", _New Society_, 29th March, 47(860), 738-40.
G.G.Kassebaum, B.O.Baumann, 1965.
"Dimensions of the sick role in chronic illness", _Journal of Health and Human Behaviour_, 6(1), 16-27.
D.Katz, K.W.Braly, 1961.
"Verbal stereotypes and racial prejudice", 40-46 of E.E.Macoby, T.M.Newcomb, E.L.Hartley (eds.), _Readings in social psychology_, Methuen. (3rd edition.)
I.Katz, D.C.Glass, D.J.Lucido, J.Farber, 1977.
"Ambivalence, guilt and the denigration of a physically handicapped victim", _Journal of Personality_, 45(3), 419-429.
I.Katz, J.Farber, D.C.Glass, D.Lucido, T.Emswiller, 1978.
"When courtesy offends: effects of positive and negative behaviour by the physically disabled on altruism and anger in normals", _Journal of Personality_, 46(3), 506-518.
H.R.Kerbo, 1976.
"The stigma of welfare and a passive poor", _Sociology and Social Research, 60(2), 173-187._
N.Kessel, H.Walton, 1965.
Alcoholism. Harmondsworth: Penguin.
J.C.Kincaid, 1973.
Poverty and Equality in Britain: a study of social security in Britain. Harmondsworth: Penguin. (Revised edition, 1975.)
C.P.Kindleberger, P.H.Lindert, 1978.
International Economics. Homewood, Illinois: Irwin. (6th edition.)
R.Kleck, 1968a.
"Physical stigma and nonverbal cues emitted in face-to-face interaction", _Human Relations_, 21(1), 19-28.
-----, 1968b.
"Self-disclosure patterns of the nonobviously stigmatised", _Psychological Reports_, 23, 1239-1248.
-----, H.Ono, A.H.Hastorf, 1966.
"The effects of physical deviance upon face-to-face interaction", _Human Relations_, 19(4), 425-436.
-----, P.L.Buck, W.L.Goller, R.W.London, J.R.Pfeiffer, D.P.Vukcevic, 1968.
"Effect of stigmatising conditions on the use of personal space", _Psychological Reports_, 23, 111-118.

R.Klein (ed.), 1975.
Social policy and public expenditure 1975: inflation and priorities. Centre for Studies in Social Policy.

N.Kogan, 1961.
"Attitudes toward old people: the development of a scale and examination of correlates", Journal of Abnormal and Social Psychology, 62(1), 44-54.

H.Land, 1966.
"Provision for large families", New Society, 24th November, 8(217), 795-6.

D.Landy, S.E.Singer, 1968.
"The social organisation and culture of a club for former mental patients", 449-459 of S.Spitzer and N.Denzin (eds.) 1968.

E.J.Langer, S.Fiske, S.E.Taylor, B.Chanowitz, 1976.
"Stigma, staring and discomfort: a novel-stimulus hypothesis", Journal of Experimental Social Psychology, 12(5), 451-463.

Law Commission, 1979.
Summary of working paper no. 74. Family Law: Illegitimacy. Law Commission.

R.Layard, D.Piachaud, M.Stewart, 1978.
The causes of poverty. (Royal Commission on the Distribution of Income and Wealth: Background Paper no. 5.) HMSO.

E.R.Leach (ed.), 1960.
Aspects of caste in South India, Ceylon and North-West Pakistan. Cambridge: Cambridge University Press.

-----, 1976.
"What should we mean by caste?", 181-186 of G.Bowker, J. Carrier (eds.), Race and ethnic relations: sociological readings, Hutchinson, 1976.

V.Lehtinen, E.Vaisanen, 1978.
"Attitudes toward mental illness and utilisation of psychiatric treatment", Social Psychiatry, 13(2), 63-68.

R.Lejeune, 1968.
Illness behaviour among the urban poor. Ph.D.: Columbia University. 69-417.

E.M.Lemert, 1951.
Social Pathology: a systematic approach to the theory of sociopathic behaviours. New York: McGraw-Hill Book Co.

E.M.Lemert, 1972.
Human Deviance, social problems and social control. Englewood Cliffs, NJ: Prentice-Hall. (2nd edition.)

G.Lenski, 1954.
"Status crystallization: a non-vertical dimension of social status", American Sociological Review, 19(Aug.), 405-413.

M.J.Lerner, 1970.
"The desire for justice and reactions to victims", 205-

229 of J.Macaulay, L.Berkowitz (eds.) Altruism and
helping behaviour: social psychological studies of some
antecedents and consequences, New York: Academic Press.
M.J.Lerner, D.T.Miller, 1978.
"Just world research and the attribution process: looking
back and ahead", Psychological Bulletin, 85(5), 1030-
1051.
P.Levinson, 1964.
"Chronic dependency: a conceptual analysis", Social
Service Review, 38(4), 371-381.
C.Levi-Strauss, (1949).
The elementary structures of kinship. (J.H.Bell, J.R.
von Sturmer, R.Needham, trans.). Eyre and Spottiswoode.
(Revised edition.)
-----, (1958).
Structural anthropology. (C.Jacobson, B.Grundfest
Schoepf, trans.). Allen Lane, 1968.
W.L.Linford Rees, 1976.
A short textbook of psychiatry. Hodder and Stoughton.
(2nd edition.)
R.Linton, 1936.
The study of Man: an introduction. New York: Appleton-
Century Co.
A.Lipman, R.Slater, 1978.
"Homes for old people: toward a positive environment",
199-217 of V.Carver, P.Liddiard (eds.) 1978.
J.Locke, (1791).
"Report of the Board of Trade to the Lords Justices in
the year 1697, respecting the relief and employment of
the poor", 101-152 of An account of the origin,
proceedings and intentions of the Society for the
Promotion of Industry, Louth: R.Sheardown. (3rd edition.)
London Medical Group, 1978.
'The stigma of mental illness': symposium held at King's
College Medical School, 28th November.
S.Lukes, 1977.
"Alienation and anomie", ch.4 of Essays in social theory,
Macmillan.
M.Luther, (1536).
"Ordinance for a common chest", in F.R.Salter (ed.) 1926.
G.Lyketsos, C.Panayotakopoulos, 1970.
"Prejudices against the mental patient", British Journal
of Social Psychology and Community Health, 4(3), 175-183.
A.Lynes, 1979.
"The cost of justice for lone parents", New Society, 25th
October, 50(890), 189-190.
R.Lynn, (1969).
"Comprehensives and equality: the quest for the
unattainable", 285-295 of H.Silver (ed.), Equal
opportunity in education: a reader in class and
educational opportunity, Methuen 1973.

B.Q.Madison, 1968.
Social welfare in the Soviet Union.   Stanford,
California: Stanford University Press.
D.R.Mandelker, 1973.
Housing subsidies in the United States and England.   New
York: Bobbs-Merrill.
G.Marcus, 1928.
"Social attitudes as they are affected by financial
dependency and relief-giving", The Family, 9(5), 135-140.
R.P.Marinelli, A.E.DellOrto (eds.), 1977.
The psychological and social impact of physical
disability. New York: Springer Publishing Co.
D.Marsden, 1973.
Mothers alone: poverty and the fatherless family.
Harmondsworth: Penguin Books. Revised ed.
D.Marsden, E.Duff, 1975.
Workless: some unemployed men and their families.
Harmondsworth: Penguin Books.
P.Marris, 1958.
Widows and their families. Routledge and Kegan Paul.
T.H.Marshall, 1963.
Sociology at the crossroads. Heinemann.
J.H.Masserman, (1943).
Behaviour and neurosis: an experimental psychoanalytic
approach to psychobiologic principles. New York: Hafner,
1964.
D.Matza, 1964.
Delinquency and drift. New York: John Wiley and Sons.
-----, 1967.
"The disreputable poor", 289-302 of Bendix, Lipset (eds.)
1967.
D.Matza, H.Miller, 1976.
"Poverty and proletariat", 639-675 of RK Merton, R Nisbet
(eds.), Contemporary social problems, New York: Harcourt
Brace Jovanovich. (4th edition.)
M.Mauss, 1925.
The Gift: forms and functions of exchange in archaic
societies. (I.Cunnison, trans.). Cohen and West, 1966.
C.Mayo, R.G.Havelock, 1970.
"Attitudes toward mental illness among mental hospital
personnel and patients", Journal of Psychiatric Research,
7, 291-298.
M.Meacher, 1972.
Rate rebates: a study of the effectiveness of means
tests. Child Poverty Action Group.
M.Meacher, 1974.
Scrounging on the welfare: the scandal of the four week
rule.Arrow.
K.P.Meadow, 1969.
"Self-image, family climate and deafness", Social Forces,
47(4), 428-439.

D.Mechanic, 1974.
   Politics, medicine and social science.   New York: John
   Wiley and Sons.
R.K.Merton, 1968.
   Social theory and social structure.   New York: Free
   Press.
N.Middleton, S.Weizman, 1976.
   A place for everyone: a history of state education from
   the end of the 18th century to the 1970's.   Victor
   Gollancz.
D.Miller, W.H.Dawson, 1965.
   "Effects   of   stigma   on   re-employment   of   ex-mental
   patients", Mental Hygiene, 49, 281-287.
D.Miller, 1976.
   Social justice.   Oxford: Oxford University Press.
S.M.Miller, F.Riessman, 1968.
   Social class and social policy.   New York: Basic Books.
S.M.Miller, P.Roby, 1968.
   "Poverty: changing   social   stratification",   64-84   of
   D.P.Moynihan   (ed.),   On   understanding   poverty:
   perspectives from the social sciences.   New York: Basic
   Books.
Ministry of Pensions and National Insurance, 1966.
   Financial   and   other   circumstances   of   retirement
   pensioners: report on an inquiry by the Ministry of
   Pensions and National Insurance with the co-operation of
   the National Assistance Board.   HMSO.
R.Minns, 1972.
   "Homeless families and some organisational determinants
   of deviancy", Policy and Politics, 1(1), 1-21.
T.Moriarty, 1974.
   "Role of stigma in the experience of deviance", Journal
   of Personality and Social Psychology, 29(6), 849-855.
R.M.Moroney, 1976.
   The family and the state: considerations for social
   policy.   Longman.
M.R.Mosely, 1973.
   Attitude difference toward disabled persons as a function
   of   educational   integration.   Ed.D.:   University   of
   Houston.   73-22925.
P.Morris, 1969.
   Put away: a sociological study of institutions for the
   mentally retarded.   RKP.
P.Moss, 1970.
   Welfare rights,   project two.   Liverpool: Merseyside
   Poverty Action Group.
C.L.Mulford, 1968.
   "Ethnocentrism and attitudes toward the mentally ill",
   Sociological Quarterly, 9(1), 107-111.
C.L.Mulford, J.B.Murphy, 1968.
   "Selected correlates of the stigma associated with mental

illness", Journal of Social Psychology, 74(1), 103-110.

S.F.Nadel, 1953.
"Social control and self-regulation", Social Forces, 31(3), 265-273.
National and Local Government Officers Association, undated.
Report of the Housing Working Party: Housing - the way ahead.NALGO.
New Society, 1978.
"Roll call", 6th April, 44(809), p.3.
H.Newby, 1977.
The deferential worker: a study of farm workers in East Anglia. Allen Lane.
O.Newman, 1972.
Defensible space: people and design in the violent city. Architectural Press, 1973.
P.Niesewand, 1980.
"The harrying of the Harijans", The Guardian, 9th April.
J.R.Noonan, J.R.Barry, H.C.Davis, 1970.
"Personality determinants in attitudes toward visible disability", Journal of Personality, 38(1), 1-15.
T.J.Northcutt, 1959.
The relation of social class membership to opinions regarding welfare services and recipients. Ph.D.: Florida State University. 59-1762.
D.W.Novak, M.J.Lerner, 1968.
"Rejection as a consequence of perceived similarity", Journal of Personality and Social Psychology, 9(2), 147-152.
J.C.Nunally, 1961.
Popular conceptions of mental health: their development and change. New York: Holt, Rinehart and Winston.

S.Olshansky, 1970.
"Work and the retarded", 29-46 of N.R.Bernstein (ed.), Diminished people: problems and care of the mentally retarded Boston: Little, Brown and Co.
J.H.Orley, 1970.
Culture and mental illness: a study from Uganda. Kampala: East African Publishing House.
C.Orlik, 1978.
"Cat meat trail", New Society, 9th November, 46(840), 339.
George Orwell, (1937).
The road to Wigan Pier. Secker and Warburg, 1959.

S.Page, S.Page, 1974.
"What is psychiatric stigma?", Psychological Reports, 34(2), 630.
S.Papper, 1970.

"The undesirable patient", Journal of Chronic Diseases, 22, 777-779.

L.E.Pardo, 1974.
Stigma and social justice: the effects of physical disability vis-a-vis moral turpitude. Ph.D.: York University, Toronto.

L.D.Park, 1977.
"Barriers to normality for the handicapped adult in the United States", 25-33 of Marinelli, DellOrto (eds.), 1977.

J.Parker, 1975.
Social policy and citizenship. Macmillan.

R.A.Parker, (1967).
"Social administration and scarcity", 204-212 of Butterworth, Holman (eds.) 1975.

T.Parsons, 1951.
The social system. Routledge and Kegan Paul.

-----, 1958.
"Definitions of health and illness in the light of American values and social structure", 165-187 of E.G.Jaco (ed.), Patients, physicians and illness: sourcebook in behavioural science and medicine, Glencoe, Illinois: Free Press.

M.Payne, 1980.
"Strategies for the management of stigma through social work", British Journal of Social Work, 10(4), 443-456.

B.H.J.Pehrsson, 1972.
The blind as dependent or independent: a study of the socialization of the blind. Ph.D.: Fordham University. 73-1489.

H.H.Perlman, (1951).
"Are we creating dependency?", Social Service Review, 34(3), 323-333.

D.L.Phillips, 1963.
"Rejection: a possible consequence of seeking help for mental disorders", American Sociological Review, 28(6), 963-972.

-----, 1966.
"Public identification and acceptance of the mentally ill", American Journal of Public Health and the Nation's ·Health, 56(5), 755-763.

-----, 1967.
"Identification of mental illness: its consequences for rejection", Community Mental health Journal, 3(323), 262-266.

M.H.Phillips, 1972.
The impact of the declaration procedure upon the perceptions and attitudes of mothers receiving Aid to Families with Dependent Children. D.S.W.: Columbia University. 72-28079.

A.F.Philp, N.Timms, 1957.

The problem of 'the problem family': a critical review of
the literature concerning the 'problem family and its
treatment'. Family Service Units.
D.Piachaud, 1979.
   The cost of a child: a modern minimum.   Child Poverty
   Action Group.
G.Piers, M.B.Singer, 1953.
   Shame and guilt: a psychoanalytic and a cultural study.
   Springfield, Illinois: Charles C.Thomas.
I.Piliavin, A.E.Gross, 1977.
   "The effects of separation of services and income
   maintenance on AFDC recipients", Social Service Review,
   51(3), 389-406.
W.T.Pink, M.E.Sweeney, 1978.
   "Teacher nomination, deviant career lines, and the
   management of stigma in the junior high school", Urban
   Education, 13(3), 361-380.
R.Pinker, 1971.
   Social theory and social policy. Heinemann.
-----, 1973.
   Dependency and welfare. Unpublished draft paper for the
   Social Science Research Council.
F.Piven, R.Cloward, 1971.
   Regulating the poor: the functions of public welfare.
   Tavistock, 1972.
L.Podell, 1968.
   Families on Welfare in New York City. New York: Center
   for the Study of Urban Problems, Baruch College, City
   University of New York.
S.Pollack, D.Huntley, J.G.Allen, S.Schwartz, 1976.
   "The dimensions of stigma: the social situation of the
   mentally ill person and the male homosexual", Journal of
   Abnormal Psychology, 85(1), 105-112.
R.Pomeroy, H.Yahr, L.Podell, 1970(?).
   Studies in public welfare: reactions of welfare clients
   to social service. New York: Center for the Study of
   Urban Problems, Baruch College, City University of New
   York.
D.Porteous ('A citizen of Glasgow'), 1783.
   A letter to the citizens of Glasgow. Glasgow: Robert
   Chapman, Alexander Duncan.
A.Power, 1979.
   Tenant co-ops or tenant management corporations in the
   USA. North Islington Housing Rights Project.
J.R.Poynter, 1969.
   Society and pauperism: English ideas on poor relief 1795-
   1834. Routledge and Kegan Paul.

L.Rainwater, 1967.
   "The lessons of Pruitt-Igoe", The Public Interest,
   1967(8), 116-126.

------, (1970).
   Behind ghetto walls: black families in a Federal slum.
   Allen Lane, 1971.
H.E.Ransford, 1972.
   "Blue collar anger: reactions to student and black
   protest", American Sociological Review, 37, 333-346.
R.Rawlinson, (1864-65).
   Appendix 3 of the 17th Annual report of the Poor Law
   Board. 158-160 of M.E.Rose (ed.), 1971.
N.Raynsford, 1979.
   "Cold water on homeless myths", New Society, 16th
   October, 50(889), 133.
M.Reddin, 1977.
   Universality and selectivity: strategies in   social
   policy. Dublin: National Economic and Social Council
   (Eire).
R.Redner, 1980.
   "Others' perceptions of mothers of handicapped children",
   American Journal of Mental Deficiency, 85(2), 176-183.
S.Rees, 1975.
   "How misunderstanding occurs", 62-75 of R.Bailey, M.Brake
   (eds.), Radical Social Work, Edward Arnold.
D.A.Reisman, 1977.
   Richard Titmuss: welfare and society.   Heinemann
   Educational Books.
P.Richards, 1977.
   The medieval leper and his northern heirs.   Cambridge:
   D.S.Brewer.
A.Richardson, J.Naidoo, 1978.
   The take-up of Supplementary Benefits: a report on a
   survey of claimants. Unpublished (prepared for DHSS).
S.A.Richardson, A.H.Hastorf, N.Goodman, S.M.Dornbusch, 1961.
   "Cultural uniformity in reaction to physical
   disabilities", American Sociological Review, 26, 241-7.
H.Riffault, J-R.Rabier, 1977.
   The perception of · poverty in Europe.   Brussels:
   Commission of the European Communities. (V/171/77-E).
J.Ritchie, P.Wilson, 1979.
   Social security claimants: a survey amongst the customers
   of a local social security office carried out on behalf
   of the Department of Health and Social Security.   Office
   of Population Censuses and Surveys.
A.Rodgers, 1977.
   A comparative study of self-esteem attitude factors
   between welfare beneficiaries and non-welfare middle-
   income respondents. Ph.D.: University of South Carolina.
   DBJ77-22430.
B.N.Rodgers, A.Doron, M.Jones, 1979.
   The study of social policy: a comparative approach.
   George Allen and Unwin.
H.Rodman, 1965.

"Middle-class misconceptions about lower-class families",
213-230 of Marriage, family and society: a reader, New
York: Random House.
-----, 1971.
Lower-class families: the culture of poverty in, Negro
Trinidad. Oxford University Press.
L.Rogler, A.B.Hollingshead, 1965.
Trapped: families and schizophrenia. New York: John
Wiley.
M.Rokeach, S.Parker, 1970.
"Values as social indicators of poverty and race
relations in the United States", The Annals, 388, 97-111.
E.Romano, 1968.
The impact of mental retardation upon the self-concept of
the mother: a comparative study of the self-regarding
attitudes of mothers of trainable children and selected
mothers of nonretarded children. Ph.D.: Syracuse
University. 68-13856.
I.Rootman, 1972.
"Social class and attitudes toward mental illness: a
study of a Canadian prairie community", Canadian review
of Sociology and Anthropology, 9(1), 21-32.
H.Rose, 1975.
"Who can delabel the claimant?: welfare rights from the
claimant's perspective", 143-154 of M.Adler, A.Bradley
(eds.), Justice, discretion and poverty: Supplementary
Benefit Appeal Tribunals in Britain. Professional Books.
M.E.Rose (ed.) 1971.
The English Poor Law 1780-1930. Newton Abbot: David and
Charles.
G.Rosenberg, 1974.
Attitudes toward mental illness and upward social
mobility in working-class adolescents. Ph.D.: New York
University. 74-17,153.
M.Rosenberg, 1965.
Society and the adolescent self-image. Princeton, NJ:
Princeton University Press.
Z.Rubin, L.A.Peplau, 1975.
"Who believes in a just world?", Journal of Social
Issues, 31(3), 65-89.
M.Rutter, N.Madge, 1976.
Cycles of disadvantage. Heinemann.

C.Safilios-Rothschild, 1970.
The sociology and social psychology of disability and
rehabilitation. New York: Random House.
M.Sahlins, 1972.
Stone age economics. Tavistock.
P.Sainsbury, 1955.
Suicide in London: an ecological study. Institute of
Psychiatry.

F.R.Salter (ed.), 1926.
Some early tracts on Poor Relief. Methuen.
V.D.Sanua, 1970.
"A cross-cultural study of cerebral palsy", Social Science and Medicine, 4(5), 461-512.
T.R.Sarbin, 1970.
"The culture of poverty, social identity, and cognitive outcomes", 29-46 in V.L.Allen (ed.), Psychological factors in poverty, Chicago:Markham.
W.Scarfe, A.Scarfe, 1974.
Victims or bludgers? Case studies of poverty in Australia. Malvern, Victoria: Sorrett Publishing.
W.E.Schafer, C.Olexa, 1971.
Tracking and opportunity: the locking-out process and beyond.Scranton, US: Chandler Publishing Co.
T.Scheff, 1966.
Being mentally ill: a sociological theory. Weidenfeld and Nicolson.
S.Schifferes, 1978.
"Homes rule in Ireland", Roof, November, 179-181.
T.J.Schmid, 1977.
Parental reactions to the affiliational stigma of mental retardation. Ph.D.: University of Minnesota. 77-19036.
M.E.Schiltz, 1970.
Public attitudes towards Social Security, 1935-1965. Washington DC: US Department of Health, Education and Welfare - Social Security Administration.
C.G.Schwartz, 1956.
"The stigma of mental illness", Journal of Rehabilitation, 4(Jul-Aug), 7-29 passim.
R.A.Scott, 1967.
"The selection of clients by social welfare agencies: the case of the blind", Social Problems, 14(3), 248-257.
-----,1969.
The making of blind men: a study of adult socialisation. New York: Russell Sage Foundation.
-----, 1972.
"A proposed framework for analysing deviance as a property of social order", 9-35 of Scott, Douglas (eds.) 1972.
R.A.Scott, J.D.Douglas, 1972.
Theoretical perspectives on deviance. New York: Basic Books.
M.Seeman, 1959.
"On the meaning of alienation", 401-414 of L.Coser, B.Rosenberg (eds.) Sociological theory: a book of readings, Collier-Macmillan (3rd. ed., 1976).
D.R.Segal, M.W.Segal, D.Knoke, 1970.
"Status consistency and self-evaluation", Sociometry, 33(3), 347-357.
S.P.Segal, 1978.

"Attitudes toward the mentally ill: a review", _Social Work_, 23(3), 211-217.

H.D.Seibel, 1972.
"Social deviance in comparative perspective", 251-281 of Scott, Douglas (eds.), 1972.

A.Seldon, H.Gray, 1967.
Universal or selective social benefits?   Institute of Economic Affairs.

G.B.Shaw, 1928.
The intelligent woman's guide to socialism, capitalism, sovietism and fascism. Harmonsdworth: Penguin Books, 1937.

N.Shenton, 1976.
Deneside - a council estate.   York: University of York Department of Social Administration and Social Work.

E.Shils, 1968.
"Deference", 103-132 of J.A.Jackson (ed.), _Social stratification_, Cambridge University Press.

S.Shoham, 1970.
The mark of Cain: the stigma theory of crime and social deviation. Jerusalem: Israel Universities Press.

W.Shore, 1981.
"When drink is a deadly stigma ...", _Nottingham Evening Post_, 21st February, p.9.

J.Siller, 1962.
"Personality determinants of reaction to the physically handicapped", _American Psychologist_, 17(6), 338.

J.Siller, A.Chipman, L.T.Ferguson, D.H.Vann, 1967.
Attitudes of the nondisabled toward the physically disabled. New York: New York University School of Education.

G.Simmel, (1908).
"The poor" (trans. C.Jacobson), _Social Problems_, 13, 118-139.

-----, 1950.
The sociology of Georg Simmel. (K.H.Wolff, trans. and ed.). New York: Free Press.

J.L.Simmons, 1965.
"Public stereotypes of deviants", _Social Problems_ 13(2), 223-232.

R.Simpson, 1978.
Access to primary care. (Royal Commission on the National Health Service Research paper no. 6). HMSO.

S.Singha, S.Donnan, 1980.
"Who uses VD Clinics?", _New Society_, 16th October, 54(935), 115-116.

E.O.Smigel, 1953.
"Public attitudes toward 'chiselling' with reference to unemployment compensation", _American Sociological Review_, 18(1), 59-67.

G.Smith, T.Smith, 1974.

"The community school - a base for community development?", 186-198 of Jones, Mayo (eds.) 1974.

A.T.Soares, L.M.Soares, 1969.
"Self-perceptions of culturally disadvantaged children", American Educational Research Journal, 6(1), 31-45.

R.Sommer, R.Hall, 1958.
"Alienation and mental illness", American Sociological Review 23(4), 418-420.

D.A.Sorensen, 1972.
Attitude change toward epilepsy as a function of viewing a seizure episode. Ph.D.: University of Connecticut. 73-9844.

D.Soyer, 1961.
"Reaching problem families through settlement based casework", Social Work, 6(3), 36-42.

-----, 1975.
"The right to fail", 53-64 of F.E.McDermott (ed.), Self-determination in social work, RKP.

J.C.Spencer, 1963.
"The multi-problem family", 3-54 of B.Schlesinger (ed.), The multi-problem family: a review and annotated bibliography. Toronto: University of Toronto Press.

J.Spencer, 1964.
Stress and release in an urban estate: a study in action research. Tavistock.

S.Spitzer, 1975.
"Toward a Marxian theory of deviance", Social Problems, 22(5), 638-651.

S.P.Spitzer, N.K.Denzin (eds.), 1968.
The mental patient: studies in the sociology of deviance. New York: McGraw-Hill.

M.N.Srinivas, 1962.
Caste in modern India and other essays. Asia Publishing House.

L.Srole, 1956.
"Social integration and certain corollaries: an exploratory study", American Sociological Review, 21(1), 709-716.

G.Y.Steiner, 1971.
The state of welfare. Washington DC: Brookings Institution.

W.J.Stephen, 1979.
An analysis of primary medical care: an international study. Cambridge: Cambridge University Press.

C.Stevens, 1973.
Public assistance in France. Bell.

O.Stevenson, 1973.
Claimant or client?: a social worker's view of the Supplementary Benefits Commission. Allen and Unwin.

C.St.-John Brooks, 1980.
"Boarding out", New Society, 31st July, 53(924), 222.

218   References

J.D.Stoeckle, 1975.
"The reorganisation of practice in the community", 351-
396 of J.Kosa, I.K.Zola (eds.) 1975, Poverty and health:
a sociological analysis, Cambridge, Mass.: Commonwealth
Fund (Harvard University Press).
E.V.Stonequist, 1935.
"The problem of the marginal man", American Journal of
Sociology, 41(1), 1-12.
A.Stuart, 1975.
"Recipient views of cash versus in-kind benefit
programmes", Social Service Review, 49(1), 79-91.
------, 1971.
Means tests and the poor: opinions and attitudes of
recipients of five means-tested services. Ph.D.:
Brandeis University (Florence Heller Graduate School for
Advanced Studies in Social Welfare). 72-1584.
K.Stubbs, 1980.
The press and social security: an analysis of popular
press coverage of the social security system and its
clients. Unpublished B.Sc. dissertation: London School
of Economics and Political Science.
P.J.Sullivan, 1971.
Perception of and reaction to 'welfare stigma' and the
influence of programme participation, life conditions and
personal attitudes. Ph.D.: Catholic University of
America, Washington DC.
Supplementary Benefits Commission, 1978.
Takeup of Supplementary Benefits. HMSO.
M.B.Sussman, 1969.
"Dependent disabled and dependent poor: similarity of
conceptual issues and research needs", Social Service
Review, 43(4).383-395.
N.S.Sutherland, 1976.
Breakdown: a personal crisis and a medical dilemma.
Weidenfeld and Nicolson.
T.S.Szasz, 1971.
The manufacture of madness: a comparative study of the
inquisition and the mental health movement. Routledge
and Kegan Paul.
J.A.Szuhay, 1961.
The development of attitudes toward the physically
disabled. Ph.D.: University of Iowa. 61-5615.

H.Taine, 1874.
"Notes on England", 169-171 of M.E.Rose (ed.) 1971.
R.H.Tawney, 1936.
Religion and the rise of capitalism: an historical study.
John Murray.
P.F.Taylor-Gooby, 1976.
"Rent benefits and tenants' attitudes: the Batley rent
rebate and allowance study", Journal of Social Policy,

5(1), 33-48.
J.tenBroek, F.W.Matson, 1966.
"The disabled and the law of welfare", 485-516 of tenBroek, California Law Review (eds.), The law of the poor, San Francisco: Chandler, 1966.
J.A.K.Thomson, 1953.
The ethics of Aristotle. Harmondsworth: Penguin.
The Times, 19.4.1834.
R.M.Titmuss, 1950.
Problems of social policy. HMSO/Longmans, Green and co.
-----, 1955.
"The social division of welfare: some reflections on the search for equity", in Essays on the Welfare State, George Allen and Unwin, 1963. (2nd edition.)
-----, 1968.
Commitment to welfare. George Allen and Unwin.
-----,1970.
The gift relationship: from human blood to social policy. Harmondsworth: Penguin.
-----, 1974.
Social policy: an introduction. George Allen and Unwin.
J.Townsend, 1788.
Observations on various plans offered to the public for the relief of the poor. C.Dilly.
P.B.Townsend, 1963.
The last refuge: a survey of residential institutions and homes for the aged in England and Wales. Routledge and kegan Paul.
-----, 1976.
"Selectivity - a nation divided?", 121-127 of Sociology and social policy, Harmondsworth: Penguin.
-----, 1979.
Poverty in the United Kingdom: a survey of household resources and standards of living. Harmondsworth: Penguin.
-----, B.Abel-Smith, 1965.
The poor and the poorest: a new analysis of the Ministry of Labour's family expenditure surveys of 1953-54 and 1960. Bell.
H.C.Triandis, L.M.Triandis, 1965.
"Some studies of social distance", 207-217 of I.D. Steiner, M.Fishbein (eds.), Current studies in social psychology, New York: Holt, Rinehart and Winston.
H.M.Trice, P.M.Roman, 1970.
"Delabelling, relabelling, and Alcoholics Anonymous", Social Problems, 17(4), 538-546.
J.L.Tringo, 1968.
The hierarchy of preferences: a comparison of attitudes and prejudice toward specific disability groups. Ph.D.: University of Connecticut. 70-01321.
-----, 1970.

"The hierarchy of preference toward disability groups", _Journal of Special Education_, 4(3), 295-306.
M.S.Tseng, 1972.
"Attitudes toward the disabled - a cross-cultural study", _Journal of Social Psychology_, 87(2), 311-312.
J.Tucker, 1966.
Honourable Estates. Victor Gollancz.
M.Turner, 1960.
Forgotten men. National Council of Social Service.
R.H.Turner, 1972.
"Deviance avowal as neutralisation of commitment", _Social Problems_, 19(3), 308-321.

S.Uttley, 1980.
"The welfare exchange reconsidered", _Journal of Social Policy_ 9(2), 187-205.

P.Vellender, 1980.
Letter to _The Guardian_, 18th February, p.10.
G.Velho, 1978.
"Stigmatisation and deviance in Copacabana", _Social Problems_, 25(5), 526-530.
J.L.Vives, 1531.
"The Ypres scheme of poor relief (Forma subventiones pauperum)" (trans. 1535), 36-76 of .F.R.Salter (ed.), 1926.
G. de Vos, 1967.
Seminar report in A. de Reuck, J. Knight (eds.) _Caste and race: comparative approaches_, J. and A. Churchill.

C.Wadel, 1973.
Now, whose fault is that?: the struggle for self esteem in the face of chronic unemployment. - : Institute of Social and Economic Research, Memorial University of Newfoundland.
A.Walker, 1980.
"The social creation of poverty and dependency in old age", _Journal of Social Policy_, 9(1), 49-75.
E.J.Walsh, 1974.
Job stigma and self-esteem. Ph.D.: University of Michigan. 74-25354.
J.P.Walsma, 1970.
Attitudes and knowledge of the aged regarding Old Age Insurance and Old Age Assistance. D.S.W.: University of Southern California. 71-02540.
R.A.Ward, 1977.
"The impact of subjective age and stigma on older persons", _Journal of Gerontology_, 32(2), 227-232.
D.Watson, 1980.
Caring for strangers: an introduction to practical philosophy for students of social administration. RKP.

R.L.Watson, E.Midlarsky, 1979.
"Reactions of mothers with mentally retarded children: a social perspective", Psychological Reports, 45(1), 309-310.

B.Webb, 1948.
Our partnership. (B.Drake, M.I.Cole, eds.). Cambridge University Press.

S.Webb, (1889).
"The basis of socialism: historic", in Fabian Essays, Fabian Society/ George Allen and Unwin, 1931.

S.Webb, B.Webb, 1929.
English Poor Law history. Part 2: the last hundred years. Frank Cass, 1963.

M.Weber, (1904-5).
The protestant ethic and the spirit of capitalism. (T.Parsons, trans.) George Allen and Unwin, 1930.

-----, 1967.
"The development of caste", 28-36 of Bendix, Lipset (eds.) 1967.

B.A.Weisbrod, 1970.
On the stigma effect and the demand for welfare programmes: a theoretical note. Madison, Wisconsin: University of Wisconsin Institute for Research on Poverty.

K.Westergaard, 1979.
Seminar at LSE, 26th April: 'Scandinavian policies and the employment crisis'.

F.R.Westie, M.L.Westie, 1957.
"The social distance pyramid: relationships between caste and class", American Journal of Sociology, 63(2), 190-196.

H.L.Wilensky, C.N.Lebeaux, (1958).
Industrial society and social welfare: the impact of industrialisation on the supply and organisation of social welfare services in the United States. New York: Free Press, 1965.

H.W.Williams, 1944.
"Benjamin Franklin and the Poor Laws", Social Service Review, 18(1), 77-91.

W.M.Williams, 1956.
The sociology of an English village: Gosforth. Routledge and Kegan Paul.

J.B.Williamson, 1974a.
"Beliefs about the welfare poor", Sociology and social research, 58(2), 163-175.

-----, 1974b.
"Beliefs about the motivation of the poor and attitudes toward poverty policy", Social Problems, 21(5), 634-648.

-----, 1974c.
"The stigma of public dependency: a comparison of alternative forms of public aid to the poor", Social

Problems, 22(2), 213-228.
T.A.Willis, 1978.
"Perceptions of clients by professional helpers", *Psychological Bulletin*, 85(5), 968-1000.
D.Wilson, 1979.
"The Swedish dream grows tired", *New Society*, 6th December, 50(896), 544-546.
W.Wolfensberger, 1969.
"The origin and nature of our institutional models", 59-171b of RB Kugel, W Wolfensberger (eds.), *Changing patterns in residential services for the mentally retarded*, Washington DC: President's Committee on Mental Retardation.
M.Wolins, 1967.
"The societal function of social welfare", *New Perspectives*, 1(1), 1-18.
B.F.Wootton, 1959.
Social science and social pathology. Allen and Unwin.
M.E.Worthing, 1974.
"Personal space as a function of stigma effect", *Environment and Behaviour*, 6(3), 289-294.
B.A.Wright, 1960.
Physical disability: a psychological approach. New York: Harper and Row.
N.L.Wyers, 1975.
On the effect of stigma and other deterrents on three rural means-tested programmes. Ph.D.: Columbia University. 75-25746.

M.R.Yarrow, J.A.Clausen, P.R.Robbins, 1955.
"The social meaning of mental illness", *Journal of Social Issues*, 11(4), 33-48.
H.E.Yuker, J.R.Block, J.H.Young, 1970.
The measurement of attitudes toward disabled persons. Albertson, New York: Human Resources Center.

M.Zavalloni, 1973.
"Social identity: perspectives and prospects", *Social Science Information*, 12(3), 65-91.
R.C.Ziller, J.Megas, D.DeCencio, 1964.
"Self-social constructs of normals and acute neuropsychiatric patients", *Journal of Consulting Psychology*, 28(1), 59-63.
M.Zuckerman, 1975.
"Belief in a just world and altruistic behaviour", *Journal of Personality and Social Psychology*, 31(5), 972-976.
U.Zwingli, (1525).
"Ordinance and articles touching almsgiving", 99-103 of F.R.Salter (ed.) 1926.

British Government Papers.

British government papers are listed in chronological order.
All papers are published by HMSO.

Hansard, 1834a.
    Hansard's Parliamentary Debates, Third Series: vol.24.
    Commons, June 10th: 324-352.
-----, 1834b.
    Hansard's Parliamentary Debates, Third Series: vol.25.
    Lords, 31st July: 777-787.
Poor Law Commissioners, 1834.
    Report: Appendix F.
Hansard, 1870.
    Hansard's Parliamentary Debates, Third Series: vol.199.
    Commons, 17th February: 438-498.
Cd.2852, 1906.
    Report of the Departmental Committee on Vagrancy. Vol.1.
Cd.4499, 1909.
    Report of the Royal Commission on the Poor Laws and the
    Relief of Distress.
Cd.4625, 1909.
    Royal Commission on the Poor Laws and the Relief of
    Distress: Appendix. Vol.1: Evidence.
Cmd.3585, 1930.
    Poor Law. Report of a special inquiry into various forms
    of test work.
Cmd.6404, 1942.
    Social insurance and allied services.
Cmnd.169, 1957.
    Royal Commission on the Law relating to Mental Illness
    and Mental Deficiency: Report.
Cmnd.3703, 1968.
    Department of Health and Social Security. Report of the
    Committee on Local Authority and Allied Personal Social
    Services.
Cmnd.7320, 1978.
    Department of Health and Social Security. Review of the
    Mental Health Act 1959.
Cmnd.7357, 1978.
    Department of Health and Social Security. Report of the
    Committee of Inquiry into Normansfield Hospital.

Index